D1607959

Race, Maternity, and the Politics of Birth Control
in South Africa, 1910–39

Frontispiece 1 "The Viljoen family," a poor white family in rural Transvaal. Mrs. Viljoen is an example of the poor white mothers that the birth-control movement attempted to reach in the 1930s. The portrait was taken in 1929 by E.G. Malherbe during his work for the *Carnegie Commission of Investigation on the Poor White Question* (1929–32).

Source: E.G. Malherbe Manuscript Collection, Killie Campbell Africana Library, University of Kwa-Zulu Natal, Durban.

Frontispiece 2 "Angela with her daughter," in Rooiyard, an African slumyard in Doornfontein, a neighbhorhood near central Johannesburg. The portrait was taken in the 1930s by Ellen Hellmann in the course of research for her study, *Rooiyard: A Sociological Survey of an Urban Native Slum Yard* (not published until 1948). In 1937 the Race Welfare Society began to offer birth-control services through a clinic for African and Coloured women on Buxton Street in Doornfontein in hopes of attracting women like Angela.

Source: Historical Papers, University of the Witwatersrand, Johannesburg.

Frontispiece 3 Mother and baby, St. Monica's Home, Cape Town, in the 1930s. In 1917 the Anglican Church in Cape Town established St. Monica's Home as a maternity home for poor women, and in 1921 expanded its services to include an ante-natal clinic. St. Monica's served poor "Coloured," Muslim and white women in Cape Town, including Woodstock and Salt River, two neighbourhoods also served by the Cape Town Mothers' Clinic. Thus, this mother represents the many Coloured women who visited the Mothers' Clinic in the 1930s.

Source: Historical Papers, University of the Witwatersrand, Johannesburg.

Race, Maternity, and the Politics of Birth Control in South Africa, 1910–39

Susanne M. Klausen

palgrave
macmillan

First published in 2004 by
PALGRAVE MACMILLAN
Houndmills, Basingstoke, Hampshire RG21 6XS and
175 Fifth Avenue, New York, N.Y. 10010
Companies and representatives throughout the world.

PALGRAVE MACMILLAN is the global academic imprint of the Palgrave Macmillan division of St. Martin's Press, LLC and of Palgrave Macmillan Ltd. Macmillan® is a registered trademark in the United States, United Kingdom and other countries. Palgrave is a registered trademark in the European Union and other countries.

ISBN 1–4039–3452–5 hardback

This book is printed on paper suitable for recycling and made from fully managed and sustained forest sources.

A catalogue record for this book is available from the British Library.

Library of Congress Cataloging-in-Publication Data

Klausen, Susanne Maria, 1965–
    Race, maternity, and the politics of birth control in South Africa, 1910–39 / Susanne M. Klausen.
        p. cm.
    Includes bibliographical references and index.
    ISBN 1–4039–3452–5 (cloth)
    1. Birth control – South Africa – History – 20th century. 2. Birth control – Political aspects – South Africa. 3. Eugenics – South Africa – History – 20th century. 4. South Africa – Population policy. I. Title.

HQ766.5.S6K53 2004
304.6'66'0968—dc22   2004042095

10 9 8 7 6 5 4 3 2 1
13 12 11 10 09 08 07 06 05 04

Printed and bound in Great Britain by
Antony Rowe Ltd, Chippenham and Eastbourne.

To Brian Egan

Contents

List of Maps

List of Tables

List of Abbreviations

ACVV	*Afrikaanse Christelike Vroue Vereniging* (Afrikaans Christian Women's Union)
CAVS	Cape Association for Voluntary Sterilization
CBC	Society for Constructive Birth Control and Racial Progress
CHO	Chief Health Officer
CYL	Congress Youth League
DPH	Department of Public Health
DRC	Dutch Reformed Church
ESSA	Eugenics Society of South Africa
GNP	*Gesuiwerde* (Purified) Nationalist Party
ICU	Industrial and Commercial Workers' Union
MC	Mothers' Clinic
MCC	Mothers' Clinic Committee
MOH	Medical Officer of Health
MP	Member of Parliament
MPH	Minister of Public Health
NBCA	National Birth Control Association
NEUM	Non-European Unity Movement
NP	National Party
OFS	Orange Free State
PPASA	Planned Parenthood Association of South Africa
RWS	Race Welfare Society
SAIRR	South African Institute for Race Relations
SAAAS	South African Association for the Advancement of Science
SAMJ	South African Medical Journal
SANCBC	South African National Council for Birth Control
SANCMFW	South African National Council for Maternal and Family Welfare
SAP	South Africa Party
SPH	Secretary of the Department of Public Health
TB	Tuberculosis
UP	United Party
VD	Venereal Disease
WFAVS	World Federation of Associations for Voluntary Sterilization

List of Birth-Control Clinics Established in South Africa in the 1930s

Benoni

- A birth-control clinic established in 1933. In 1938 it was taken over by the municipal health department.

Cape Town

- The Mothers' Clinic opened at 234 Main Road in Observatory on February 15, 1932 and moved to 354 Main Road the following year.
- In 1936 a birth-control clinic was established in the Divisional Council VD and TB clinic in Grassy Park.
- In 1938 the Cape Town City Council established a birth-control clinic in Maitland under the supervision of the Mothers' Clinic Committee (MCC).
- In 1939 a birth-control clinic was established in a Divisional Council clinic in Hout Bay.

Durban

- A birth-control clinic, the Mothers' Clinic, was open for a few months in 1936.

East London

- The East London birth-control clinic opened in 1936.

Johannesburg

- The Women's Welfare Centre opened in Sauer's Building on Loveday Street on February 4, 1932. It was renamed the Central Clinic in 1937 and moved to Welfare House on Fox Street in 1940.
- The Traveling Clinic for white women opened in Vrededorp and Jeppe in 1937.

- A birth-control clinic for Coloured women opened in the Methodist Church in Ferreira in August 1935. It closed in January 1936.
- A birth-control clinic for Coloured and African women opened on Buxton Street, Doornfontein, in January 1937.
- A birth-control clinic for Indian women was opened by July 1935, location unknown. In June 1939 the clinic was moved to Crown Road in Fordsburg.

Pietermaritzburg

- The Pietermaritzburg Mothers' Welfare Society opened the Mothers' Welfare Clinic in October 1933.

Port Elizabeth

- The Port Elizabeth Married Women's Welfare Centre opened in 1933. By April 1938, the Port Elizabeth Committee had seven clinics under its supervision, two in the city, one at New Brighton, and rural clinics at Uitenhage, Addo, Kirkwood and Longmore.

Pretoria

- A birth-control clinic was established in July 1932.

Acknowledgments

This book is based on my doctoral dissertation and therefore has been many years in the making. From conducting research in South Africa in 1997 to revising the thesis into a manuscript in 2004, many friends and colleagues in Canada, Britain and South Africa have made invaluable contributions to this project. It is with great pleasure that I acknowledge their assistance.

For their expertise and encouragement I would like to thank Helen Bradford, Karen Dubinsky, Alison Forrest, Ben Greene, Janice Griffiths, Lesley Hall, Helen Harrison, Geoff Hudson, Jonathan Hyslop, Lara Marks, Jeremy Martens, Angus McLaren, Patti Phillips, Neil Roos, Marijke du Toit, and Carol Williams. Alan Jeeves provided wonderful guidance as my doctoral supervisor at Queen's University.

Heartfelt thanks also to those friends overseas whose generous hospitality and guidance in unfamiliar cities and archives made many research trips successful, including Mary Caesar, Natasha Erlank, Kate Fletcher, Julia Grey and Rehana Rossouw and the kids, Mairi Johnson and Ali Parsadoust, Claudia Kasten, Cynthia Kros and Alan Mabin, Simone McCallum, and Sandra Petersman.

I am very grateful to Queen's University, the Social Sciences and Humanities Research Council, and the Hannah Institute for the History of Medicine for their financial support during my doctoral candidacy. I am also deeply grateful to the Hannah Institute for the History of Medicine for awarding me the 2001 Hannah Millenium History of Medicine Doctoral Dissertation Award, a prize that was gratifying and sustaining in that anxious phase between graduation and employment. Finally, I am grateful to the Department of History at the University of Victoria for making me feel welcome as a postdoctoral fellow from 2000 to 2002, and to the Wellcome Trust Centre for the History of Medicine at UCL in London, where I spent many happy months as a visiting scholar in 2001 and 2002. The support and recognition of all of these institutions greatly aided me to complete this project.

I have benefited enormously from the expertise and intellectual generosity of a number of wonderful archivists and librarians in South Africa, including Carol Archibald, Michelle Pickover, and Kate Abbott at the Historical Papers at the University of the Witwatersrand Library;

Carol Leigh of the Africana Collection of the Johannesburg Library; and Nellie Somers at the Campbell Collections at the University of KwaZulu Natal. I was also fortunate to secure the research assistance of a number of talented scholars, including Felicitas Becker, Koni Benson, and Ellena Hahn.

Thanks also to those people who had been involved in the South African birth-control movement, or else knew leading members, who shared their memories and insights with me: Marcia Berger, Lorna Brounell, Mary Carson, Dorothea Douglas-Henry, Elin Hammar, the family of J.L. Hardy, Patricia Massey, Anne Ramsey, Isobel Robertson, Geoffrey Scott, Nan Trollip, and Joan Wessels. The staff at the head office of the Planned Parenthood Association of South Africa (PPASA) in Johannesburg was remarkably helpful in locating sources, for which I will be forever grateful. As an ideal example of what "the new South Africa" can be, Audrey Elster and the office staff at PPASA provided me with unlimited access to their historical documents. I would also like to acknowledge the generosity of the late Dr Elin Hammar who gave me access to the Race Welfare Society's papers and agreed to donate them to the Historical Papers at the University of the Witwatersrand where they will be available to future researchers.

During 2003 I was fortunate to be able to present papers at three academic seminars at which scholars posed stimulating questions and offered insightful comments that broadened my understanding of the political significance of the South African birth-control movement: the WISER Seminar Series at the University of the Witwatersrand in Johannesburg, the History Seminar Series at the University of KwaZulu Natal in Durban, and the Social Studies of Medicine Seminar Series at McGill University in Montreal.

I gratefully acknowledge the permission to include portions of this book that were previously published as follows: " 'Poor Whiteism,' White Maternal Mortality, and the Promotion of 'Public Health': The Department of Public Health's Support for Contraceptive Services in South Africa, 1930–1938," *South African Historical Journal*, 45 (2001); "The Imperial Mother of Birth Control: Marie Stopes and the South African Birth-Control Movement, 1930–1950," in Greg Blue, Martin Bunton and Ralph Crozier (eds) *Colonialism and the Modern World* (Armonk, NY: M.E. Sharpe, 2002); "The Race Welfare Society: Eugenics and Birth Control in Johannesburg, 1930–1939," in Saul Dubow (ed.), *Science and Society in Southern Africa* (Manchester: Manchester University Press, 2000); and "Women's Resistance to Eugenic Birth Control in Johannesburg, 1930–1939," *South African Historical Journal*, 50 (May 2004).

My parents, Willy and Karen Klausen, and my brother and sister-in-law, Steven and Debby Klausen, offered me unstinting moral support. I am fortunate to have a family that values intellectual achievement and that encouraged me at difficult moments in my graduate studies to "hang in there."

Finally, to my partner Brian Egan I offer a thousand thank yous for his steadfast patience and faith in me, his generous assistance in editing the manuscript and, last but by no means least, the fabulous cooking that sustained me in body and soul over the years. I know how profoundly blessed I am to have you in my life.

Susanne Klausen,
Ottawa

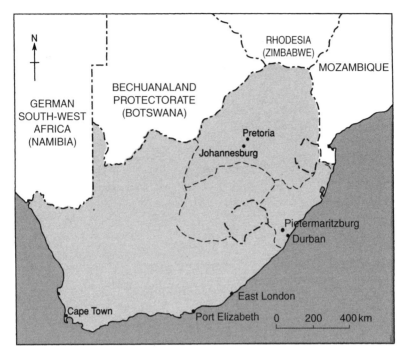

Map 1 Map of Union of South Africa, 1910.

Introduction

The existence of the white race in Africa is by no means assured, and unless we mend our ways we may go the same way in the south that the Roman and the Greek, the Carthaginian and the Vandal did in the north.

John X. Merriman, 1913[1]

I

In 1993, while an undergraduate and reproductive rights activist living in Victoria, I made my first trip to Southern Africa as the Canadian delegate to an international conference on youth and AIDS in Windhoek, Namibia. After the conference, I spent some weeks traveling around the country, which had obtained its freedom from South African rule a few years previously, and met Namibians from all walks of life with whom I chatted about my reasons for visiting their country. When I told them it was to share experiences with youth from around the world engaged in HIV/AIDS education and activism, I was repeatedly dumbstruck by peoples' comments and stories related to contraception. One young African man, for example, said he never used condoms because they were part of the CIA's plan to reduce the African population. As a student interested in the history and politics of reproduction I had read about population control in Asia but had learned nothing about it in relation to Africa; indeed, I do not think Africa had ever figured in my undergraduate studies. Consequently, his response intrigued me. Perhaps, I thought, his story was an example of gender politics; maybe he simply justified avoiding condoms by drawing on popular anti-American/imperial sentiments.

Later, on the same trip, I caught a ride with a white obstetrical nurse from Swakopmund who was soon cheerfully regaling me with tales of injecting African women who had just given birth in hospital with Depo Provera, without first informing them let alone obtaining their consent. She even described pursuing African women down hospital hallways and jabbing them from behind with the long-term contraceptive. Whether she was telling the truth or not I had no way of verifying, but what struck me at the time was her blatant assumption that a white Western woman like me would appreciate her efforts to "liberate" African women from what she considered "too many" pregnancies. Sitting in the *bakkie* as we drove across the Namib desert my mind returned to that African fellow and I wondered with keener interest what more he could have told me about the history and politics of contraception in Southern Africa. My curiosity piqued, I decided to look into these matters when I returned home.

During my graduate studies at Queen's University I found research by scholars such as Barbara Brown and Barbara Klugman that condemned the efforts from the 1960s to the 1980s of the racist regime of the National Party (1948–90) to hitch contraceptive services to an authoritarian population control program intended to curb the population growth of blacks.[2] Here I am drawing upon David Goldberg's definition of "racism" as "the irrational (or prejudicial) belief in or practice of differentiating population groups on the basis of their typical phenomenal characteristics, and the hierarchical ordering of the racial groups so distinguished as superior and inferior," a definition appropriate for the ideology and practices of the South African Government until the democratic transition in 1994.[3] By the 1970s, disenfranchised blacks, by far the majority in South Africa, were becoming increasingly militant, and the (white) political elite was ever-more anxious about the threat they posed to the state. In addition to numerous other repressive programs and practices, the Government in 1974 established the Family Planning Program to provide free contraceptives to black women, sometimes under coercive circumstances, and precious little else in the way of accessible medical services.[4] Indeed, J.H.O. Pretorius, a senior civil servant in the Ministry of Health in the 1990s, admitted to the South African Truth and Reconciliation Commission, established to ascertain the extent of human rights abuses perpetrated under *apartheid* (the National Party's policy of "separate development" for the "races"), that family planning services had been "directed at controlling the size of the black population."[5] At the same time as the state and members of the medical profession were taking steps to curb black fertility, officials exhorted whites to increase their birth rate, either explicitly or through incentives such as tax breaks for married couples with numerous children. In 1960, for example, the Minister of Bantu Administration and Development urged married white women to have babies in celebration of the founding of the Republic.[6]

When trying to trace the roots of the Family Planning Program it quickly became apparent that there was virtually no research into the history of medicalized contraceptive services in South Africa. In fact there were few studies on the history of fertility control (which includes a wide range of practices, such as contraception, abortion, infanticide and child abandonment) generally, with important exceptions such as the historian Helen Bradford's path-breaking work on the history of abortion.[7] This contrasted sharply with the rich historiography on fertility control available in other national contexts, including European and Scandinavian countries, the United States, Great Britain, and the former British settler colonies of Australia, New Zealand, and Canada, to cite a few examples.[8] Beginning in the 1970s, many historians of medicine and women in these regions were inspired by the new social history that examined social relations "from below" and second-wave feminism to investigate fertility control practices. But in South Africa critical medical historians were primarily concerned to trace the drastic deterioration of health among the disenfranchised African majority in the modern era. This political economy approach was a necessary corrective to the previous, celebratory historiography of Western biomedicine in Southern Africa, which had exaggerated the achievements of colonial medicine and overlooked indigenous African healing systems.[9] Such studies demonstrated the negative impact of the erosion of pre-colonial social systems on Africans' health and productivity.[10] Profound changes in African societies in the region were the result of epic historical processes that began in the nineteenth century, from imperial conquest through to the development of capitalist farming and mining, the emergence of the migrant labor system, urbanization, political exclusion, and segregation.[11] However, these studies in medical history paid little attention to reproductive politics, women's health, or state-sponsored preventive health policies and programs in the pre-*apartheid* era, including contraceptive services. Therefore, in 1997, I returned to the region to trace the origins of medicalized birth control in South Africa, and this book presents the findings of my research.

II

In common with the rest of the British Empire, South Africa experienced the "first round" of the national debate about birth control in the inter-war era.[12] During the early 1930s, extra-state birth-control organizations emerged around the country and, in the face of controversy and criticism, opened private clinics. Soon they sought financial support from the state and in order to lobby effectively, in 1935 they formed a national coalition, the South African National Council for Maternal and Family Welfare (SANCMFW). Only three years later the Department of Public Health (DPH) awarded the coalition a grant-in-aid of £1000 pounds that was renewed annually.

These were remarkable developments. Compared to the rest of the British Empire, the South African state was quick to support birth control. Only in Great Britain, where the Ministry of Health reluctantly approved the distribution of contraceptive information through maternal welfare centers in 1930, did the state endorse birth control at an earlier date. The South African state funded contraceptive services decades ahead of the other dominion governments: for example, in Australia and New Zealand, governments only began subsidizing the extra-state birth-control movement in the early 1970s. In Canada it was still a federal crime to advertise contraceptives until 1969.[13] The South African Government's early embrace of birth control is all the more surprising in light of the widespread stigmatization of the practice in white society during the early part of the century. As Chapter 1 shows, for two decades after Union (in 1910), the Anglican, Catholic and Dutch Reformed Churches, as well as leading members of the medical profession, condemned preventing pregnancy by using "artificial" means (contraceptive technologies) as immoral. Moreover, outspoken doctors, politicians, and other elites opposed birth control out of fear that the proportion of whites would shrink relative to the far larger and subordinate black population, putting white minority rule in even greater jeopardy. Given the conservatism regarding birth control in the early years of Union, why did the practice become acceptable in the 1930s? Why was there such a rapid shift in the dominant perception of birth control from a tainted moral issue to a respectable matter of public health policy?

To answer this question, we must understand the social and political context in which these developments took place. As Chapter 1 explains, by the 1930s, elites – industrialists, capitalist farmers, merchants, politicians, and professionals such as teachers, journalists, lawyers, priests, academics and the upper ranks of the civil service – were experiencing a crisis of confidence in the future of the young nation and their ability to maintain a "white civilization" in a region dominated numerically by blacks. Ever since Union, South Africa's colonial project had been vulnerable.[14] The state faced serious challenges on a variety of fronts, including emergent African nationalism, black and white worker militancy, a stagnating economy, a large "poor white problem," and deteriorating health among both African and white populations. South Africa was not alone in fearing national decline. Starting in the late nineteenth century, a period of intensifying political and economic rivalry between Western nations and empires, there was a palpable sense of anxiety in Europe and its colonies, at both "the outer edge of white settlement and at the centre of empire," about whites' ability to maintain imperial rule.[15] This sense of vulnerability was especially sharp in South Africa where, in contrast to other settler colonies like Australia, colonists comprised a small population in relation to the colonized. Moreover, the South African economy was uniquely dependent on the colonized majority as the source of labor on white-owned farms and in the gold mines. Even before Union, the political leadership was worried about the demographic imbalance between the races. For example, during the Reconstruction Era, the years of negotiation following Britain's defeat of the Boers in the South African War (1899–1902) until Union, John X. Merriman wrote to the Afrikaner leader Jan Smuts, "Above all we must constantly keep in mind that as Europeans we are but a handful in the face of an overwhelming mass of an inferior race."[16] Clearly, even before the formation of South Africa, whites were already experiencing a keen sense of racial and national fragility. However, the Great Depression (1929–32) intensified their anxiety dramatically. The global crisis in capital accumulation unleashed a wave of social upheaval and hardship in South Africa that led to increased cross-racial militancy among the unemployed, a rising rate of white maternal mortality, a sharp rise in desperation and hunger among Africans on reserves, and, some believed, further degeneration of the white race. By the late 1920s elites were gripped by doubts about the future of their young nation. It was the crisis of the 1930s that paved the way for the public's rapid acceptance of contraceptive services, although in ways that some readers may find surprising.

Because of the South African Government's desire for black population control during *apartheid*, one might expect that the state's initial interest in supporting contraceptive services was to curb the fertility of blacks. But this was not the case. During the interwar era, the state showed no concern for regulating Africans' fertility, let alone taking steps to reach blacks with contraceptives. This lack of interest was not because of the gold mining industry's anxiety about the "recruitment crisis" of the 1930s, as a recent study has suggested.[17] Though mine owners and the state were clearly concerned about the declining health of Africans as conditions on rural reserves rapidly deteriorated and the shrinking supply of male African workers for the mines during the post-1933 expansion of the industry, they had no interest in intervening in African fertility. Instead, the state was entirely preoccupied with regulating the fertility of an entirely different social group that was an even greater political problem, namely the "poor whites."

The "poor white problem" was the predominant social and political problem in South Africa from Union until the Second World War. The term "poor whites" referred to the rural Afrikaans-speaking whites who were pushed off the land and pulled into the cities in a steady stream from the late nineteenth century by a series of economic depressions and natural disasters. Even before Union, elites were concerned about the increasing population of impoverished whites, but by the 1920s poor whites were becoming increasingly noticeable in mixed-race urban slums where they lived "cheek by jowl" with blacks – too close to the "non-Europeans," according to their upper-class counterparts, both literally and figuratively. By "sinking" to the level of the "Native," poor whites were considered an ominous sign of the fragility of the white race.[18]

Whites who failed to attain a proper standard of "civilized" whiteness, meaning a standard of living higher than and separate from the colonized, were a source of anxiety throughout the colonial world. As the anthropologist and historian Ann Laura Stoler argues, colonial authority rested on two false premises: one, that Europeans in the colonies "made up an easily identifiable and discrete biological and social entity," and two, that "the boundaries separating colonizer from colonized were thus self-evident and easily drawn."[19] In the already vulnerable settler colony of South Africa, poor whites were living, disturbing proof of the permeability of racial boundaries, thus they shook the tenuous twin ideological pillars of white supremacy. By the late 1920s, the poor white problem had already reached crisis proportions, but the Depression, which hastened the urbanization of poor whites, greatly intensified elites' racial insecurity and loathing of poor whites, and soon there were calls on the state to take steps to limit the fertility of poor whites.

At the height of the economic crisis of the early 1930s, social reformers from around the country felt compelled to propose birth control as the solution to the perceived state of national decline. They included members holding two distinct ideological perspectives: eugenists and maternal feminists. Eugenists, the focus of Chapter 2, believed that the proliferation of poor whites was threatening the quality of the white race and, by extension, the very survival of white civilization. In 1930, a group of eugenists based in Johannesburg formed the Race Welfare Society and began promoting the perception of poor whites as inherently unfit and an expensive burden on the taxpaying middle classes. The Race Welfare Society argued that poor whites should be persuaded or compelled to have fewer children. Those who were mentally defective should be sterilized while others capable of being responsible should be taught to use contraceptives, and on February 4,1932, the group opened the country's first birth-control clinic for the purpose of reigning in poor whites' fertility.

Though eugenists opened South Africa's first birth-control clinic, they were marginal in the nascent birth-control movement in comparison to the second, much larger, ideological wing that was comprised of maternal feminists. These middle-class, mostly Anglophone women also advocated birth control as a solution to the nation's crisis, but they defined the nature of the crisis differently. As Chapter 3 shows, they believed that the main threat to the nation was the tremendous suffering to which mothers were subjected during the harsh years of the early 1930s, evident in the rising number of maternal deaths from abortion. Providing mothers with birth control, they believed, would strengthen the role of mothers in the home and thereby buttress the family and stabilize the nation. By far the most successful group of maternal feminist birth-control activists was the Cape Town Mothers' Clinic Committee, which also opened a clinic in February 1932, just ten days after the Race Welfare Society, though neither knew of the other's existence until months later. The Mothers' Clinic Committee was a liberal organization that from the start served poor white and black women, albeit in segregated sessions, as did the other maternalist groups that emerged around the country in subsequent years. Though primarily concerned with helping South Africa's mothers, the maternalists and eugenists shared elements of white supremacist thought. As Leila Reitz, South Africa's first female member of Parliament and vocal supporter of the birth-control movement told the second meeting of the SANCMFW in 1936, "There was the problem of the Native population. A white healthy life is of great value in this country."[20]

In highlighting the role of white racial insecurity in the development of medicalized contraceptive services in South Africa, this book contributes to the growing body of work on the political salience of whiteness, meaning a white racial identity, in the nation's modern history. Today it is widely accepted that "race" is a social construction. Like other categories of identity such as gender and class, race is a product of ideological and cultural struggle that is given meaning through the agency of human beings in social relations. Thus it is profoundly political in character. In recent years, historians have demonstrated that the social construction and malleability of race applies equally to whites as it does to the "others."[21] Until recently in South Africa, the thrust of radical social historical inquiry was directed towards elucidating the dynamics of black society and black identity within the context of industrialization. Social historians who were inspired by British and American historical materialists, most notably E.P. Thompson, Eric Hobsbawm, and Eugene Genovese, sought to recover the history of the marginalized, dispossessed and potentially revolutionary subjects, by far the largest number of whom were black.[22] Moreover, radical social historians tended to employ the structuralist, class deterministic analysis of their Marxist predecessors of the 1970s by viewing the arrangement of class relations on a straightforward "oppressor/oppressed" continuum, which meant they disregarded the intraracial tensions among whites of different ethnicities and classes that contributed to the construction of whiteness.[23] Studies of elites also took their subjects' whiteness as a given that did not need to be unpacked or explained. But scholarly interest in the meaning and political import of whiteness is growing, as recent work on scientific racism, whites' changing self-perception in the post-*apartheid* era, and working-class white men's experiences during and after the Second World War, to cite a few examples, demonstrates.[24]

With regards to terminology, it is crucial to understand the multiple and contested meanings of "race" that existed in South Africa the 1930s. After Union, South Africans were officially divided into oppositional categories of "European" that comprised white settlers and their descendents, and "non-European." The latter category was divided into three sub-categories: "Natives," (also called "Bantus") comprising indigenous Africans; "Coloureds," descendents of mixed-race unions between the original white settlers at the Cape, indigenous Khoikhoi, and slaves from West Africa and the East Indies; and "Asiatics," made up of Indians, Malays, and Chinese. All three groups were subjected to a range of discriminatory laws and economic forces. It is a sign of the racism of the day that such a heterogeneous group of peoples were covered by the single, negative term "non-European." In the 1970s "non-Europeans" started transcending the state's divisive racial categorization by claiming a single "black" identity out of recognition of their shared interest in overthrowing the race-based, discriminatory regime and creating in its place a just and humane society for all citizens regardless of skin color. In this book I continue this tradition and employ the term "black" to refer to these people collectively. This is not intended to overlook the varied histories and cultures within these social groups, which are referred to by their official racial categories when discussing their particular experiences in relation to fertility politics.

Though this book is concerned with a national story, it situates events in the broader context of European imperialism. In doing so it contributes to the growing recognition that in many fundamental respects South African history is not exceptional. Instead it shares numerous features in common with other colonial societies committed to settlement and was embedded in a wide set of transnational relationships. By 1930 birth-control movements were active in at least thirty countries around the world, in and beyond the West, and advocates of modern, medicalized contraceptives were communicating across national and racial boundaries.[25] These advocates were participants in a global circulation of ideas and technologies that originated in the West but quickly spread, and they drew upon international connections in their local work. By placing the colony and metropole "in a single analytic field," I analyze the intense, productive connection between the colonial advocates of birth control and their metropolitan counterpart, Marie Stopes, Britain's leading birth-control advocate in the 1920s.[26] Stopes and the South Africans had a long-lasting relationship that illustrates what recent postcolonial theorists have identified as the mutually constitutive nature of relationships between the metropole and the periphery.[27] (The South African Department of Public Health also turned to Britain for advice on birth control.) As Chapter 3 illustrates, while the South Africans drew upon Stopes for inspiration and advice, as well as for more mundane but critical matters such as obtaining contraceptive supplies, Stopes also benefited from the relationship. Moreover, in the process of looking to Britain for direction and guidance, the South Africans affirmed their dual identity as Britons as well as South Africans. On the one hand they were proud citizens in a "Greater Britain," the global British community comprised of Great Britain, India, and the colonies of British settlement, Canada, Australia, New Zealand, and Southern Africa, and they were loyal to the imperial project.[28] Yet on the other hand, their Britishness could be subordinated to their South African identity as they gained confidence in the colonial context. In addition, the birth-control advocates shared a cosmopolitan worldview and investment in modernity, for they believed they were part of a cutting-edge, progressive, international movement for "scientific" social reform.

In Chapters 4 and 5, I analyze the operation of South Africa's first birth-control clinics. I compare encounters that occurred between the clinic users and service providers in the clinics operated by the Race Welfare Society in Johannesburg and the Mothers' Clinic Committee in Cape Town. By contrasting women's response to the two clinics I highlight the importance of the ideology of the service providers. In contrast to the providers, it is difficult to reconstruct the experience of the thousands of so-called ordinary women who utilized the clinics. The primary sources for this study are the records of the birth-control organizations, the archives of the three levels of Government, newspapers, and other artifacts produced in self-conscious fashion by literate members of the middle classes and political elite. The clinics' users left no written record of their experience or opinion. Only oral history methodology can recover in any substantive way the perceptions and opinions of poor women and couples of all races who struggled to control their fertility and raise families under grinding conditions of poverty.[29] Nevertheless, reading the records against the grain provides valuable clues about women's reactions to the clinical encounter and their attempts to utilize contraceptives. These two chapters, like the previous chapter's discussion about Stopes and the South Africans, attempt to decenter the locus of power in analyses of relationships. They argue that providers did not unilaterally determine the direction of the development of contraceptive services in South Africa; women's utilization of the clinics was also crucial to the expansion of services, an argument that reinforces recent claims that medicalization is produced by the medical profession in conjunction with consumers of medical services.[30] The relationships under investigation, whether between metropole and colony on the macro-level or service providers and users on the local level, were interdependent and negotiated.

In the final chapter I examine the Department of Public Health's decision to endorse birth control (1935) and to subsidize the extra-state agencies that provided the services (1938). Of singular importance was Sir Edward Thornton, the Secretary for Public Health and Chief Health Officer of the Union from 1932 to 1938. Thornton, along with colleagues in the civil service, reacted to the (white) public's anxiety over racial and national decline by moving to strengthen the health of the population. In doing so, he was receptive to new opportunities for improving public health services, including endorsing the birth-control movement. He paid close attention to the efforts of birth-control advocates on the

frontline of public debate and their clinics. Once convinced of its efficacy, Thornton skillfully set about cultivating the public's and leading
Churches' approval of birth control, and by the second half of the 1930s
he felt able to take concrete steps towards expanding access to contraceptive services. Finally, analyzing Thornton's relationship to local birth-
control organizations challenges analyses of maternal health and welfare
policies and services that focus only on national actors and politics pertaining to their development, and take insufficient account of the local
context in which such services were often devised and implemented.[31]
In this study I try to show the interconnections between local and
national actors and their motives in the development and provision of
contraceptive services in South Africa.[32]

For years after 1910 birth control was controversial and stigmatized.
By 1936, Henry Britten, president of the Race Welfare Society, summed
up the receptive mood in Government, social welfare circles and
the (white) public when he stated at a meeting of the SANCMFW that
"the Clinics were making great progress, by getting more cooperation
and less opposition."[33] By the outbreak of the Second World War, birth
control was deemed a matter of public health. The subsequent chapters
trace and explain this rapid transformation.

1
Fears of National Decline and the Politics of Birth Control

> Some of us ... feel that we are going to have the greatest difficulty in upholding our white civilisation in this country, and this is a point upon which we must concentrate if we are going to pull through.
>
> Leila Reitz, first woman member of Parliament, member of the Interdepartmental Committee on Destitute, Neglected, Maladjusted and Delinquent Children and Young Persons, Honorary Vice-President of the National Conference on Social Work, and advocate of accessible contraceptive services, 1934[1]

I

For two decades after Union, the Government of South Africa largely avoided the issue of birth control. It did not prohibit the importation, manufacture, sale or use of "mechanical devices" intended to prevent conception. Nevertheless, the lack of legislation regulating the use of technologies of fertility control was no indication that utilizing them was socially acceptable in the settler society. To the contrary, and in parallel with the rest of the British Empire (including Great Britain and the Dominions of Canada, Australia, and New Zealand), birth control was highly stigmatized in South Africa. Sex, at least officially, was intended for procreation, not recreation, thus any method of controlling fertility other than abstinence was condemned. The Anglican Church declared its disapproval of birth control at the Lambeth Conference (the decennial international gathering of Anglican bishops) of 1908, and ten years later reaffirmed its opposition to using "unnatural" means to prevent conception.[2] The South African Dutch Reformed Church (DRC) and the

Catholic Church were equally unequivocal.[3] Until 1934, the former regularly condemned birth control without qualification and the latter continues to do so today.

It was primarily for conservative moral reason that a committee of the South African Senate considered, in 1917, drafting legislation intended to curb access to contraceptives. During the Senate Select Committee's hearings for the proposed Medical, Dental, and Pharmacy Bill, senators expressed concern that contraceptives, specifically "Malthusian sheaths" (condoms), had become far too available to whites at pharmacies and "low shops." Committee members were particularly anxious that white youths were using contraceptives for "immoral" sexual activity outside of marriage.[4] Representatives from the medical profession also voiced concern over unregulated access to contraceptives. Among the doctors who deplored the widespread, unregulated practice of birth control were such prominent figures as Dr. J.A. Mitchell, Assistant Health Officer for the Union, C.F.K. Murray, President of the South African Medical Council, W.T.F. Davies, President of the Transvaal Medical Council, and A.J. Anderson, Medical Officer of Health for Cape Town. In the words of C.T. Anderson, a general practitioner, doctors objected to making "medical men ... intermediaries for the sale of these articles," because contraceptives encouraged immorality.[5] The Council of the Witwatersrand Branch of the British Medical Association also opposed legislation that would permit the sale of contraceptives to women and men on the basis of prescriptions from doctors: "any legislation," the Council declared, "which purports to associate the medical profession in any manner with the traffic in contra-conceptives [sic] would be most objectionable."[6] Moreover, Dr. William Darley-Hartley, editor of the *South African Medical Record (SAMJ)* from 1903 to 1927, a particularly outspoken opponent of birth control, wrote numerous articles and editorials condemning the practice.[7] One doctor writing in the 1930s claimed that contraception was still so deeply stigmatized by association with illicit sex that most general medical practitioners were actually ignorant of modern methods of birth control.[8]

There was, however, an additional, distinctly South African racial dimension to the senators' and doctors' hostility at the 1917 hearings for the proposed Medical, Dental, and Pharmacy Bill. They were anxious about the ability of whites to maintain their rule over the far larger black population. After Union, whites comprised only about twenty percent of the population. The first census, conducted in 1910, enumerated a population of 5 878 000, with 1 257 000 whites (of whom about 700 000 were Afrikaners and about 500 000 were Anglophones) and 4 621 000 blacks (3 956 000 Africans, 517 000 Coloureds and 148 000 Asians). By 1930, the proportions were roughly the same: 1 801 000 whites as compared to 5 585 000 blacks.[9] Nervous about the relatively small size of the white population, senators noted the racial implications of taking steps to limit family size. They felt the number of whites needed to expand, not remain static let alone shrink, and therefore it would be in the interest of "the national well-being" to curtail access to contraceptives.[10] Doctors concurred with this view. Anderson, for one, believed that the use of contraceptive technologies was already preventing white population growth, and many of his colleagues agreed. In 1932, for example, a doctor condemned both birth control and abortion because "we have in South Africa a small white population with all the dangers of a strongly increasing black race."[11] (During the Senate deliberations, the regulation of black reproduction was never considered.) Yet in end, the Government did not pass a law prohibiting access to contraceptives. Apparently politicians and doctors could not agree on a process that would withhold contraceptives from "immoral" and selfish whites while still allowing access to medically legitimate cases, such as women who were too frail for pregnancy and men who were afflicted with venereal disease. But official disapproval of accessible contraceptives continued nevertheless. In 1931, the South African Minister of Public Health, Dr. D.F. Malan, flatly rejected a proposal by a group of eugenists in Johannesburg to open a free-standing birth-control clinic (see Chapter 2).

Of course, the moral prohibition against using contraceptives did not actually prevent South Africans from taking steps to control their fertility. For centuries women of all races and classes in the region found ways to rid themselves of unwanted pregnancies. Prior to colonization African women employed herbal abortifacients and emmenagogues to regulate their fertility, and they continued to do so for decades after Union in both rural and urban areas. Among white women, surgical abortion was commonplace by the turn of the twentieth century and perhaps the most prevalent form of fertility control.[12] In terms of preventing conception in the first place, Africans in Nguni, Tswana and Sotho speaking communities across Southern Africa practiced non-penetrative "thigh sex," though many ceased to practice this traditional form of contraception after the transition from rural to urban life in the twentieth century.[13] Among whites during the first two decades after Union, middle-class women often obtained commercially produced contraceptive technologies like the diaphragm from their private doctors; many others had them sent from Britain by mail or else obtained them during visits "Home." As for men, they could easily find condoms in urban centers, just as the Senate Sub-Committee had feared. A manager of "a large firm of wholesale and distributing chemists" told the *Cape Times* newspaper in 1939 that contraceptive appliances and chemicals were widely used by 1930: "There is an enormous demand for these things in Cape Town. Although we do not ourselves push the sale of contraceptives, we do a considerable trade ... [and] small retail chemists in side streets do an astonishing business."[14] Whatever steps white couples took to prevent pregnancy, they did so privately, secretly, and often shamefully, knowing full well their actions transgressed the moral standards of the day.

By the late 1930s, however, the attitude toward birth control in South Africa had changed dramatically. In 1938, just seven years after Malan had opposed a proposal for a birth-control clinic, and decades prior to the other dominions in the empire, Jan Hofmeyr, Malan's successor as Minister of Public Health, called on local authorities around the country to expand access to contraceptive services. Also in that year the central Government provided the nascent national birth-control coalition, the South African National Council for Maternal and Family Welfare, with a grant-in-aid of £1000 to be renewed annually. What factors led to the change in attitude toward birth control? Why did the central Government change its position on birth control from disapproval to enthusiastic support in such a short period of time?

II

The rapid shift in the state's stance was bound up in the pervasive feeling among elites in the 1930s that South Africa had entered a phase of national decline. This perception was far from unique to South Africa. As historians have shown in recent years, by the late nineteenth century, there was a palpable sense of anxiety throughout the European empires regarding the ability of the imperial "race" to maintain colonial rule. At a time of heightened competition between the European powers and of social upheaval caused by modernization, elites turned to the new racial science based on ideas adapted from Darwinism to confirm fears that the imperial race was declining. One manifestation of this anxiety in the early twentieth century was the keen interest among elites in improving the quality, and increasing the quantity, of European populations. In Britain, for example, where imperialists were nervous about lagging behind Germany in terms of fitness, the pioneering eugenist and biometrician Karl Pearson gave voice to this growing sense of dread when he imagined a global conflict in which races with superior scientific knowledge and military prowess would "overwhelm" the inferior races, which he defined as those less fit in physical and moral terms.[15]

Throughout the British Empire, fears of racial and national decline were prevalent during the first four decades of the twentieth century. In both colonial and imperial contexts, politicians, the medical profession, and other managers and participants in the colonial project were concerned about the quality of health and falling birth rates among the colonizers, and talk of "race suicide" and "race degeneration" was commonplace.[16] In Australia in 1936, for example, the National Health and Medical Research Council, established in response to concern about the declining health of settlers, declared that whites must "populate, or perish."[17] In New Zealand, settlers were fearful that white rule was vulnerable in the face of the rapidly growing Maori population.[18] In Canada, eugenists tried to stem the influx of "degenerate" immigrants that were contributing to "racial degeneration."[19]

Similar preoccupations existed in the Dominion of South Africa. During the first-third of the twentieth century, the middle classes and ruling elite were worried about the strength of "white civilization" and questioned whites' ability to maintain control over the far larger African population. They had good reason to do so, for even before Union there were serious challenges to the colonial social order. One such challenge was the bitter division between Boers and Britons that weakened whites in the face of the disenfranchised African majority. As far back as 1885 in the Cape Colony the Dutch newspaper *De Zuid-Afrikaan* warned that the two white ethnic groups must transcend their divisions and "toe one line in the struggle for existence against the natives." White supremacy was not guaranteed and it was "not absolutely certain that the colonists rather than the natives would prevail in the great struggle."[20] The term "swamping," which was commonly used in the early twentieth century to refer to whites being overwhelmed numerically by blacks, was deployed as early as 1887. After Union, threats to the young nation multiplied. In the 1910s, the state faced serious challenges from the militant white workforce, which organized major strikes in 1913, 1914 and 1922. In 1914–15 the Afrikaner rebellion against fighting for the British in the First World War, in the words of the long-time political leader Jan Smuts, threatened "the very foundation of our national existence."[21] Moreover, as discussed further below, white poverty was rapidly increasing. As Hermann Giliomee observes, the crises of the 1910s "nearly brought the fledgling South Africa to its knees."[22]

The situation only worsened in the 1920s. From the end of the First World War until 1933, the national economy was listless. The gross domestic product declined and white unemployment surged. In 1922 the Unemployment Commission estimated the number of unemployed poor whites at 120 000 out of a total of 540 000 "economically active" whites.[23] Also beginning in the 1920s the state and industrialists began to perceive disease and debility among Africans, whose labour on the mines was the backbone of the industrial economy, as a major threat to the economy. A sickly African population also raised fears of contamination of white society.[24] In addition, African nationalism became a serious challenge to the state as African political leaders, angry over blacks' political exclusion, began to organize in the cities and countryside. In 1912 the South African Native National Congress was formed (renamed the African National Congress in 1923), and in the years immediately following the First World War, Africans implemented a campaign against the pass laws and a series of strikes in Cape Town and on the Witwatersrand (or Rand), the industrial region surrounding Johannesburg. In the countryside, the Industrial and Commercial Workers" Union (ICU) emerged in 1919 as a trade union but it quickly flourished as a mass movement of protest against rural workers" poor living and working conditions. By the late 1920s the ICU had 250 000 members.[25] In the early 1920s, the "Natives," in the words of Prime Minister Smuts, had been deeply affected by the "Bolshevistic tendencies of labour" and by dangerous ideas about racial equality.[26]

In the 1920s urban whites also became increasingly nervous about being "swamped" as Africans fled rural areas and settled in cities in order to secure a livelihood. Though authorities tried to halt the flight of Africans from the countryside where their labour was sought by capitalist farmers and mines owners, they were unsuccessful. The epic process of incorporating Africans into the capitalist economy that developed in the wake of the discovery of diamonds in Kimberley in 1867 and gold deposits on the Rand in 1886 inexorably eroded Africans' pre-colonial societies. The mineral revolution led to the widespread proletarianization of African men and a massive expansion in the system of labour migration.[27] Clements Kadalie, the leader of the ICU in the 1920s, summarized the situation facing Africans: "From a comparatively free husbandman the Native has been converted into a modern wage-slave, with only his labour power to sell."[28] As rural "Native Reserves" began collapsing under the weight of overexploitation and agricultural disasters such as droughts and locust plagues, men and women fled the countryside for the cities in search of livelihoods. Alarmed, the state reacted in 1923 with the *Native (Urban Areas) Act* that designated urban centers as "white areas," allowed Africans to live in cities only if they ministered to the needs of whites, and obliged them to carry passes indicating their places of employment.[29] By the mid-1920s, J.A. Mitchell, the Secretary for Public Health, called the threat of being "swamped" by urbanizing Africans the "real racial danger" facing South Africa.[30] In 1929, anxiety over the prevalence of Africans in the cities was reflected and exploited during the notorious "Black Peril" national election. Officials also became increasingly concerned about black population growth. In 1923 the Drought Investigation Committee reported that in the Karoo (a rural region in the Cape), the white population was on the decline while the number of Africans on "Native Reserves" was rapidly rising, because of forced repatriation in combination with a relatively high birth rate.[31] During the 1920s the Government became increasingly preoccupied with the "Colour Question" – the problem of what to do with the African majority – and the "segregationist solution" assumed political prominence.

However, the greatest challenge to the viability of the new nation was the "poor white problem." "Poor whites" were a group of impoverished Afrikaans-speakers who emerged in South Africa during the uneven development of capitalism. They were descendants of the *voortrekker* (pioneer) Boers who, starting in the 1830s, migrated from the Cape Colony northwards into the sub-continent where most subsisted for more than a century as *trekboere* (itinerant pastoralists), *bywoners* (squatters and tenant labourers), or as small-scale farmers. With the advent of the mineral revolution, the Boers' rural way of life was severely undermined. The development of commercial agriculture to service the growing cities centered on the mining industry curtailed *trekboere*'s access to land, as owners fenced their properties and cut off grazing land for stock. Moreover, as the value of arable land increased, *bywoners* increasingly fell into poverty. By the turn of the century, the devastation wreaked by the Anglo-Boer War (1899–1902), the rinderpest (a cattle disease that entered South Africa in 1896), the Boers' Roman–Dutch law of inheritance requiring equal division of land among male heirs, and recurring droughts and agricultural crises in the 1880s, 1900s and 1920s further loosened the Boers' marginal hold on land. (African rural communities were also severely affected by many of these events.) Impoverished Boers, like rural Africans, were pushed off the land and pulled to the cities in search of means to survive. Unable to compete in the burgeoning industrial economy with European immigrants, who had greater education and skills, and unwilling to compete with Africans for low-paid manual labour – what they called "*kaffir*" work – the urban "poor white" failed to gain entry to the respectable white working class. Instead they constituted an underclass comprised of a fractured group of self-employed petty commodity producers, such as brick-makers, trolley drivers, casual service-providers, as well as the "truly destitute."[32] In popular and official parlance they became known as the "poor whites."[33]

The middle classes had long perceived poor whites as a threat to white supremacy because they displayed such a shocking lack of whiteness – a white racial identity based on a sense of essential difference from and superiority to blacks. In rural and urban working-class districts alike, poor whites flagrantly flouted the segregationist ethos and lived cheek by jowl with blacks.[34] "The coloured people are mixed up among the whites like plums in a pudding," remarked *The Star*, a major Johannesburg newspaper representing the opinion of the mining companies.[35] Through fraternizing with blacks, poor whites eroded the color line that demarcated white from black, as numerous commentators exclaimed. One newspaper claimed in 1916 that South Africa's slums posed double the moral and social dangers of "ordinary" slums in Europe because in them poor whites were "dragged down to a still lower level" by contact with "natives."[36] As early as 1894, John X. Merriman, the Minister for Agriculture for the Cape Colony, made it clear in a speech given to the Cape Parliament that it was absolutely necessary to instill in poor whites a sense of racial superiority, or else face an end to white supremacy itself:

> ... the European race in this country [is] the garrison. They held the country in the interests of civilization, and in the interests of good government and general enlightenment to South Africa ... The question of ... the poor whites was the most important ever brought before Parliament ... it was impossible that these people could be left alone ... .The white population was in a minority in the country, but they must be a dominant minority if they were to live there at all, and if their brethren were to sink into the slough as they saw them doing it would be impossible for the rest to maintain their position of dominance.[37]

Via intimate contact with blacks, poor whites were also considered dangerous vehicles for importing African diseases into the white community: "... increase in disease among them ["Non-Europeans"] is bound to be reflected eventually in its increase among Europeans, spreading of course from the lower strata upwards," warned Dr. P.W. Laidler, Medical Officer of Health for East London.[38] As E.G. Malherbe, a prominent

Afrikaner social scientist, stated in 1929, poor whites were "a skeleton in our cupboard, raising questions about the capacity of the ruling white race to maintain its dominance."[39] Looking back at the troubled inter-war years, the liberal Margaret Ballinger noted in her autobiography, "It is difficult now to remember or to appreciate the dark shadow which poor whiteism cast over this country in the 1920s and 1930s ... Yet it was the formative force in standardizing the relationship of black and white."[40]

Miscegenation was a particularly horrifying phenomenon for "respectable" whites whose reactions to the idea of race mixing highlight the fragility of whiteness and the "South Africanist nation" that was built on the political marginalization and exploitation of blacks.[41] To colonizers throughout the European empires, miscegenation was the clearest testimony of whites' lack of racial loyalty, for as Ann Laura Stoler notes, blurring the color line also muddied the political "boundaries on which [white] power rested."[42] In the early twentieth century managers of colonial state projects abhorred "carnal practices" that blurred the distinction between colonizer and colonized.[43] In South Africa, miscegenation also sparked fear of biological taint as elites abhorred exposing the white "race" to contact with black blood.[44] Poor whites who crossed the color line sexually were loathed, a reaction exemplified by historian C.W. De Kiewiet in 1941 when he wrote, "[t]he poor whites were on the frontier between the Europeans and the native. Through their weakness might pour a debasing stream of uncivilized blood."[45] The influential Carnegie Commission of Investigation on the Poor White Question (1929–32), funded by the Carnegie Corporation in New York to study the causes of and propose solutions for poor whiteism, lamented that the leveling effect of poverty on the races was causing miscegenation: "Long-continual economic equality of 'poor whites' and the great mass of non-Europeans, and propinquity of their dwellings, tend to bring them to social equality. This impairs the tradition which counteracts miscegenation, and the social line of colour division is noticeably weakening."[46] Yet the widespread fear of miscegenation was unfounded: by 1937 there were only 101 marriages registered across the color line, "the vast majority between white men and coloured women."[47]

In order to instill a proper sense of whiteness into poor whites, the Dutch Reformed Church, colonial, and, after 1910, Union Governments implemented a series of relief schemes explicitly intended to raise the standard of living of poor whites above that of blacks. As early as 1889, the Cape Government voted funds for an irrigation scheme in an effort to provide work for landless white farmers.[48] In an attempt to rescue the poorest members of the flock, the DRC began establishing labor colonies in order to draw them out of Babylon and "back to the land." After Union in 1910, the central Government established a series of policies and programs aimed at returning as many poor whites as possible to the land. Yet despite state intervention, rural whites continued to flee the countryside and the problem continued to swell. By 1924 the poor white problem had gained sufficient political prominence to defeat Smuts' South African Party (SAP) in the national election, as voters felt Smuts had not done enough to tackle the issue.

With the assumption of the Afrikaner National Party (NP) to power in 1924 and, with the support of the (whites-only) Labour Party, the central Government stepped up its efforts to rehabilitate poor whites. By the early 1920s it was clear that poor whites were becoming permanently urbanized, so the Government turned its attention to providing them with a "firm-footing" in the cities with protective legislation such as the *Wage Act* (1925) that offered minimum wage rates that allowed whites a "civilized" standard of living, and the *Colour Bar Act* (1926) that legalized the job color bar to safeguard the jobs of semiskilled and skilled white workers. The Government also established in 1924 the "civilised labour policy" that led to the replacement of "non-European" workers in Government-funded sectors like the harbours, post offices and railways with unemployed whites. Also in 1924 the Government created the Department of Labour with the explicit object of finding work for whites, with additional preferential legislation to follow. In bolstering the position of poor whites, the state inevitably undermined blacks' even further. Between 1924 and 1933 the number of white laborers on the railways increased from 4760 to 17 683 (from 9.5 percent to 39.3 percent of the labor force) while the number of African workers fell from 37 564 to 22 008 and of Colored workers from 5628 to 4663.[49] Appalled by these developments at a time when Africans faced starvation on the collapsing Native Reserves, the liberal historian William Macmillan in 1930 observed angrily, "[g]estures from the Government of white masters show ... that they have chosen this of all moments to decide that poor whites in particular must be protected against the "Native menace."[50]

For all of these reasons – labor militancy, African nationalism, a listless economy, the deteriorating health of Africans, African urbanization, and the intractability of the poor-white problem – elites' faith in the promise of their new nation was vulnerable by the late 1920s. Then, beginning in 1929, white anxiety erupted into fear that South Africa was in decline.

III

The catalyst that congealed white anxiety into a new, despondent discourse of national decline was the Great Depression (1929–32). Though short in duration when compared to other industrializing nations, the global crisis in capital accumulation wreaked havoc on South Africa, unleashing a wave of economic devastation, class conflict, and social upheaval. Agricultural export prices plummeted, the value of livestock products fell by half, wool prices collapsed, total income from industrial manufacturing dropped by 20 percent, and bankruptcies were common. In 1932, the value of South African goods was 38 percent of their 1928 value. By 1933 the price of maize, the country's major agricultural product, had fallen by half since 1929. The crisis, along with the prolonged drought that also struck the country in the early 1930s, compounded the already widespread poverty among black and white workers and peasants throughout the country. Twenty-two percent of white and Coloured men were officially unemployed (statistics do not exist for women's and Africans' unemployment), and poverty among Africans was endemic. Government reports warned of the possibility of "mass starvation" among rural Africans who were crowded into the desperately poor "Native Reserves."[51] As the Depression ravaged the rural economy, more poverty-stricken blacks and whites were driven off the land and, in search of livelihoods, thousands streamed into cities where they settled in already overcrowded, mixed-race slums.[52] In 1927, the slumyard population in just Johannesburg, the country's largest city, had already risen to over 40 000 and the Depression witnessed "a massive growth" of unemployed blacks and whites in the cities.[53] The white population in the Witwatersrand almost doubled between 1921 and 1936, from 230 657 to 402 223.[54] One indication of Africans' imploding rural economy was the dramatic rise in the number completely dependent on waged work in the cities, from 75 000 in 1925 to 155 000 in 1936.[55]

The economic crisis resulted in a dramatic resurgence of worker militancy, which had faded by the early 1920s. In 1931 and 1932, Johannesburg, for example, saw the greatest number of strikes in more than a decade with 6 284 and 4 011 workers involved respectively.[56] Furthermore, strikers displayed a remarkable degree of class-based, interracial solidarity, which indicated that white workers' loyalty to the white supremacist nation state was weakening.[57] As a consequence, authorities perceived the slumyards as both a threat and embarrassment, as "fertile fields" for subversive propaganda and leftist sympathizers as well as "convincing evidence of how a capitalist society failed to provide good homes for the very poor."[58] While slums had been deplored as "storm centres" of popular militancy since the early 1920s, in the economic crisis of the Depression authorities became increasingly nervous about white workers and "Native Bolsheviks" forging a class-based alliance across the racial divide.[59]

The economic crisis and social upheaval crystallized into a discourse of national decline. In the early 1930s, the idea took hold that South Africa had fallen backwards from an A1 (first class) to a C3 (third class) nation on the international stage. Fear of this dangerous development was palpable in Parliament throughout the decade and into the early 1940s. In 1934, for example, Member of Parliament (MP) Leila Reitz demanded the clearance of slums in order to segregate poor blacks and whites, which, she claimed, would "go a long way towards making our nation an A1 instead of a C3 nation."[60] But most politicians pointed to the drastic deterioration in health among blacks as well as whites as proof of national decline. In 1935, MP C. Bain-Marais, in introducing legislation compelling the medical examination of African domestic servants who were considered primary vectors of disease among whites, stated "I think the time is most opportune to examine every channel through which diseases, which may frustrate our endeavours for a cleaner and healthier nation should be examined."[61] Dr. H. Reitz, another member of Parliament, summed up the prevailing mood succinctly when he told the Legislative Assembly in 1935: "We want to make the South African nation an A1 nation. We do not want a C3 nation here, and the only way to get an A1 nation is to have a healthy population."[62] In 1942, MP Mr. Labuschagne, arguing in favor of a comprehensive state public health system, declared "if we had spent £1 000 000 per year [on medical services] we would have had a very different type of people here in South Africa today. We would have had a people which could have called itself an A1 people and which could have prided itself on being among the foremost nations of the world. Unfortunately we are not an A1 people today,"[63] and other members of Parliament, such as Dr. A.M. Moll, made a similar point the following year.[64]

During the 1930s there was a steady supply of research indicating that Africans" health was declining at an alarming rate.[65] Marks and Andersson have argued that the state's growing awareness of this health crisis was because of "medical men outside of the mines and by members of the Department of Public Health ... who were beginning to be aware of the deteriorating conditions in the rural areas and the appalling social conditions in the towns."[66] In the early 1930s the *Native Economic Commission* (1930–32), which was established to investigate the social and economic conditions of Africans in urban areas, warned that the deterioration of the reserves could lead to a poor black problem on a larger scale than the poor white problem and that this would pose a social and political threat to white supremacy.[67] Nutritional surveys taken in the late 1930s, first of white schoolchildren and then on a smaller scale of blacks, revealed a generally poor state of health.[68] In 1937 Smuts warned that "the natives of this country are becoming rotten with disease and a menace to civilization."[69]

But new knowledge indicating that whites were losing their vitality was even more alarming proof of national decline, for it suggested that the white race might soon lose its grip on the nation.[70] Statistics indicating a crisis in white health abounded. Politicians highlighted studies on the high rate of rejection of military recruits (26 percent) and the large proportion of white children, as much as 65 percent of the student population in the Orange Free State, were deemed "defective."[71] One particularly ominous sign of white racial decline was the rise in white maternal mortality during the Depression.[72] Between 1921 and 1928, white maternal mortality accounted for an average of 5 deaths per 1000 live births in South Africa.[73] By 1934 it had climbed to 5.99, amongst the highest recorded internationally.[74] By comparison, between 1930 and 1934 the maternal mortality rate was relatively low in the Netherlands (3.15) and Scandinavia (e.g., 3.74 in Denmark). In New Zealand it was 4.62; in Australia 5.45; and in England and Wales, a common reference for South Africans, it was 4.3.[75]

Concern regarding white maternal mortality dates back to the beginning of Union. As had long been realized, the main cause of death associated with pregnancy and childbirth was a shortage of medical and midwifery services for women in rural areas and for poor women in urban areas.[76] Maternal mortality in rural areas had been perceived as a "pressing" problem as early as 1911, when the King Edward VII Memorial Order of Nurses was established with the express purpose of addressing it.[77] Also in 1911, the Johannesburg Health Committee, pressed by the Women's Reform Club, hired women health visitors to visit poor white mothers who had recently given birth in order to provide medical care for mothers and babies.[78] In the 1920s, concern about maternal health grew, leading to developments such as the establishment of a chair of Gynaecology at the Witwatersrand University Medical School. In 1928 a "large conference on the crisis in maternity care" was also held in Johannesburg and that year new procedures and regulations for midwives were established by the central state.[79]

In the early 1930s, doctors began to report that there was an increasing incidence of maternal deaths from botched abortions. In an article published in the *South African Medical Journal* (*SAMJ*) in 1932, doctors noted that abortion was "a subject which has aroused considerable public interest in recent years," adding "[t]here seems to be a general opinion that the practice of intentional abortion is on the increase, and that the maintenance of the maternal death-rate at its present high figure ... may be due to this cause."[80] They also cited a study by the British Ministry of Health (1930) that estimated ten to twelve percent of maternal deaths were caused by abortion, suggesting the same could apply to South Africa. Another crucial source of new knowledge about maternal mortality was the highly influential Carnegie Commission. In 1929 Marie Rothmann, the sole female investigator on the Commission, interviewed dozens of poor white women in the countryside and vividly described the hardship they experienced during childbirth. She reported that women, often mothers and their daughters, helped each other during labor, engaged lay midwives, or else gave birth alone or with the assistance of their husbands. As she pointed out, women often died as a result of the lack of professional care. She remarked, "It strikes a visitor in the thinly populated areas that there are more husbands with second or third wives than wives with second and third husbands ... It can be readily understood ... that the family strength has been maintained by the accession of fresh mothers."[81] The rise in the number of deaths of white women contained the threat of the disintegration of the family and decline of the nation.

The threat to white motherhood became prominent and politicized. By the 1920s both Afrikaners and Anglophones regarded women as responsible for mothering the South African nation by ensuring the moral and physical health of the family. As Doctor Mathew Porter declared in 1920, "The quality of a nation's home life is one of the determining factors of a nation's strength."[82] For Afrikaners, women were *volksmoeders* (mothers of the nation) who were equally responsible for maintaining the health of the *volk* as well as the health of their own families. Anglophones and Afrikaners alike agreed on the necessity of strengthening the family by addressing maternal health needs. In 1930, Dr. W.P. Steenkamp pressed Malan, the Minister for Public Health, in Parliament to establish a commission to investigate the problem of white maternal mortality. He replied that the matter was already receiving careful consideration from the Department of Public Health (DPH), which indeed it was.[83] In 1932 the *Official Year Book of the Union* acknowledged that "Infant and maternity welfare ... have, in the past, been neglected, but during the last few years a greatly increased amount of interest has been taken in these and kindred matters."[84] Indeed, as we will see, political preoccupation with saving white motherhood would ultimately lead the DPH to support a number of national public health measures.

Related to the crisis of motherhood was the troubling news that the white birth rate was continuing to fall. In a move that signaled official concern about the implications of a low white birth rate, the DPH in 1936 released statistics demonstrating that the "European" birth rate had been falling relentlessly since 1911, shown in Table 1.1.

Nervousness over the falling white birth rate was a symptom of whites' sense of vulnerability about their numerical inferiority: in 1936 whites comprised 21 percent of the population whereas Africans were 69 percent, Coloureds 8 percent and Asians 2 percent.[85] The DPH pointed

Table 1.1   Rate of natural increase among "Europeans" in the Union of South Africa, per 1000 of population, 1936

Year	Birth rate	Death rate	Natural increase
1911	32.2	10.4	21.8
1912	32.2	10.3	21.9
1913	31.7	10.3	21.4
1914	30.2	9.5	20.7
1915	29.3	10.3	19.0
1916	29.3	10.2	19.1
1917	29.0	10.3	18.7
1918	28.6	17.2	11.4
1919	26.9	11.9	15.0
1920	29.0	11.1	17.9
1921	28.4	10.4	18.0
1922	27.5	9.5	18.0
1923	26.7	9.8	16.9
1924	26.3	9.6	16.7
1925	26.5	9.4	17.1
1926	26.2	9.6	16.6
1927	25.9	9.7	16.2
1928	25.8	10.2	15.6
1929	26.1	9.5	16.6
1930	26.4	9.7	16.7
1931	25.4	9.4	16.0
1932	24.2	10.0	14.2
1933	23.5	9.3	14.2
1934	23.4	9.7	13.7
1935	24.5	10.6	13.9

Source: *Annual Report of the Department of Public Health, for the Year Ended June 30, 1936* (Pretoria: Union of South Africa, 1936), p. 16.

out that in 1934 the white birth rate had fallen precipitously to an all-time low point. It tried to reassure the public that "European" South Africans still had a relatively high birth rate in comparison to western European countries, but this was small comfort since European birth rates were so low that they "face[d] the threat of extinction."[86] In 1937 the DPH called the worldwide decline in European population growth one of the most serious social problems of the day.[87] The cause of the falling birth rate is unclear. What is certain is that women were taking steps, either through contraception or abortion, to limit the number of children. While some commentators, such as Marie Rothmann, felt empathy for poor women's predicament during the harsh economic times of the early 1930s, others blamed "selfish" middle-class women for neglecting their responsibility to the nation to produce fit, white babies. In 1937, D.F. Malan, now leader of the Opposition and a *predikant* (minister) in the DRC, reflected the sense of crisis about the low white birth rate, and inflected the discourse of white anxiety with patriarchal moralizing about women's duty to propagate the nation:

> We notice in all countries in the world ... that the process of propagation of the different peoples has been tremendously impeded, in other words, that the birthrate is dropping tremendously ... and the most serious thing that we notice about the matter is that the rate is dropping just with those people that are most highly developed, just with the people who were the creators and exponents of European civilisation. This is an extremely serious phenomenon ... Women formerly considered it as their function par excellence and not only as their function but as their duty and honour, as their responsibility, to take upon themselves the duty of propagating and protecting the survival of the people ... I think that the time has come to make a plea that the women should appreciate their duty and responsibility for the propagation of the people. I ask whether the time has not come to take steps to help her in the fulfillment of her functions ... So in Germany and Italy they have done much to promote the increase and protection of the population by promoting family life and to make it possible for women, especially poor women, to have and to build up families. This, as a matter of fact, is a most necessary work today.[88]

Malan was not alone in suggesting in Parliament that the breakdown of the family was putting the white race at risk of being "swamped." MP Col. J. Wilkens of the United Party called (unsuccessfully) for legislation

Table 1.2   Population size and rate of growth in South Africa, by race, 1921–36

Year	Europeans	Bantus	Coloureds	Asiatics
1921	1 519 488	4 697 813	545 548	165 731
1936	2 003 512	6 597 241	767 984	219 928
% Increase	31.85	40.43	40.77	32.7

Source: *Debates of the House of Assembly*, vol. 23, April 1, 1937, p. 4042.

requiring a minimum of five children per white couple and the imposition of a tax on unmarried men to compel them to marry and start a family.[89] MP S.P. le Roux also painted a bleak future for whites if couples continued to avoid having children. First he cited statistics (shown in Table 1.2) demonstrating that between 1921 and 1936 "non-Europeans" had increased their population size at a faster rate than "Europeans." Next he made population projections for 15 years hence based on current population trends. In light of these disturbing figures, le Roux called on the Government to encourage middle class whites to have larger families:

> There is another point, which I hope the Government will give serious attention to. It is a problem which is vexing many parts of the world and especially in South Africa, I refer to the growing difference between our European and Non-European population ... At the same rate of increase in 15 years we will have about 2 650 000 Europeans, 9 300 000 Bantu, 290 000 Asiatics and 1 100 000 Coloured, making a total of 13 340 000 and in 30 years, only one generation, we shall have about 3 500 000 Europeans, 13 000 000 Bantu, 385 000 Asiatics and 1 550 000 Coloured. I think for this country that is a very serious matter and we have to consider the best means of overcoming it, whether by wholesale immigration of selected immigrants or in some other way. In my view we have too many motor cars and garages and too few children and nurseries.[90]

Yet another cause for worry regarding white racial vitality was the high incidence of white infantile mortality. In 1929 the death rate per 1000 births was 64.19 – much higher, according to the DPH, than in other "civilized" countries (meaning countries ruled by whites) and almost double the figure for New Zealand that year (see Table 1.3).[91]

Government and community leaders had long realized that taking steps to decrease the infantile mortality rate would increase the size and

Table 1.3 European infantile mortality rate
in the Union of South Africa, 1919–36

Year	Infant mortality rate per 1000 births
1919	81.81
1920	90.07
1921	77.09
1922	72.91
1923	74.42
1924	73.73
1925	68.39
1926	64.82
1927	70.63
1928	70.49
1929	64.19
1930	66.84
1931	63.07
1932	68.57
1933	61.01
1934	60.79
1935	62.81
1936	59.06

Source: *Annual Report of the Department of Public Health, for the Year Ended June 30, 1937* (Pretoria: Government Printer, 1937), p. 72.

productivity of the white community. In large part to this end, the Union Government passed the Children's Protection Act (1913) that set out to protect neglected and orphaned children by regulating and subsidizing private child welfare organizations.[92] In 1924 there were 42 child welfare societies offering a range of services, including infant consultation bureaus that provided free meals for expectant mothers, free medical care for infants and free milk for babies, and Government provided over half their revenues.[93] In 1926 the South African National Council for Child Welfare and in 1928 the DPH allocated the new coalition of 62 welfare centers an annual grant-in-aid of £1000.[94] Whether or not these initiatives had an impact, the infantile mortality rate did drop dramatically, from a peak of 90.07 in 1920 to 62.81 in 1935. Nevertheless, in the climate of anxiety that prevailed in the wake of the Depression, the drop was not enough to appease the white community. In 1937, MP Leila Reitz noted with alarm that the South African rate of white infantile mortality was 70 per 1000, almost double New Zealand's figure of 37 per 1000.[95] Such evidence convinced authorities that whites were losing their vitality.[96] The racism inherent in this concern emerges in stark relief when the rate of white infantile mortality is compared to that of the African population, which was much higher: in 1943, for example, the death rate among Africans in Alexandra (an African township located a few miles north of Johannesburg) was an estimated 380 per 1000 births.[97]

However, once again the most disturbing sign that whites were degenerating was the seemingly inexorable growth of the poor white problem. Despite decades of state intervention, the Government had failed to eliminate poor whiteism. To the contrary, during the Depression the problem worsened dramatically as the economic devastation accelerated the exodus of small-scale farmers from the land. By 1930 as many as 400 000 whites in a total white population of just over two million (20 percent) were believed to be living in destitution.[98] The swelling numbers of poor whites who were conspicuously failing to thrive in the modernizing economy deeply undermined elites' fragile belief that South Africa was a modern nation in a "progressive Empire."[99] In 1937, Leila Reitz gave voice to the widespread concern that white civilization was imperilled by poor whiteism:[100]

> We all know that the problem always at the back of the minds of everyone in this country is how to maintain ... our white civilization. Some look at the problem from the liberal point of view, and others look at it from the repressive point of view, but our aims are the same: to protect our white civilization and to give our white children that quality that will make them, shall I say, the aristocrats of this country. If we do not remain the aristocrats of this country our white civilization is doomed. This country is especially interested not only in the quantity of the children that will grow up, but also in their quality. We are vitally interested in the quality. We know perfectly well that the children of our poor lack vital energy ... and without that they will sink below the level at which they can keep themselves apart as a separate race.[101]

Janie Malherbe, wife of E.G. Malherbe, made the same point in the clearest terms while speaking to a women's organization in Victoria, Australia the same year:

> We have for the whole Union of South Africa a small population of one and three-quarter million whites, which is your population for Victoria alone. In contrast to this our black population outnumbers

the white by nearly four to one, which is a blessing as far as the general question of domestic labour is concerned, but brings many responsibilities and difficult situations in its train. The fact that nearly 400 000 of our small white population are so poor that they are dependent on state and charitable aid for their very existence, is however our gravest cause for concern. These people are known as "poor whites," a term which owes its origin to the presence of a large black population below whose standards of living that of white man must not be allowed to drop.[102]

Poor whites seemed to threaten the very basis of white rule in the young nation.[103]

Feeding the elites' sense of urgency was the growing conviction that poor whites might well be biologically inferior. Until the 1930s, agencies attempting to "rehabilitate" the poor whites interpreted their predicament in environmentalist terms. Exposure to blacks in the countryside and urban slums caused poor whites to "sink" to an unacceptable level. But during the Depression, as the poor white problem reached crisis proportions, a competing interpretation of the cause of poor whiteism arose that attributed their condition to inherent, biological inferiority. Eugenists responded to the national crisis by inflecting the pre-existing discourse of anxiety about the poor white problem with biological determinism.[104] As late as 1941 the historian C.W. de Kiewiet captured the pessimistic mood of the day when he wrote of poor whites, "at the base of white society had gathered, like a sediment a race of men so abject in their poverty, so wanting in their resourcefulness, that they stood dangerously close to the natives themselves ... If the economic historian could adopt the classification of the botanist or the biologist, he would say that poor blacks and poor whites belonged to the same species."[105] The Carnegie Commission repeatedly suggested that there were poor whites who were inherently inferior and that their numbers were growing. Marie Rothmann, one of five commissioners, remarked on the prevalence of poor whites with "subnormal intelligence" and called the "propagation of the unfit" a "very urgent problem."[106] "Unfit" parents, she stated, were breeding a lazy, stupid and criminal type of poor white.[107] Another commissioner, E.G. Malherbe, a prominent Afrikaner social scientist and catalyst in the formation of the Carnegie Commission, argued in a much more elaborate fashion that poor whites were less intelligent than the middle classes. As a result, he warned, their high fertility was threatening the survival of "Europeans." Their "lack of intelligence" was caused at least in part by bad heredity, he said, and he predicted that their rapid proliferation would lead inevitably to a drop in the general level of intelligence of the white population. This would leave South Africa unable to meet the future requirements of an industrial economy.[108] His observations were included in the *Joint Findings and Recommendations of the Carnegie Commission*:

> Poor families tend to be markedly larger than more prosperous ones, and the children of the former more often show lack of intelligence (as determined by retardation and poor progress at school). This fact has bearings on the quality of our future European population. More than half of our school children are from poor families, and not only is the development of their intelligence often hampered by unfavourable circumstances, but in some cases there are also chances of the child's heredity being poor.[109]

As subsequent chapters explain, the biological interpretation of poor whiteism ultimately lost out to the interpretation of the problem in terms of environmental factors such as urbanization and lack of education. Nevertheless, the biological argument was sufficiently legitimate in the early 1930s to mobilize eugenists to advocate accessible contraceptive services, a subject explored in the next chapter.

Soon elites began calling for a restriction of poor white fertility. In his report for the Carnegie Commission, Malherbe wrote a chapter entitled "Education, Poverty and Size of Family," which began with the statement that, "The fact that there are different rates of increase in population at different socio-economic levels of society lies probably at the bottom of most of our social and economic problems."[110] Marie Rothmann, too, remarked repeatedly on the large numbers of children in her study of women and the poor white family for the Commission. Their concern was included in the Commission's Report:

> *If this process is not counteracted and stopped* it points to a future possibility of the numbers of the lowest section becoming so large that the burden placed on the shoulders of the more prosperous part of the population ... may be too heavy to bear. ... Education and industry will have to reckon with this in the future. Similar processes are, naturally, also taking place in other countries, but is [sic] deserves special attention in our case, since it affects our relatively small European population as [the] bearer of European civilization in South Africa (emphasis added).[111]

Dr. A.W. Murray, an Assistant Health Officer for the Union appointed to the Carnegie Commission as a Research Officer to study the influence of health factors on the poor white problem, evidently also believed that the unrestrained fertility of poor whites was dangerous. In 1929 he quietly solicited the opinion of magistrates and doctors from districts around the country on the matter, and respondents urged the DPH to support birth control because, as one doctor wrote, " ... *the supply of poor whites must be arrested ...* they live and breed beyond their means" (emphasis in original).[112] Another respondent, a magistrate, was equally blunt in expressing the alarm of middle-class whites:

> The poor white has no ... sense of responsibility. He marries young and has numerous children who have around them from infancy squalor, shiftlessness and incompetence. He is not worried at all, by the number of his children. He gets free doctors, free nurses, free medicine, and he knows that the Government will find work for him and pay him for that work more than he is worth, and besides he can always ask for rations. And so it is that the intelligent citizens who have backbone and a sense of independence are restricting their numbers whilst the unworthy are multiplying beyond desirable limits. ... The early marriages and irresponsible breeding are the causes of the cancer. ... And as irresponsible and unrestricted breeding is the cause of the spread of poor whiteism, so would restricted breeding be the cure. I can think of no other cure. ... After all no woman wishes to be turned into a rabbit, which is what the average poor white makes of his wife. I think it imperatively necessary that the women be instructed in birth control.[113]

Many members of the public agreed. In 1930 South Africa had its first public debate about birth control, an event provoked by the 1930 Lambeth Conference's resolution to allow the use of contraceptives within marriage. The resolution passed with 193 votes in favor and 67 votes against (with 40 abstentions) and was essentially a pragmatic accommodation of an irreversible trend by couples to practise birth control. (None of the South African bishops in attendance voted in favor of the resolution. In explaining why, one bishop invoked whites' "civilizing mission" in Africa, claiming that permitting birth control would foster illicit sexual activity among Africans.[114]) The Lambeth Conference's amended position unleashed a bitter controversy in South Africa, as dozens of articles and letters on birth control flooded the English press for weeks.[115] One important consequence of the debate was increased public knowledge about the appalling conditions under which the poor were raising their families. For example, a member of the Child Life

Protection Society, when asked her opinion about birth control, replied:

> ... from our large experience of tubercular and other disease in families we feel that, provided birth control clinics were run under very strict control and by a competent public body, and provided those who went to them had medical certificates to show that they had a disease which made it undesirable for them to have more children, we should be able to support it ... These are people who are not physically fit to have children, but go on having them, and every child they have is liable to be born with the same disease. We have cases on our books of parents, one or both in the last stages of consumption, who are living in one room with their children, and are still having children.[116]

Graphic descriptions of consumptive mothers and unemployed fathers with large broods of sickly children led to a flood of calls for birth control for poor whites. As one letter writer to the *Cape Times* stated, "It is a heartless act to bring into the world helpless innocent children doomed to lives of misery, poverty, ignorance, and crime, owing to their parents' inability to make the necessary provision for them. Everyone, including the State, should regard the begetters of such children as criminal ... Birth Control may, therefore, be deemed to be the very first and highest of all duties."[117] Some argued in neo-Malthusian terms that having fewer children would rehabilitate the poor; others were maternalists who claimed helping destitute mothers would buttress the family and nation. All correspondents in favor of birth control hoped to stem the tide of white poverty and ill health that burdened the taxpayer and threatened the viability of the nation. A social worker summed up the prevalent fear that the poor, unfit and criminal sections of society were "flooding out the educated middle class which was limiting its families."[118] She continued:

> There is no question that indiscriminate breeding of children is directly related to overcrowding, unemployment, disease and similar social evils. These women often produce mentally defective or diseased children, who themselves marry and have children and so the same conditions are created over again. There is a most urgent and emphatic need for a birth control clinic in the City to which poor parents, who cannot afford to have many children, but do not know how to prevent them, can go for help and information.[119]

The *Cape Times* summed up the public mood with the observation that there was a general "feeling in favour of instruction in birth control to those classes of people who stand most in need of it," the poor and sickly.[120]

A minority of participants in the debate that took place in the letters section of the *Cape Times* opposed the Anglican Church's new position mainly out of fear for the future of the white race. (The Roman Catholic Church condemned the resolution on patriarchal moral grounds, arguing sex was for procreation only.) Some claimed it would lead the white race to "depopulate," or die out, by hastening the "swamping" by blacks.[121] One woman lamented that accessible birth control means "it will indeed be – as far as we are concerned – a black man's country in a few years' time."[122] Critics of accessible birth control repeated this claim throughout the decade. In 1937, a medical sociologist writing in the *South African Medical Journal* urged doctors to educate couples about the need for more white babies, not fewer, since they were unlikely to "independently understand the situation and take the initiative in sufficient numbers just to ensure the maintenance of European civilization."[123] South African "depopulationists" did not invent the discourse, they merely drew upon the terms of a debate that had raged in Britain from the end of the First World War through to the Second World War. During this period of intense international rivalry and nationalism there was widespread anxiety in Britain about the declining birth rate throughout the Empire. Between 1876 and the early 1930s, the British birth rate dropped dramatically from 36.3 per thousand to 15, and the average size of families fell by nearly two-thirds. Given the prevailing climate of anxiety, such statistics sparked the National Birth Rate Commission to investigate the problem, and its two Reports (1916 and 1920) recommended encouraging the production of more children.[124] The historian Jeffrey Weeks argues that in Britain during the 1930s the attempt to define birth control as a health issue was "stymied by a renewed anxiety over the decline in the birth rate."[125] Weeks' observation can easily be extended to South Africa. However, the unique, racialized social and political arrangements that prevailed in South Africa, gave rise to a locally specific politics of birth control, where opposition was inflected and energized by the fear of being "swamped" by blacks.

Another, intimately related, dimension of whites' hostility to birth control was the fear of "race suicide," meaning the middle classes would disappear while poor whites proliferated. Proponents of the theory argued that only the middle classes had the prudence and self-discipline to utilize contraceptives, as demonstrated by their relatively low birth rate. In contrast, poor whites were reckless and self-indulgent and incapable or unwilling to practice self-restraint. Thus, some argued, making contraceptives available would inevitably hasten the dangerous trend in birth rate differentials between the classes. In the words of a doctor writing to the *Cape Times* in 1930:

> ... the trouble with birth control was that the wrong people were using it. The people who could provide the best human stock were limiting their families to an extent which repair the wastage in population, while the people over-breeding and producing an excess of inferior children were the very people, such as drunkards and "poor whites," whom it was practically impossible to induce to use contraceptives, even if they were provided for them free ... South Africa is underpopulated, but it is children of the better-class people that we want, and it is these people, unfortunately, who are practising birth control.[126]

A member of the Cape Town Women's Municipal Association concurred with this view in a letter to the *Cape Times*: "I am afraid [birth control] is calculated to decrease the population we really want and make no difference to that we do not want."[127] She added there was one form of fertility control she *did* favor, namely "absolute sterilization of mental defectives and degenerates," and stated that most members of her association would agree.[128] Another letter writer went so far as to claim that a dropping middle-class birth rate, caused by the evil practice of birth control, was already causing the "decay" of South Africa.[129] Once again, South Africans were drawing upon a population panic that broke out first in the metropole and adapting it to the South African context. Fear of "race suicide" flourished in Britain during the first few decades of the twentieth century and was also a powerful source of opposition to the British birth-control movement.

Anti-feminists also lashed out against the increasingly prevalent practice of birth control. Some men, seemingly apoplectic over white women's acquisition of the franchise in 1930, saw birth control as women's latest move to shirk motherhood. One doctor condemned suffragists ("the shrieking sisterhood") who "threaten[ed] the overthrow of civilisation itself" by practicing birth control:

> There should be a clause in any Woman's Suffrage Bill granting the vote only to women who have done their duty by the State in producing a sufficiency of children for maintaining the integrity of the State ... Cannot women realise that their most glorious crown is that of motherhood? ... Some [women] who have written to the papers,

have given the impression that the average wife is a housekeeping nymphomaniac with social ambitions ... Let them apply to themselves the masculine test of "fitness for the job." If they are not fit to be good wives and mothers for God's sake let them hide their shame rather than influence for evil others whose ideals are higher and purer ... We want children and fine ones.[130]

In light of the intense controversy surrounding the practice in the early 1930s, the Government decided to maintain its unwillingness to endorse birth control. The DRC was still strictly opposed to birth control. Even the Carnegie Commission had made only oblique references to birth control for poor whites and the final report avoided openly advocating it. (This did not prevent Rothmann and Malherbe from becoming key Afrikaner proponents of birth control, as subsequent chapters will show.) This was likely because the DRC played such a prominent role in Commission: it was the DRC that formally requested the Carnegie Corporation to fund a study on the poor white problem in 1929 and, after the request was granted, it was the main body represented on the board of control supervising the study. Moreover, one of the investigators, J.R. Albertyn, was a *predikant*; his volume on the sociology of the poor white problem displayed the church's conservative ideology on questions of marriage, family, and morality.[131]

Given that the DRC's membership comprised four fifths of the Afrikaans-speaking population, Government approval of birth control in the face of DRC opposition would have been politically impossible. As Saul Dubow argues, for the first third of the twentieth century the dominant form of racial antipathy in South Africa was between the two white ethnic groups; it was not until the 1930s that "the definite association of race with colour" occurred and race tensions shifted in the main to between whites and blacks.[132] Even before Union, British imperialists had made known their unhappiness over the rapid population growth of the Boers and their hopes to attain numerical superiority in the nascent South Africa. Sir Alfred Milner, High Commissioner of British South Africa and Governor of the two former Boer republics, was prepared to withhold political power from the newly acquired colonies of Transvaal and the Orange Free State (OFS) until the British population dominated: "On the political side, I attach the greatest importance of all to the increase of the British population ... If, ten years hence there are three men of British race to two of Dutch, the country will be safe and prosperous. If there are three of Dutch and two of British, we shall have perpetual difficulty."[133] Milner did not get his wish, for

Afrikaans-speakers continued to predominate in the two former Boer Republics. (He also dreadfully miscalculated the "congruence between culture and class" in South Africa, as William Beinart notes; Anglophones were deeply divided along class lines, as was clearly indicated by white mineworkers' strikes in the immediate post-First World War era.[134]) Winston Churchill also evinced concern over Boer population growth. In 1906, the year before the Transvaal and the OFS were granted self-government by the British, Churchill wrote in a secret memorandum that the British Government was absolutely determined to maintain "a numerical majority of a loyal and English population" in the colonies.[135] Despite these official soundings of alarm over British–Boer demographics, the British Government refrained from implementing an official population policy in South Africa, just as it had in Britain itself. By the 1930s, Anglophones and moderate Afrikaners were united in trying to forge a bi-cultural nation based on black subordination. Therefore, endorsing birth control for poor whites – who were mostly Afrikaans-speakers – without the approval of the Afrikaners' Church was politically unthinkable.[136]

In the face of such staunch opposition to birth control, during the Depression the Government focused its efforts and resources on expanding the already-existing rescue programs for poor whites. This resulted in increased intervention in the economy on behalf of unemployed white men, the "centerpiece" of the rehabilitation policy during the early 1930s.[137] Between the end of 1929 and the beginning of 1934, the central Government more than doubled the number of unskilled whites employed by the state. White men employed on temporary works such as road construction, dam building, and the National Soil Erosion Scheme "radically increased," and by April 1933 the total number peaked at 46 453.[138]

Yet, despite the controversy surrounding it, the idea of establishing birth-control clinics had taken hold. At the height of the economic and social crisis of the early 1930s, a small but determined group of middle-class social reformers began to propose birth control as the solution to the perceived state of national decline. Members of this group shared the conviction that the nation was fragile and its future in doubt. However, birth control advocates diverged in their interpretations of the nature of the crisis. One wing was comprised of eugenists who were convinced that the problem was a race matter. They believed that the white race was losing its vitality and blamed the proliferation of "inferior" poor whites for this trend. Whites must curb the fertility of poor whites, according to the eugenists, if white civilization was to survive.

As Stoler argues, colonial eugenists in the early twentieth century were preoccupied with "the vulnerabilities of white rule and new measures to safeguard European superiority."[139] In South Africa, colonial elites targeted "degenerate" members of the ruling race with birth control in a bid to maintain white supremacy. The second, much larger wing was made up of maternal feminists (or maternalists) from around the country who perceived poverty as the main threat to the nation because of its eroding effects upon the family. Alarmed over the rise in maternal mortality, and inspired by the Lambeth Conference and the success of the South African suffragists in obtaining the vote in 1930, maternalists set out to strengthen the nation by helping its mothers, "European" and "non-European" alike. They believed that uplifting families of all races was key to sustaining the nation, and agreed that helping women to have fewer children was the best way to assist families to survive under harsh economic and social conditions.

In subsequent chapters I will discuss how these qualitatively different interpretations of the cause of South Africa's instability led to distinctly different approaches to birth control, in rhetoric as well as in practise. Nevertheless, despite their differences, in the subsequent decade the eugenists and maternalists who publicly advocated birth control together succeeded in legitimizing contraceptive services in the eyes of elites. Their work would ultimately enable the state to promote contraceptive services.

2
Birth Control and the Poor White Problem

> In South Africa, large families, often 10 to 12 and even 20 children, occur among the poor whites. It is the slum-dwellers, the feeble in will, the careless, the shiftless and indifferent who have the large families and, consequently, in the future, a larger proportion of the population will have the hereditary characteristics of these classes … In South Africa there must be limitation of the "poor white" element.
>
> Herbert Fantham, President of the Race
> Welfare Society, 1930[1]

I

Though the middle classes and ruling elite had long been uneasy about the future of South Africa, the Great Depression sparked fears that the country had begun to decline because of the rapidly deteriorating health of the population. Within the social movement that emerged in 1930 to offer birth control as a solution to the national crisis, social reformers clustered into two discernible groups that reflected distinct ideologies. One group was made up of women who believed that poverty posed the greatest danger to the nation because of its devastating impact on the family, examined in the next chapter. This chapter analyzes the second group, the eugenists that were convinced that the primary threat to the social order was "racial" in nature. Eugenists argued that "white civilization" was in jeopardy, which was threatening the viability of the young nation. Certainly the line dividing the two approaches was often blurred, as maternalists evinced complacency regarding South Africa's unequal racial order and some eugenists were genuinely attempting to eliminate poverty and suffering among whites. Nevertheless, they were

40

sufficiently different ideologically to have markedly different degrees of success as providers of contraceptive services on the one hand and, on the other hand, as lobbyists of the state.

Popular during the first third of the twentieth century, eugenics was simultaneously a science of heredity and a social movement dedicated to improving physical, mental, or moral qualities in human populations. [2] Eugenists were educated middle-class professionals who believed that science should guide social policy in areas involving human biological reproduction and population health. They also assumed that they were equipped with the requisite knowledge and skills to put biological theories about racial health into practice. Therefore they set out to understand the hereditary basis of individuals' moral, mental, and physical qualities, and then to apply new knowledge through programs and policies intended to maximize the production of the "fit" (positive eugenics) whilst minimizing the numbers of "unfit" (negative eugenics).

In contrast to the impression given in the literature, which has tended to focus predominantly on Anglo-American and German contexts, eugenics was a popular manifestation of unease over the social consequences of modernization and existed in at least thirty countries in the late-nineteenth and early-twentieth centuries.[3] As William Schneider notes, the roots of this pervasive phenomenon lay in the massive consequences of rapid industrialization (including class differentiation and related social conflicts), the extreme economic cycles endemic to capitalism, growth of government, mass urban in-migration, and the increasing authority of science.[4] Eugenics was a prime example of hereditarian thought during the early part of the twentieth century; indeed it was an expression of the biological worldview that permeated modernizing societies. As such it was a manifestation of the longstanding interaction between the social and natural sciences whose origin can be traced back to crucial moments in the development of modern science, such as Charles Darwin's assertion in *Origin of Species* (1859) that evolution was implicated in human history. Darwin had developed his theory of natural selection in light of Thomas Malthus's 1798 essay on population and *laissez faire* utilitarianism, thus biology and political economy merged in the production of the revolutionary scientific paradigm itself.[5] After Darwin, popular conservatives such as Herbert Spencer and Francis Galton adapted the theory of natural selection to explain and justify the extreme social inequality and poverty that had emerged in Britain during the industrial revolution. Thus eugenics was part of a pre-existing tradition of interpreting society in biological terms.[6]

In each national context, eugenics was articulated within the dominant political ideology, from fascism in Germany and Japan to capitalist democracy in Britain and the United States, and social democracy in Sweden and Denmark. Its tenets were absorbed and promoted by advocates as disparate as reactionary Nazi doctors and progressive Brazilian public health officials.[7] Therefore the ideological content of a eugenics movement can only be ascertained by analyzing its theory and practice in historical and cultural context. In South Africa, scholars have begun to analyze the relationship between eugenics and the entrenchment of white supremacy.[8] To date, this work has focused primarily on the development of eugenic theory in elite institutions such as the academy and medical profession whereas little is known about its implication and deployment in popular culture. This examination of eugenics in the birth-control movement helps address this knowledge gap.

In South Africa, eugenists were white supremacists preoccupied with maintaining an unequal social and racial order. They believed that the white race was experiencing a drastic erosion in quality, which, if undeterred, would inevitably render it unable to withstand "swamping" by the far larger black population. For example, in 1933 E.G. Malherbe, fresh from his research for the Carnegie Commission of Investigation on the Poor White Question, warned of such dangers in a speech that was reported by the *Star* newspaper under the alarmist headline, "Future of the White Race in Question."[9] The cause of white degeneration, he and other eugenists argued, was the proliferation of poor whites, a biologically inferior population whose growing numbers were draining the race of strength and vitality, and, by "sinking" to the level of the African, eroding the line dividing white from black. Already anxious about whites' numerical inferiority nationally and internationally, eugenists were convinced their race could ill afford erosion from within, and so they set out to curb the fertility of poor whites. In the words of P.W. Laidler, the Medical Officer of Health for East London, poor whites must practice birth control in order that whites would be fit enough to ward off "the yellow and black men ... massed in over-populated countries looking for expansion."[10]

In common with their international counterparts, eugenists in South Africa saw themselves as modernizers improving their society. Therefore they were not content to merely alert authorities regarding the threat poor whites posed to whites' racial strength; rather, they wanted to intervene in the problem by implementing programs to limit their reproduction. The organization that led the way in this endeavor was the Race Welfare Society (RWS), established in Johannesburg in 1930.[11]

The RWS initially comprised 13 professionals who came together to undertake "the study, investigation and application of eugenics with especial reference to South African problems."[12] Their leaders were Herbert Fantham and his wife Annie Porter, two highly respected scientists with considerable professional reputations. Fantham, President of the RWS, was born in England and educated at Cambridge. He immigrated to South Africa in 1917 in order to take up a position as professor of zoology and comparative anatomy at the University of the Witwatersrand. He was the founder of the Department of Zoology and dean of the faculty of science from 1923 to 1926.[13] On his own and in collaboration with Porter, Fantham produced numerous scientific papers on the heritability of physical and "racial" characteristics that they presented at meetings of the South African Association for the Advancement of Science (SAAAS) and elsewhere throughout the 1920s and early 1930s.[14] He was also president of the Eugenics Society of South Africa (ESSA), an intellectual study group based in Pretoria, of which he was a founding member.[15] In 1917 Porter established the Department of Parasitology at the South African Institute for Medical Research, and was its head until 1933. She also served as a senior lecturer in parasitology at the University of the Witwatersrand. She was dedicated to projects with a public health dimension, and was noted for becoming personally involved in her research. In one instance she deliberately infected herself with tapeworm in the course of a study on abattoirs and measly meat.[16] Together Fantham and Porter conferred legitimacy on the RWS and were instrumental in its early success.

Fantham and Porter drew readily upon the authority of science to justify their social prejudices and prescriptions. Both were extreme biological determinists who believed, in Fantham's words, that "Mental and moral differences are almost entirely due to the influence of heredity and ... are but slightly affected by environment."[17] They were outspoken in their opposition to social welfare programs, which they felt were "naïve" philanthropic measures that interrupted natural selection. Such interventions merely preserved the "unfit" in society and, even worse, aided social undesirables to reproduce their kind. As Fantham explained in a public lecture in 1930,

> In the earlier stages of civilized society, man interfered little with nature's method of selection, the result being that the incapable, the foolish, mentally or physically weak died out or were eliminated by the tribe. To-day, philanthropic measures, preventive measures against disease, better medical services have resulted in the rearing to

maturity of many individuals, inadequate mentally, physically and socially, and allowing them to reproduce offspring as inadequate as themselves.[18]

Porter was equally pessimistic: "Philanthropists," she said, "fall all over themselves to help the afflicted and obviously unfit. We have cripple schools, deaf and dumb schools, special schools for the mentally disturbed, for the truant, the thief and for all sorts of unfit. In these costly special schools, every effort is made to do the often impossible and turn the inadequate into adequate citizens."[19]

Both scientists reflected and fostered middle-class fears that whites were in jeopardy of losing, in Fantham's words, their position as "torch-bearers of progress and civilization" as a result of the rapid growth of poor whites. They shared the ideology promulgated by the conservative English Eugenics Society that, as the historian Greta Jones explains, accounted for poverty not "in terms of economic or social structure" but as "the natural consequence of the existence of a stratum of low mental endowment."[20] They extended this theory to South Africa where they biologized poor whiteism, explaining the presence of inferior whites in terms of their innately low intelligence. Alarmed by the fall in the white birth rate among "the more educated and better paid classes" while poor whites seemed to them to breed uncontrollably, the two scientists sought to ensure the rational selection of superior qualities in society. Their solution was a two-pronged strategy. First they would bring contraceptive knowledge and technologies to poor white women with sufficient intelligence to utilize them; and second, they urged authorities to approve the sterilization of the mentally unfit, the so-called "feebleminded." As Fantham declared in 1930, "Only the nobler, more intelligent, energetic and healthier citizens of the present should be the ancestors of future generations."[21] Porter concurred: "The State needs all the *good* children it can get. But it does not need the under-nourished, mal-adjusted brood of the overworked and under-paid slum dweller or the feebleminded, and so the woman eugenist would extend to them the knowledge of birth control" (emphasis in original).[22]

During the 1920s, this husband and wife team garnered little support for eugenics. The Great Depression, however, with its attendant social and economic crises created a far more amenable ideological climate. In 1930, the year the Depression hit South Africa, their message began resonating among the middle classes. Soon others were inspired to work with them, such as Edward Mansfield, a prominent and active member of the RWS whose interest in birth control was motivated solely by the desire to limit the fertility of social undesirables. It was he who instigated the formation of the RWS and recruited Fantham and Porter to lead it.[23] He was closely involved in establishing the RWS's first birth-control clinic in 1932 and was central to the formation of the South African national birth-control coalition in 1935. Other key members were respected liberal social welfare reformers, such as Henry Britten (1878 –?) and John Lawton Hardy (1879–1941). Britten, chair of the RWS from late 1932 until 1944, was Chief Magistrate of Johannesburg until he retired in 1932 and thereafter pursued on a full-time basis his self-described hobby of social welfare work, a passion that appears to have been bound up with his long-standing involvement in the Anglican Church. He was awarded a prestigious Coronation Medal in 1937 for philanthropy.[24] Hardy was the RWS's treasurer and auditor.[25] He was a founding member of the Johannesburg Board of Charities and was active in the South African Institute for Race Relations as well as other social agencies interested in "Native" welfare.[26] He also took a leading role in the establishment of the Rand hostels for (white) juvenile delinquents in need of housing and employment. Years of combating juvenile delinquency probably stimulated his interest in birth control, for he believed that delinquents were created in unstable homes comprised of poor families with too many children. Hardy was sufficiently prominent in social reformist circles to be appointed treasurer of the 1936 National Conference on Social Work.

The medical profession was also well represented from the start: at the 1932 annual general meeting, eight of the fifteen members elected to the RWS's executive were doctors.[27] Because the group wanted to promote birth control, a controversial undertaking in the early 1930s, it courted the participation of sympathetic doctors who could help win the support of the medical profession and the Department of Public Health (DPH).[28] It also sought the approval of the South African Medical Council before it engaged medical staff to devise clinic procedures, manage clinics, and train District Surgeons in contraceptive techniques.[29] Moreover, the RWS sent pamphlets to all District Surgeons in Transvaal and the Orange Free State inviting them to visit its birth-control clinic (which many did), and requesting that they send eligible women (namely married poor whites) to Johannesburg for contraception.[30] For their part, doctors agreed that birth control would mitigate the social problems that contributed to the nation's decline, such as poor whiteism and the high maternal mortality rate, and believed that contraceptive services should be placed firmly under their profession's control.

There were a number of ideological threads that bound members of the RWS together into a relatively cohesive whole. First, they shared an assumption of race and class superiority that was broad enough, if not uniformly deep, to accommodate the extreme views of someone like Fantham as well as liberals like Hardy. Second, they held in common a worldview that explained social problems in biological terms, though there was a distinction between those who did so in an intellectually systematic, rigorous fashion and others who were merely fellow travelers. Third, all wished to intervene in their society's massive problems and combined a common concern to stabilize the existing social order with a genuine, deeply felt desire to eliminate human suffering. Fourth, they shared a faith in the efficacy of science over politics and religion as the arena in which to pursue their social goals. Finally, members perceived themselves as participants in an international, progressive social movement. Fantham, for example, represented South Africa to the International Federation of Eugenics Organisations, and members followed developments in eugenics and birth control overseas and collected works by Margaret Sanger, the American birth-control activist.[31] Simultaneously they, just like the maternalist birth-control activists elsewhere in the country, saw themselves as imperial citizens of a Greater Britain. The RWS named its first birth-control clinic the Women's Welfare Centre, the name given to the Malthusian League's clinic that opened in London in 1921 and was in touch with the English Eugenics Society and the National Birth Control Association, both of which sent upon request pamphlets for circulation in South Africa.[32]

Initially the RWS also found a popular audience; 318 people attended its first annual general meeting in 1931, and 220 people the following year.[33] In this period it mounted an impressive propaganda campaign by promoting eugenics at public lectures on subjects ranging from the ethics of birth control to the inheritance of mental defect, events that were also well-attended and widely reported.[34] The popularity was a reflection of the widespread anxiety provoked by the Depression that quickly congealed into acute loathing of poor whites. The popularity of this sentiment points to the fragility of whiteness in this period, for the increasing number of members of their race "sinking" to the level of blacks suggested that a white racial identity was weak and vulnerable to absorption. At the same time, it was a manifestation of the middle classes' deep resentment at having to subsidize this failing population that appeared to be incapable of attaining a proper sense of whiteness regardless of the extent to which public assistance was given them.

As noted in the previous chapter, public relief schemes had been developed for poor whites streaming to the cities even before Union in 1910, and yet the problem only grew in size during the course of the 1910s and 1920s, much to the frustration of taxpayers, especially those in Johannesburg. By 1920 there were 2300 unemployed white men on the Witwatersrand (or the Rand), with an additional 750 on relief works, largely the result of a major drought affecting the country and extensive lay-offs in the mining sector. Unemployment continued to rise as a depression set in. According to the Inspector for White Labour for Johannesburg that year: "Although the various relief schemes inaugurated by the Government absorbed a large number of men out of work on the Rand, the places of these men have been more than filled again by new arrivals from the outside Districts."[35] Then, in 1922, a major mine strike broke out on the Rand that lasted for months. By 1922 the Rand Aid Association was providing charity relief for 25 000 people per week, until the mining industry began to improve in August of that year.[36] The situation worsened again in 1923 when drought and locusts caused havoc for rural whites in the western Transvaal, creating another major wave of immigrants to the Rand. By 1927, municipal authorities estimated that over 40 000 people were living in Johannesburg's slums.[37] Then, during the Great Depression, white unemployment skyrocketed again. Among men in the city, unemployment rose over 400 percent between 1926 and 1932–33 (from 17 000 to 72 000).[38] In 1930 alone the Rand Aid Society received over 200 requests each month for employment from whites newly arrived to the city.[39] By 1932 the rate of rural white impoverishment in South Africa was most rapid in the Transvaal.[40] Their extreme poverty was shocking to respectable residents with a fragile sense of whiteness. One family was described by an Anglican missionary doctor in 1930 as "living in native hovels, the father out of work, the mother lying in bed with acute rheumatic fever and heart disease, and six children fed only on mealie meal, one of which lives on a mattress in the corner of the room covered with flies and prostrate with pneumonia."[41]

As the slum problem grew, middle-class resentment intensified. Because the city's fiscal base was small – taxes on mining and manufacturing industries went to the central state – the burden of providing municipal services for a growing population of poor whites fell on increasingly impatient whites that owned homes in the city. Taxpayers were also stridently opposed to the slums because they dragged down property values.[42] In 1933, white ratepayers in Doornfontein, a working-class district close to downtown, were on the "verge of a revolution" because slum conditions had degenerated to a shocking degree.[43]

In addition to the seemingly inexorable poor white problem, residents of Johannesburg watched nervously as blacks began once again to organize during the late 1920s. Even more alarming, poor whites and blacks started protesting against their harsh situation in mixed-race demonstrations. In 1928, industrial unions representing black workers on the Rand banded together to form the Federation of Non-European Trade Unions that had 10 000 members in the clothing, mattress, furniture, meat, dairy, and numerous other industries.[44] The following year a demonstration of 4000 people of "every colour and nationality" marched through the streets of the city.[45] In 1931, 3000 black and white workers took to the streets demanding bread and jobs before clashing with police, and in 1933, 2000 unemployed workers of all colors staged another mass protest.[46]

Moreover, the black population was growing rapidly on the Rand during the 1930s, fuelling elites' insecurity and stimulating an openness to eugenic ideas. After 1932, the push of extreme rural poverty and the pull of a growing number of manufacturing and other semi-skilled jobs (the result of South Africa's booming economy beginning in 1933) caused a rapid influx of Africans to the Rand. In the southern Transvaal, the African industrial labor force grew from 36 153 to 80 722 between 1932 and 1936.[47] Between 1928 and 1936, the number of African women on the Rand almost quadrupled, rising from 29 000 to 107 000; the number of white women rose moderately by comparison in the same period, from 112 000 to 196 000. (There were only 15 000 coloured women on the Rand by 1936.) By 1936 there were more blacks than whites in Johannesburg.[48] This intensified racial interaction in the crowded slums, which heightened fears of miscegenation that Fantham claimed would "dilute the creative energetic blood" of whites and result in an inferior "hybrid" coloured population that "has not the energy nor the persistence of the white."[49]

The RWS tapped into whites' anxiety and resentment, and Fantham was particularly effective at voicing and exploiting such sentiments. In 1930, for example, he vilified poor whites at a public lecture in no uncertain terms:

> The less socially adequate are those largely temperamentally unfit, the careless, inefficient, idle, intractable, slack and self-indulgent. In South Africa we have the poor whites ... forming about eight percent of the population. These less fit do not sustain their burdens themselves, but they are passed on to the community in unemployment doles, free meals at school, payment of less than their fair share of taxation, etc.[50]

Fantham became a national authority on the cost to the taxpayer of supporting poor whites. In 1934, for example, a doctor cited him in the *South African Medical Journal*: "Professor Fantham, of Witwatersrand University, has stated that approximately £5 000 000 out of an annual Budget of £32 000 000 is spent in the endeavour to cope with the socially inadequate."[51] Members of the RWS explicitly appealed to taxpayers' frustration at public events by arguing that a lower poor-white birth rate would reduce the burden of taxation imposed by government to provide for the diseased and improvident. James Davidson, a member of both the RWS and Rand Aid Society, for example, reported that one poor white family who was dependent on charity "had cost the Rand Aid Society £1000 to support since 1910."[52] Birth control, promised the eugenists, would change all that. Anxious to apply eugenics as soon as possible, the RWS immediately made opening birth-control clinics their top priority. As the 1934 annual report of the RWS noted, "Members hardly need to be reminded that the Race Welfare Society is eugenic in intention and that its main purpose is to secure the physical and mental betterment of the race. To achieve this aim the most practical course appears to lie in the wise direction of the Birth Control movement."[53] Birth control was the single most important way to "lessen the stream of recruits to the poor-white class" and the number of feebleminded, who were "a scandal and menace to the community."[54] As Fantham bluntly explained, "Eugenists desire that the unfit shall not procreate and that their taint shall die with them."[55]

II

In February 1931 the RWS informed the DPH of its intention to open a birth-control clinic for social undesirables, for eugenic reasons discussed above; women's needs were never mentioned. But the Minister of Health, D.F. Malan, opposed the proposal, likely for moral reasons; Malan was a puritanical *predikant* in the Dutch Reformed Church (or DRC).[56] However, the Secretary for the DPH, Edward Thornton, was receptive to the idea, for he thought birth control might mitigate poor whiteism and white maternal mortality, both of which were high pro-file health problems demanding the Government's attention. Therefore, Thornton suggested that the RWS open what he called an Outpatient Gynecological Clinic where mothers could obtain medical attention for **all** their gynecological problems; distributing contraceptives would only be one aspect of the proposed clinic's services.

With his counter proposal, Thornton, not the RWS, raised the issue of maternal health. Unlike contemporary birth-control movements elsewhere, such as the United States, Britain, and Germany, and even other South African birth-control organizations such as the Cape Town Mothers' Clinic Committee, the RWS initially lacked a feminist component. Certainly some members of the organization, as well as of the public at large, were attracted to the RWS in hopes it could mitigate the high white maternal mortality rate afflicting South Africa. At the inaugural public meeting, for example, a medical member of the RWS told the audience that birth control was necessary in light of the "appalling maternal and infantile death rate" in South Africa, which was double that of New Zealand.[57] The following year another member of the RWS, the Labour Party Member of Parliament Geoffrey Hills, reported that the working class had nowhere to go to obtain birth-control advice and as a result "the health of thousands of women suffered."[58] Henry Britten also added his voice to the chorus when he declared that "Women ... should have the right to say whether or not birth control should be practiced."[59] In 1936, the RWS affiliated with the South African National Council of Women, suggesting that it had evolved into a maternal health organization during the course of the decade.[60] However, in its initial dealings with the DPH, the RWS evinced no concern for women *qua* women. The shift in mandate to include a focus on maternal health was imposed on the RWS by the DPH.

Anxious to meet with the DPH's approval, the RWS amended its strictly eugenic mandate and incorporated all of Thornton's suggestions. As a result, the RWS's clinics provided gynecological health care for women seeking contraceptives by referring them to clinics for venereal disease as necessary. Nevertheless, in its revised mandate the RWS managed to retain its primary emphasis on negative eugenics: "The Centre [will] serve the purpose of (a) *Counselling mothers of subnormal physique or intelligence*, (b) Giving advice on contraceptive measures when required in the interest of the Mother's health and the well-being of the family, (c) A clearing house for cases of disease requiring medical or surgical care, (d) Introducing Mothers to Societies which provide post-natal aftercare" (emphasis added).[61] In a landmark step, the RWS opened South Africa's first birth-control clinic, the Women's Welfare Centre for white women, on February 4, 1932 in downtown Johannesburg. The clinic's operation is examined in Chapter 4.

In the climate of anxiety over "race suicide" and "swamping" by blacks, the creation of the RWS's first clinic was controversial. In his appearance before the Commission Appointed by the Provincial

Council in 1933 to enquire into the work of charitable organizations, Edward Mansfield was asked by commissioners "whether further spread of Birth Control information might not reduce the Birth rate among well-conditioned families."[62] Mansfield replied that the RWS considered a birth-control clinic for the impoverished "to be all the more necessary" in order to counterbalance the widespread use of contraceptives among the better classes. He also stated "personally he could not imagine why diminution of [the] subnormal class should be accompanied by diminution of the Super-normal class."[63] As the RWS bluntly explained a few years later, "We are faced with the startling fact that whilst all social classes from the well-to-do to the very poor are practicing ... spacing and regulation of their families, the retarded and feeble-minded are left to perpetuate their unhappy kind in ever increasing numbers."[64] Another sign of the controversial nature of birth control was the RWS's complaint in 1935 that some newspapers in Johannesburg would not accept advertisements for the Women's Welfare Centre.

In its defense the RWS emphasized users' extreme poverty, reporting, for example, that "a large portion of clients was unable to pay the modest clinic fee."[65] Indeed, the RWS provided little else in the way of biographical information about the white women who attended the Women's Welfare Centre beyond their material circumstances. Typical RWS reports claimed that "practically all the women assisted belong to the very poor class – the class which the Centre was designed to help."[66] The RWS also observed that, "A large number of the [users'] husbands belong to the ranks of the unemployed. It is obvious that in many of these cases the birth of more children would have thrown an additional burden on the State and the various charitable organizations. Meantime, the mothers, already hard put to maintain the existing families, are relieved of the incessant fear of 'another mouth to feed.' "[67] In his presentation to the Medical Council of South Africa in Cape Town in 1934, Dr. I.J. Block, a member of the RWS, also emphasized women's economic distress, reporting that 25 percent of the Women's Welfare Centre users' husbands were unemployed and remarking that this was a very common and "laudable" reason women gave for wanting to avoid pregnancy.[68] The RWS also tried to reassure the public that it did not serve women "anxious to avoid parenthood for selfish reasons."[69] Instead, as R.F.A. Hoernle, president of the RWS, claimed at the 1939 annual general meeting, "healthy Mothers have more children and the ultimate aim of our Society is to keep mothers healthy."[70] The RWS also exhorted fit and prosperous whites to have larger families; by the decade's end it still wanted 'healthy, well-conditioned people' to have larger families.[71]

Thus it claimed that the Women's Welfare Centre was of "National, as well as Individual benefit."[72]

Despite ongoing public suspicion towards birth control, the RWS found approval where it most wanted it: with the DPH. Dr. E.H. Cluver, an Assistant Health Officer for the Union, visited the RWS's Women's Welfare Centre a few months after it opened and expressed his "appreciation of the work being done," which was extremely gratifying to the RWS.[73] Moreover, during the course of the decade the RWS forged fruitful institutional linkages with other social welfare agencies, members of parliament, and the Department of Social Welfare, and received regular coverage in the press.[74] By 1939 the Children's Aid Society, Rand Aid Society, and District Nurses Association were sending the RWS names of women deemed appropriate for birth control.[75] Also in 1939, at the RWS's annual general meeting, Cluver, now Secretary for Public Health and Chief Medical Officer for the Union, once again paid a compliment.[76] At that meeting, Dr. Henry Gluckman, a member of Parliament and leading exponent of expanded public health services in South Africa, expressed his appreciation of the RWS's work, saying he supported it on "social grounds" and thanking Cluver for his "wise support" of the organization.[77] Endorsements were accompanied by financial support. Beginning in 1934 the city council of Johannesburg made annual grants to the RWS and in 1938 Dr. A.J. Milne, the Medical Officer of Health for Johannesburg, joined the RWS's executive.[78] In sum, by the late 1930s the RWS was perceived as a legitimate public health and social welfare organization by official and private social welfare agencies. Its growing credibility was symbolized most vividly by the decision in 1940 to move the Central Clinic (as the Women's Welfare Centre was renamed in 1937) to the newly built Welfare House at 158 Fox Street in order to facilitate cooperation with other social service agencies.[79]

In Afrikaner circles, Malherbe was also finding success in promoting eugenic birth control. After completing his work for the Carnegie Commission, Malherbe set out to win the approval of the DRC for birth control. This was after a few years of actively promoting contraception at public events by arguing in eugenic terms that "the poor and weaker classes" should restrict their fertility. In 1932, for example, he presented his findings on the dangers of poor white fertility to the annual meeting of the SAAAS, and the meeting passed "by a large majority" a resolution, proposed by Fantham, urging the DPH to establish birth-control clinics in rural and urban areas as a means of social reform.[80] The joint effort of Malherbe, a moderate Afrikaner nationalist, and Fantham, an Anglophone, to promote eugenic birth control for poor whites illustrates how little separated middle class members of the two historically antagonistic white ethnic groups regarding the poor white problem. Both were committed to maintaining white supremacy and both believed doing so required curbing "inferior" poor whites' fertility. Racism and class resentment combined to create common ground between eugenists regardless of ethnicity.

In addition to speaking to the SAAAS, Malherbe spoke at the annual meeting of the Pretoria birth-control clinic (established in 1932 and of which his wife Janie was a member), where he made "a powerful plea for the use of birth control as a potent weapon" to stop the advance of poor whites. Otherwise, he warned, "the white race in South Africa would lose that stamina and virility so essential for the maintenance of a white civilisation." The "crude" preoccupation with "mere quantity" of whites, he said, must give way to concern about quality:

> To be lured into condoning or even approving the high birth rate in the poor white population ... because on purely quantitative grounds we fear a dwindling white population, is to make the most danger-ous of all errors. We say this particularly because we recognize the fact that we are in South Africa a small white population living in the midst of overwhelming numbers of a black population. The thing which will enable us to survive culturally, as well as physically, is quality rather than mere quantity.

His speech was reported in the *Rand Daily Mail*, a major daily newspaper in Johannesburg, under the headline "White South Africa in Danger," as well as in the *Afrikaans Die Volkstem*.[81]

Then, in 1934, Malherbe persuaded the DRC to end its opposition to birth control. This was a major victory for those trying to rehabilitate contraceptive services from a tainted moral issue to a respectable public health matter. Malherbe, the son of a DRC minister, approached leaders of the DRC and urged them to cease condemning contraception. In response Reverend Paul Nel, Moderator of the Dutch Reformed Synod of the Transvaal (and Malherbe's father-in-law), invited him to address a closed session. With statistics and diagrams from his research for the Commission in hand, he argued before the "august, black-coated assem-bly" that there was a causal relationship between large family size and low intelligence among the poor whites.[82] Their unbridled fertility was eroding the quality of the white race, an "urgent matter for our *volk* ... [because of] the presence of the Native." He suggested that the Church continue to condemn abortion but endorse contraception for those poor whites with sufficient intelligence to practice it; for the certifiably "mentally deficient" who could not be segregated he suggested forced sterilization.[83] A debate followed after which the Synod voted "by a large majority" to refrain from passing the usual motion condemning birth control.[84] Moreover, the Synod struck a commission on birth control that concluded contraceptives were appropriate in cases in which a woman's life was in danger, a mother had given two consecutive births to children who were either blind or disabled, or a mother's children were underfed.[85] By 1937, all synods of the DRC had approved of birth control. The Transvaal Synod's precedent-setting findings reflected the work of Marie Rothmann, a eugenist and maternalist (see Chapter 6), and Malherbe in trying to convince the Afrikaner community to support birth control. Malherbe continued to raise the alarm over the high birth rate among poor whites in subsequent years. In 1938 he gave a speech to the Pretoria Women's Club and said " … it should be remembered that in South Africa we have a white population living next to a large black population. We must stress the quality of the race rather than the quantity," and the *Star* agreed.[86]

III

While eugenists were clearly making headway in their efforts to legitimize birth control for racist reasons, they had much less success with the other half of their two-pronged strategy to curb poor whiteism, namely to promote forced sterilization of the feebleminded. Throughout the decade, the RWS tried to convince authorities and the public at large that sterilization was necessary, both on its own and through the South African National Council of Maternal and Family Welfare (the SANCMFW). In 1936 a member of the RWS declared that birth control was insufficient to curb the spread of "inferior elements." Segregation and sterilization of the feebleminded, drunkard and "habitual criminal" were also necessary; for the sake of the race, according to the speaker, "some individuals must suffer for the benefit of all."[87] The RWS referred optimistically to the trend towards public support for sterilization in other countries and, in conjunction with the National Council for Mental Hygiene, held a symposium on voluntary sterilization at the University of the Witwatersrand on October 29, 1941. It also called on the Union government to establish a commission to look into developing a sterilization program.[88]

At the first meeting of the SANCMFW in 1935, the RWS proposed a resolution in favor of sterilizing "mental defectives," but the coalition did not agree, apparently because members were not certain of the legality of the procedure. At the next year's meeting, held in Pretoria, the organizing secretary of the National Council for Mental Hygiene "spoke of the need for sterilization in certain cases of feeble minded persons released periodically from institutions." Henry Britten followed the speech by asking the Council to endorse the statement that "where necessary, sterilization should be a condition for the periodic release of feebleminded persons from institutions." This time the statement was endorsed unanimously.[89] The next year, Edward Mansfield met with Ursula Scott, chair of the SANCMFW, and together they wrote to Edward Thornton suggesting the DPH assist them in reaching the "feeble-minded" with birth control.[90] Finally, at a 1938 meeting, the RWS put forward a broader resolution requesting the DPH consider sterilizing the "unfit." The motion was endorsed by Dr. P.W. Laidler, the Medical Officer of Health for East London, and again the Council unanimously agreed.[91] Nevertheless, nothing came of their efforts. Eugenists in Britain failed to win approval for the forced sterilization of the mentally unfit and so, given how closely the South African DPH followed British health policy (see Chapter 6), it is highly unlikely that the South African Government would ever allow such a controversial policy. Among the general public, the response was mixed. While some considered it desirable and necessary in such desperate times, others, especially representatives of the Catholic Church, were vocally and vehemently opposed. An anonymous letter by a self-identified Catholic to the *Cape Times* illustrates this view:

> Those who would justify this operation because thereby mental defectives are averted are clearly followers of the maxim that "the end justifies the means." Although a virile race, produced in consonance with the basic principles of morality, is much to be desired, yet the existence of mental and physical weakness afford the healthier an opportunity of showing solicitude and being of kindly service. These virtues grace mankind more nobly than does mere animal perfection. It is un-Christianlike to regard the weak-minded as a national burden or a nuisance.[92]

Ironically, while it steadily succeeded in attaining respectability for birth control, the RWS did not sustain the level of popular support it had enjoyed during the volatile years of the Depression. There were fewer public lectures after 1932, which in turn were attended by smaller audiences. The novelty of eugenics had clearly faded and popular interest in the RWS flagged as a result. Part of the reason can be attributed to the departure of Fantham and Porter for Canada in order for Fantham to take up a new position at McGill University. This deprived the RWS of a charismatic leader who was capable of effectively communicating eugenic ideas to a nonscientific audience. As Dr. Laidler lamented, "Our only prominent eugenist has had to remove to Canada to find a more congenial atmosphere."

However the main reason for the tapering off of interest in eugenics was likely economic. By the end of 1933 the financial crisis was over and the economy was once again expanding. With the return of relative social stability and prosperity, concern about poor whiteism decreased. Between 1932 and 1939, well over 100 000 whites found employment, and by the end of the decade the poor white problem was visibly shrinking, though it did not disappear until the mid-1950s when the rural exodus of whites had ceased almost completely.[93] In addition, beginning in 1933, Johannesburg City Council implemented slum clearance and a subsidized housing scheme for whites. Between 1933 and 1936 City Council cleared parts of numerous slums, including Vrededorp, Fordsburg, and all of Doornfontein, neighborhoods targeted for birth control by the RWS. Blacks were increasingly relocated to locations outside the boundaries of the city and in 1937a harsh set of amendments to the Urban Areas Act was passed that restricted Africans' access to the city. There was clearly less mixing and mingling among poor blacks and whites as the decade wore on and consequently whites were no longer in a panic over miscegenation or mixed-race political resistance. Indeed, Johannesburg's revenues increased so quickly and to such an extent after 1933 that the Ratepayers Association actually requested a reduction in township rents for blacks.[94] All in all there was less of an appetite for biologizing the poor whites.

At the same time that the eugenic message was losing its audience, the RWS began to evince concern for maternal health of women of *all* races in Johannesburg. Three new members who joined the RWS in 1934 were crucial to the organization's shift towards maternalism and liberalism. Elsa (Sallie) Woodrow, A.W.(Winifred) Hoernle and her husband R.F.A.(Alfred) Hoernle were all directly involved in opening clinics for Coloured, African, and Asian women during the second half of the 1930s. Woodrow (1900–1996) was a doctor and feminist who had been instrumental in establishing the Cape Town Mothers' Clinic which opened on February 15, 1932, a mere eight days after the RWS's Women's Welfare Centre (neither organization knew of the other's existence until several months afterwards). From the start, the Cape Town clinic was open to white and Coloured women, albeit in segregated sessions, a distinction of which Woodrow long remained proud (see Chapter 3). She imported her relatively colourblind approach to birth control to Johannesburg during the two years she resided there, from 1934 to 1936.

The Hoernles were leading liberals on the Rand. In the 1920s, in the face of growing African militancy, a liberal reform movement emerged there to direct Africans away from political activity and towards "innocent" leisure pursuits such as sports and games. Groups such as the Bantu Sports Club and Bantu Men's Social Centre were organized by liberals who were intent on philanthropic "rescue" of Africans by improving their health and housing conditions as well as depoliticizing the African political leadership.[95] Liberals were influential in developing segregationist ideas during the interwar years. They were uncomfortable with scientific racism but felt that assimilation was incapable of arresting the physical and moral decay of Africans that resulted from their contact with urban life. Their anthropological notions of culture meant that they saw Africans as intrinsically different on cultural rather than biological grounds and believed contact between Africans and whites to be destructive to the former.[96] Liberals never resolved the ideological challenge posed by segregation and some, like Alfred Hoernle, became openly resigned to its inevitability.

The Hoernles were prominent in liberal efforts to improve the health of Africans. They were co-founders of the South African Institute of Race Relations (the SAIRR), established in 1929, which advocated for social and political reforms. Each served terms as president: Alfred in 1934–43, and Winifred in 1948–50 and again in 1953–54. A noted anthropologist at the University of the Witwatersrand, Winifred Hoernle (1887–1960) was involved in numerous welfare organizations dedicated to alleviating the hardship facing children (black and white), Africans, Indians, and prisoners.[97] She was deeply troubled by the appalling conditions in the slumyards and squatter camps where newly arrived African workseekers settled. Indeed, she encouraged Ellen Hellmann in the early 1930s to conduct her now-classic study of a Doornfontein slumyard *Rooiyard*.[98] African misery, previously "invisible" in the reserves, became starkly evident in the 1930s. The African infant mortality rate in Johannesburg is estimated to have been almost ten times higher than for whites: in 1928, there were reportedly 705 deaths for every 1000 black babies as compared to 78 for whites (though statistics for the black birth rate are notoriously unreliable).[99] No doubt she had a maternalist intention of stemming this appalling loss of black child life by helping black women space their pregnancies. The impression that she joined the birth-control movement out of concern for the health and welfare of black children is strengthened by the fact that in 1932, two years before joining the RWS, she was a founding member of the Joint Committee for Non-European Work which was established under the Johannesburg Child Welfare Society to coordinate welfare work among blacks. Upon her resignation from the RWS in 1951 Hoernle took up the presidency of the Johannesburg Child Welfare Organisation and retained this position until her death in 1960.[100] She emerged as the RWS's leader in the late 1930 s and her influence was plainly evident in the greater attention paid to the health and welfare of women and children relative to the need of whites to improve their racial quality. She became a leading figure in the RWS and the first woman president in 1944.

Alfred Hoernle (1881–1943) was honorary president of the RWS from 1937 until his death six years later. He was a professor and chair of the department of philosophy at the University of the Witwatersrand from 1924 until 1943 and was made dean of the faculty of arts in 1925. A university colleague recollected that "the native problem was Hoernle's dominant interest in his Johannesburg years," and that as a liberal humanist he wished to "move the Europeans to understand the natives."[101] His interest in contraception dates back to at least 1926 when he participated in a controversial symposium on the topic at the university.[102] In the early 1940 s Hoernle was chair of the Local Authority designated to administer the Alexandra Township in northeast Johannesburg, which was home to 50 000 black inhabitants (mostly Africans and about 10 percent Coloureds). He was also chair of the Alexandra Health Committee, which opposed the City Council of Johannesburg's proposal in 1943 to abolish the township. In 1939 the University of the Witwatersrand medical school asked the RWS to open a birth-control clinic in the township, perhaps because it was widely considered to be "overpopulated" or perhaps out of concern about black infantile mortality; the reason is unclear.[103] The RWS agreed to try to do so, though the outcome is also unknown.[104] His involvement in the RWS may also have grown out of his research involvement in intelligence testing, a popular activity among researchers with strong eugenic associations.[105] In 1925 he supervised intelligence testing of 20 000 English- and Afrikaans-speaking white children on the Rand and in Pretoria as part of an assessment of the educational policy to instruct children in their mother tongue.[106]

With Fantham's and Porter's departure for Canada and the arrival of maternalists and liberals like Woodrow and the Hoernles, the RWS established contraceptive services for black women. After joining the

RWS, Woodrow and Alfred Hoernle immediately set about establishing clinics for Coloured, African and Indian women. They began by attempting to secure a room in the Bridgman Memorial Hospital for a birth-control clinic but were unsuccessful.[107] In 1935 they opened a clinic for Coloured women only at the Methodist Church on West Street, in the Johannesburg suburb of Ferreira, where the reverend offered the use of his vestry.[108] The clinic was open for one hour a week under the charge of Dr. Helen Weinbrun, but it was unsuccessful in attracting women. By January 1936 only eleven women had attended the clinic and by June the total number of visits had risen to just eighteen, so the RWS decided to close it.[109]

Next, instead of opening another freestanding birth-control clinic, the RWS opted to persuade physicians working in already established clinics to offer contraceptive services. The reason for doing so is unclear. Perhaps it was to save money and energy, or maybe to provide users with an opportunity to obtain contraceptives in secret. Dr. Grace de Krogh, who managed a general clinic on Buxton Street in Doornfontein, agreed to distribute contraceptives, so in January 1937 birth-control services were made available to Coloured and African women one afternoon a week. Again attendance was low: by February, only one Coloured and four African women had visited. As Table 2.1 indicates, until 1941 (the year records cease to be available) the clinic only attracted a few dozen women per year.

By July 1935, at the instigation of Winifred Hoernle, a clinic was established in Fordsburg for Indian women one afternoon a week under the charge of Dr. Janet Booker. Once again few women attended: only 23 women in the first six months. After one year, the number had risen to 69 but fell again in the subsequent twelve months (see Table 2.2).[110]

Table 2.1 Number of first-time visits and revisits to the Doornfontein birth-control clinic for Coloured and African women, 1937–41

Time Period	First visits	Revisits	Total
January 1937–June 30, 1937	27	0	27
June 30, 1937–June 30, 1938	34	*	*
June 30, 1938–June 30, 1939	44	31	75
June 30, 1939–March 31,1940	23	10	33
March 31, 1940–March 31, 1941	25	8	33
Total	153	49	16

Note: *Data not available.

Source: Race Welfare Society Annual Reports, 1937–41.

Table 2.2   Number of first-time visits and revisits to the Fordsburg birth-control clinic for Indian women, 1935–41

Time period	New visits	Revisits	Total
October 1935–June 30, 1936	69	n/a	69
June 30, 1936–June 30, 1937	*	*	42
June 30, 1937–June 30, 1938	28	*	28
June 30, 1938–June 30, 1939	32	58	90
June 30, 1939–March 31, 194	22	66	88
March 31, 1940–March 31, 1941	31	74	105
Total	182	198	422

Note: *Data not available.
Source: Race Welfare Society Annual Reports, 1936–41.

By June 1939 the clinic had been moved to Crown Road in Fordsburg and its hours extended to two afternoons a week, which may account for the slight increase in attendance.

There is insufficient evidence to confirm the reasons why these clinics were not popular among black women. However, we can speculate that, to begin with, African and Coloured women were probably uncomfortable receiving intimate attention from white doctors and nurses. As the historian Shula Marks points out, by the 1930s the number of Africans seeking western medical treatment had greatly increased and their fear of hospitals decreased largely because of the presence of African nurses. She cites a 1942 article in the Johannesburg *Star* that stated "The presence of a nurse of his own race by his sickbed must add considerably to a patient's confidence in his treatment and his ultimate cure."[111] African mothers, who were bringing their infants to antenatal clinics by the early 1940s, were comforted by the presence of black nurses with whom they shared a common language and culture.[112] In the late 1920s the *Star* and *Rand Daily Mail* also reported that Africans' fear of hospitals was a factor in their avoidance of medical care.[113] An obstetrician based in the Eastern Cape in the early 1930s confirmed this view with his complaints, published in the *South African Medical Journal* in 1932, that African women in labor resisted utilizing white doctors and preferred indigenous medical attention.[114] This was an international phenomenon. American historian Carol McCann, in her analysis of Margaret Sanger's birth-control clinic for black women that opened in Harlem in 1930, also argues that African-American women's suspicions "generated by an all-white staff ... would keep many women away."[115] Sanger noticed that these women were more willing to "lay their cards on the table, which means their ignorance, superstitions and doubts," if they were dealing with African American doctors.[116] The fact that the RWS clinics employed white doctors and nurses likely accounted to a great extent for the reluctance of black women to use the clinics.

Beyond African resistance to Western medicine, anthropologists studying African family life in rural and urban areas in the 1930s and who were preoccupied with the breakdown of the "Native family," noted that Africans attached far less shame to women who had children out of wedlock, as traditional forms of contraception (thigh sex and other forms of sex play that avoided penetration) were increasingly abandoned in the city. This may also account to some degree for African women's disinterest in modern contraceptive technologies only available through white-run clinics.[117] Though not condoned, Africans' attitude towards illegitimacy was relatively tolerant. In both urban and tribal conditions where an illegitimate birth was considered a disgrace, the shame was never extended to the child. Unlike the Christian mores dominating white society in South Africa, among Africans, children born out of wedlock were never stigmatized by the circumstances of their birth.[118] In addition, anthropologists noted that women's fertility and social identity as mothers were central to women's "self-valuation" and the valuation of others in their community, especially elders, husbands, and mothers-in-law.[119] For this reason, many African women may not have wished to take steps to prevent pregnancy. Finally, as mentioned in the previous chapter, African women had long practiced abortion in both rural and urban South Africa as a form of fertility control, and this was probably more common than contraception in cases where women did not wish to carry pregnancies to term. Further research is required to understand urbanized black women's attitudes towards, and experiences regarding, their capacity for reproduction in this period.[120]

IV

Despite the shift towards liberal maternalism, the RWS continued to promote birth control for eugenic reasons until the early 1940s. As late as 1938, the RWS's statement of aims still placed negative eugenics at the top of its list. The goal of ensuring that there would be fewer children from ill and "shiftless" parents took precedence over that of teaching mothers to space their families for maternal and infant health benefits, and of providing gynaecological health care.[121] But the message attracted little response from the public and none from the state. Except during the Depression, eugenics never had a mass following support in South Africa. As a small minority surrounded by an increasingly visible black majority, the white community *needed* poor whites. Ensuring they obtained a proper sense of whiteness required their rehabilitation, which, in turn, necessitated the environmentalist argument that poor whites were salvageable. Simultaneously, there was a political imperative to rescue the poorest members of the *volk* rather than sacrifice them on the altar of biological fatalism, namely the need to sustain the South Africanist political movement. In the 1920s, Anglophones and moderate Afrikaners, both of whom feared emergent extreme Afrikaner nationalism, had rallied around the vision of South Africa as a nation based on white supremacy and dedicated to ethnic equality between the two dominant white groups.[122] Maintaining the *rapprochement* between Anglophones and moderate Afrikaners meant incorporating poor whites as constituent members of South Africanism and preventing Afrikaner extremists from winning the allegiance of this substantial population.

South Africans were not unique in needing poor whites as racial allies. In the Southern United States prior to the American Civil War, non-slaveholding, landless whites comprised 30–50 percent of the white population and many subsisted as farm laborers and sharecroppers.[123] Just like in South Africa, landless whites in the American South constituted a "troubling presence" in a society where racist pro-slavery advocates equated white skin with respectability and black skin with manual labor. There too, personal, often cooperative, sometimes intimate interactions with slaves also raised doubts about racial loyalty. In an observation that can be extended to the South African context, the historian Charles Bolton notes that American poor whites undermined Southern desires to create a society "in which economic and social levels divided neatly along colour lines."[124] Moreover, in both national contexts, middle-class resentment was transposed into a negative cultural stereotype of a rural, illiterate, superstitious, lazy, shiftless, irresponsible, and *fecund* public nuisance that voluntarily chose to live life contrary to respectable society.[125] Yet, at the same time, the need to maintain white supremacy in both countries rendered poor whites' a necessary racial ally against blacks.

The environmentalist interpretation of the poor white problem effectively became official in 1932 when the Carnegie Commission submitted its report. In spite of Marie Rothmann's and especially E.G. Malherbe's dual explanation for the poor white problem – a combination of environmentalism and biological determinism – the Commission ultimately offered an overwhelmingly environmental interpretation. Poor whiteism was attributed to the twin processes of urbanization and proletarianization of rural whites. The commissioners recommended accelerating governmental efforts to rehabilitate poor whites with a host of improved social welfare measures (including, as we will see in Chapter 6, in the realm of public health). The Commission had a profound impact on the Government's response to poor whiteism in subsequent years. As General Jan Smuts, the Justice Minister, said in a speech to the National Conference on Social Work (1936), which was organized in the wake of the Commission's findings:

> What was feared was that a section of the European population, under African conditions, was degenerating but the Carnegie Commission has ... entirely dispelled that delusion. There is a certain amount of degeneration and degradation, but in the vast bulk of cases there is no deterioration of the human stuff ... . The right stuff is there, and where you are going to work at the social problems of the country you have this assurance – you are not going to work in vain, you are not going to work on stuff that is intractable.[126]

Poor whites could be rehabilitated after all. Leila Reitz distilled the public's mood in 1934 by summing up the racial imperative to do so: "And this country in particular, with its native population and its coloured population and its Asiatic population, can least of all afford to disregard the conditions under which its white people live."[127]

As the decade wore on, the eugenists' determination to improve the quality of the white race through curbing the fertility of poor whites became increasingly marginal and irrelevant. As the more hopeful environmentalist interpretation of poor whites became entrenched among both South Africanists as well as extreme Afrikaner nationalists, there was little taste for talk of "inferior" poor whites. For this reason, eugenics proved to be less acceptable to elites as a justification for accessible contraceptive services than the alternative. As the next chapter shows, the maternalists' response to the national crisis embraced, rather than blamed, the poor mothers of South Africa, an approach that dovetailed nicely with both the political imperative to "uplift" the poor whites as well as the patriarchal desire to buttress the family.

3
Strengthening the Nation's Mothers through Birth Control

It is the right of poor and struggling women to receive instruction in spacing and limiting their families so as to try to obtain health, strength and economic independence for their children and themselves, thereby contributing to the welfare of the race.

The Mothers' Clinic Committee, 1933[1]

It should be noted that not only do [the clinics] endeavour to restrict births by diseased or otherwise unfit parents, but they impress on suitable parents the duty of bearing and rearing healthy children.

South African National Council of Maternal and Family Welfare, *c.* 1940[2]

I

While eugenists responded to the social disruption unleashed by the Depression by opening a clinic for poor white women in Johannesburg, elsewhere in the country birth-control advocates with a different ideology emerged. They were maternal feminists, and during and immediately after the Depression they opened birth-control clinics in urban centers located in the Transvaal, Natal, and the Cape. Unlike the Race Welfare Society (RWS) that wanted to reign in the fertility of poor white women, the maternal feminists wished to assist women of all races who were visibly struggling under the harsh economic conditions to be better mothers. Doing so would stabilize families and, by extension, the nation as a whole. By promoting birth control as a motherhood issue, maternalists would prove to be more effective than the eugenists in shaping the central Government's position on contraceptive services and serving women who sought contraceptives from their clinics.

The first, and by far the most successful, maternalist birth-control organization in South Africa was the Mothers' Clinic Committee (MCC), which emerged in Cape Town. In November 1931, seven women "gathered round the tea table in a shady garden" in Rondebosch, a middle-class neighborhood, and decided to start a birth-control clinic. Unaware of the existence of the RWS, "an ambitious plan was hatched," in the words of one of the women present, "a plan to bring the knowledge and means of birth control to women of all race groups throughout the country."[3] Raising between them enough money to open a clinic, they set out to locate suitable rooms. Three months later, on February 15, 1932, they opened the Mothers' Clinic in a mixed-race, working-class neighborhood for "European and Coloured working mothers irrespective of creed or class."[4] The maternalists' liberal approach had a proud heritage in the Cape and was probably reinforced by the decision of the Anglican bishops of South Africa in 1930 to call for full citizenship for all South Africans, regardless of race.[5]

Throughout the 1930s, the MCC comprised a group of between ten and twenty highly educated women drawn from Cape Town's Anglophone social elite.[6] Ursula Scott (1893–1963), a founding member and chair of the MCC from 1931 to 1958, was born in Cape Town to a prominent political family. She was the niece of F.W. Reitz, who was president of the Orange Free State in the 1890s, and of Olive Schreiner, the author, feminist, and social commentator who was famous in South African and British literary and political circles early in the twentieth century.[7] Schreiner was a major figure in stimulating the South African suffrage movement, and her nonracial views, exceptional among suffragists, were adopted by Scott who was "very conscious of the Schreiner background ... very proud."[8] Scott studied at Newnham College, Cambridge, for one year and then briefly served as a Voluntary Aid Detachment nurse in France during the First World War.[9] She married in 1917 and two years later returned to South Africa with her husband. In addition to chairing the MCC, she was also the first president of the South African National Council for Maternal and Family Welfare (SANCMFW) from 1935 to 1958. Scott was instrumental in obtaining respectability for birth control in South Africa but her vision and involvement also extended beyond South Africa's borders. In 1948 she attended the pivotal international conference in Cheltenham, England, which was organized by Margaret Sanger and other leading Western birth-control advocates. This seminal event eventually led to the formation of the International Planned Parenthood Federation in 1952.[10] Unfailingly dignified in public life, Scott was a tireless yet modest leader.

Though she was the premier birth-control advocate in South Africa, her diplomatic, cautious, and self-effacing style could not be more different from the powerful and provocative personalities of some of the other leading women activists of her day, such as Sanger of the United States or Britain's Marie Stopes. Instead, she was remembered for her mild yet determined leadership. Dr. Patricia Massey, who worked at the Cape Town Mothers' Clinic in the 1930s, remembered her as "a dear sweet nice woman ... dedicated."[11] All but forgotten today, in her lifetime she was recognized and respected for her efforts, receiving the prestigious Coronation Medal in 1937 for her contribution to the Mothers' Clinic.[12]

Another founder and leading member of the MCC was Dr. Elsa (Sallie) Woodrow (1900–96), the organization's first Medical Officer. Woodrow was born in England and, after qualifying as a medical doctor at Birmingham University, emigrated in 1926 along with her husband to South Africa where she worked for a few years as a general practitioner in the Eastern Cape. In 1935, Woodrow was appointed Medical Officer to the municipal Department of Health's Maternal and Child Welfare branch and became its head in 1952. She was Chair of the Western Cape branch of the SANCMFW from 1963 to 1966, and President of the SANCMFW from 1966 to 1969. In 1975, at age 75, she founded the Cape Association for Voluntary Sterilization (CAVS) that was affiliated with the World Federation of Associations for Voluntary Sterilization (WFAVS).[13] She was also a longtime, outspoken campaigner for legal abortion in South Africa from the 1970s until her death in 1996. Woodrow claimed that she devised the idea of opening a birth-control clinic in Cape Town while working in the Eastern Cape where, through her medical practice, she came into frequent contact with women desperate to avoid having more children but had no contraceptive knowledge. She was appalled that women were either forced to endure unwanted pregnancies or else resorted to dangerous illegal abortion. She returned to Birmingham, England, in 1929 in part to obtain training in contraceptive methods and upon her return to South Africa took the lead in forming the MCC.[14]

The MCC was a maternalist organization firmly committed to the notion that mothering was a woman's primary social role. Maternalism, which has been variously defined as the "domestication of politics" or social housekeeping, was a prominent strand of international feminism in the 1920s and 1930s.[15] It was an ideology that emerged in the late-nineteenthcentury and, in the historian Pamela Scully's words, "embraced the notion that women and men had different capacities and that women's maternal instincts and domestic experiences fit them for public service."[16] Put another way, maternal feminism accepted as natural and exalted women's social identity as mothers and sought to extend their putatively higher morality beyond the private "female" realm of the home to the public sphere.[17] As historian Molly Ladd-Taylor explains, maternalists believed that there was "a uniquely feminine value system based on nurturance, that mothers perform a service to the state by raising citizen-workers ... and that ideally men should earn a family wage to support their 'dependent' wives and children at home."[18] She argues that maternalists believed "women are united across class, race, and nation by their common capacity for motherhood and therefore share a responsibility for all the world's children."[19] In addition to believing they were best qualified to legislate on matters pertaining to children, maternalists believed their role in public service was to aid the poor and sickly.

Maternalism thoroughly suffused the MCC's rhetoric. Scott, Woodrow, and their colleagues pitied women raising large families in abject poverty and whose hardships only intensified during the Great Depression, and they were eager to provide them with a safe means to control their fertility. Helping physically exhausted women space or, when medically necessary, avoid their pregnancies, the group claimed, would strengthen women's role as mothers and thereby shore up the family and nation state. "While still limited in extent," the MCC stated, "the work at the clinic is definitely recognized as a necessity in constructive family rehabilitation, and as an influence on the health of the individual, the family and the nation."[20] Helping to improve women's health "increases her parental efficiency in the home."[21] While abortion was not to be countenanced, birth control was legal, effective and publicly defensible in the name of South African motherhood. As Scott explained in 1933, "The health or environment of the majority of these mothers makes the practice of contraception essential to the welfare of the community as well as to themselves."[22] Simultaneously, they subscribed to T.R. Malthus's argument that unrestricted fertility caused poverty and that having fewer children would rehabilitate the poor. According to Woodrow, limiting the fertility of the destitute and working classes "would prove one of the corner-stones in any scheme for the reduction of crime, pauperism, drunkenness and over-crowding. It would release vast amounts of time and money now spent in alleviating distress, ill health and unemployment."[23] Birth control, the MCC claimed, would improve "unemployment, housing, health and the future welfare of the race" in addition to women's health and happiness.[24]

The MCC was a facet of the emergent, though weak, white women's movement. Members of the MCC were aware of, and some had participated in, women's struggles for access to birth control and the franchise in Britain: one was even reportedly a bodyguard for the militant suffragette Emmeline Pankhurst.[25] The most important feminist influence on the Cape Town women's ideas about birth control was Marie Stopes (1880–1958), Britain's best-known and most effective advocate of birth control as a woman's right. Stopes also made the radical claim, wrapped in scientific terminology in *Married Love* (1918), that women should enjoy sexual relations within marriage. Her message resonated widely, for the book was a spectacular success, going through seven printings in its first year.[26] Immediately after the release of the book, Stopes began receiving letters from women and men seeking advice on how to prevent conception, and as a consequence she quickly realized that freedom from fear of unwanted pregnancy was a necessary precondition for women's sexual pleasure.[27] In subsequent books and pamphlets she set out to provide women with practical advice on contraception. In 1921, she and her husband, Humphrey Verdon Roe, opened Britain's first birth-control clinic, the Mothers' Clinic, in a working-class London neighborhood. She spent the following decade boisterously lambasting government, medical, and religious authorities for frowning on birth control. In 1930, the British Government finally approved the distribution of contraceptive information through maternal and child welfare centers, a crucial, if limited, victory for which she has rightfully been given much credit. More than any other single individual, Stopes helped make birth control acceptable in Britain.[28] However, her enormous impact beyond Britain's borders has been little recognized; even her own claims to having a global influence have been mistakenly dismissed as yet another example of her legendary tendency to exaggerate her self-importance.[29] Her vast correspondence confirms that throughout the 1920s and 1930s, she was in contact with international birth-control activists, as well as thousands of ordinary men and women around the world who anxiously described a variety of sex-related difficulties. For many of these men and women she was the only person they trusted with such intimate secrets and her advice was considered invaluable.[30]

Stopes had an eager following in Southern Africa during the 1920s and 1930s. South Africans learned of her from a variety of sources, including *Married Love* and her numerous other books that became available in South Africa by being sent by family and friends, reproduced by English- and Afrikaans-language presses, or purchased during trips "Home" to Britain. Readers flocked to her books for advice on sexuality and contraception. A British social worker touring South Africa in 1932 reported, "I have been told throughout my tour that Marie Stopes's books are 'best-sellers' among all sections of the community." [31] A manager of a "leading firm of city booksellers" reported in 1930 that "there was a large and constant demand for books on sex matters generally, and particularly for those on birth control," and there can be little doubt that Stopes was the author to whom he was referring.[32] Women and men from across the region wrote to Stopes for guidance on sexual matters ranging from controlling fertility, raising children, and obtaining abortions (which she opposed).[33]

Stopes's impact on the South African birth-control advocates was direct and profound. Janie Malherbe, the wife of E.G. Malherbe of the Carnegie Commission of Investigation on the Poor White Question and a founder of the Pretoria birth-control clinic, called Stopes the person who had the greatest influence for happiness on her life.[34] E.G. Malherbe also invoked Stopes's "great" publications in his successful bid to convince the Dutch Reformed Church (DRC) to end its opposition to birth control and, as shown below, she was of material assistance to the fledgling national movement.[35] In Cape Town, Ursula Scott spaced her four children using Stopes's advice, which she acknowledged with gratitude.[36] Stopes's influence on the women of the MCC is evident in their statements invoking women's right to sexual satisfaction within marriage. In a 1932 article for the *South African Medical Journal* (*SAMJ*), Woodrow informed her mostly male medical colleagues that coitus interruptus was unsatisfying for husbands as well as for their wives: "From the man's point of view, it involves a considerable control and restraint just at a time when these should be in abeyance, and from the woman's point of view it is worse, as it frequently leaves her in an excited condition and without the natural satisfaction of the act."[37] Woodrow also discouraged douching after intercourse because "the psychological effect on the woman of having to get up out of bed and go through this sordid procedure is undoubtedly harmful and tends to render the coital act abhorrent to her."[38]

Feminism in South Africa gained momentum when the suffrage movement obtained the franchise for white women in 1930, just one year before the founding of the MCC.[39] The victory strengthened middle-class feminists' confidence and sense of entitlement to participate in the public sphere. It was with this new spirit of social activism that the women of Cape Town took up the banner for birth control. Once again Sallie Woodrow exemplified the group's feminist rejection of the subjection of women. In 1932 she protested passionately against the dominant perception of women as mere "child-bearing machines" in an article published in the *SAMJ*:

No member of the medical profession can possibly be in ignorance of the results of unlimited procreation. We have all seen the poor wrecks of humanity that crawl up to the gynaecological departments of our big hospitals, their lives one long agony of child-bearing, and each month a nightmare lest their periods should not appear. Ill and broken in spirit they come, these drudges of the world, ignored by governments and religions, reduced to a hopeless despair by the much-vaunted glories of motherhood. It is no wonder that the women of the world have revolted against such abject slavery, that they are demanding to be something more than child-bearing machines, that they are demanding as their right a fuller and healthier life with opportunities for self-development and independence.[40]

South African maternalists interested in birth control were affected by international developments. In 1930 the Anglican Church decided at the Lambeth Conference to endorse birth control within marriage, a move that provided the practice with moral legitimacy. This was reassuring for respectable women like the members of the MCC and other maternalist groups across the country that knew how controversial the issue was in South Africa. Moreover, in 1930 the British Ministry of Health approved the distribution of birth-control information through maternal health centers, another stamp of official approval from the imperial metropole. While Stopes inspired the South African birth-control activists, the decisions by the Church and British Government made their cause respectable. Moreover, as they pointed out themselves, by the 1930s the birth-control movement was already making great gains elsewhere in the Empire, Europe, Britain, and the United States. By joining the fray, they took courage from the fact that they were simply the latest members to join a successful international movement.

After forming the MCC, the fledgling advocates were intensely conscious of their lack of experience. British by birth or descent, they looked "Home" to Stopes, their hero and role model, for guidance and in doing so, affirmed their self-perception as loyal Britons as well as South Africans.[41] Sallie Woodrow wrote to Stopes asking what costs might be involved in starting a clinic, what sort of opposition they should expect, and which was the cheapest and most "foolproof" method of contraception for "poor whites" and Coloured women, whose "grade of mentality," she said, was "lower than that among the working-classes at home."[42] Stopes quickly responded with advice and assistance that shaped the Cape Town clinic in fundamental ways.[43] The MCC followed Stopes in favoring contraceptive technologies designed for women, such as the cervical cap and diaphragm, because they would enable women to gain a greater measure of control over their own reproductive capacity. The MCC also purchased Stopes's "Racial" line of contraceptive technologies (cervical caps, soluble pessaries, and rubber sponges). The Cape Town women employed suggestions found in her book *Contraception: Its Theory, History, and Practice*(1923)on managing a birth-control clinic. Woodrow also affiliated the MCC with Stopes's organization the Society for Constructive Birth Control and Racial Progress (known as the CBC). During the course of the decade Stopes became intimately involved in the MCC's project and sent practical advice, moral support, and contraceptive technologies at an affordable price. For example, after learning of the MCC's difficulties in distributing contraceptives to women who lived outside the city limits, Stopes suggested it operate through already-established health clinics, which would obviate the problem of establishing additional, expensive free-standing birth-control clinics. The MCC apparently heeded her advice, as it began in 1936 to offer services through venereal disease (VD) and tuberculosis (TB) clinics managed by the Divisional Council (see below). The MCC also provided care in a warm, friendly, and supportive atmosphere in a similar style to Stopes's own clinic.[44] Her commitment to the MCC was impressive; she even replied to a letter from Cape Town while convalescing in Dorset after an incident of carbon monoxide poisoning.[45]

The MCC was true to its word in providing services to all poor women who sought them, regardless of their race. However, in typical South African fashion, liberalism had its limits with regards to matters of race. From the opening of the clinic and throughout the 1930s the MCC provided service in strictly segregated sessions, a policy that incorporated and reinforced the racial divisions in their society. Members never explained their decision to racially segregate users, an omission which in and of itself belied its unquestioning acceptance of racial difference, and they certainly left unchallenged the hardening lines of racial division in South Africa during the course of the decade and afterwards. Similarly they never questioned the structural class divisions that caused the poverty they witnessed. Members of the MCC, like white women in settler societies generally, were accepted in public life so long as they expended their efforts on uplifting and reforming the poor among the both the colonized and colonizing races rather than on working for social equality between whites and blacks.[46]

II

From the start, members of the MCC were fully aware of stringent opposition to birth control from a variety of groups, including religious bodies, proponents of "race suicide" (the belief that the middle class was on the verge of extinction), the medical profession, and whites who feared "swamping" by blacks.[47] Each of these groups registered its objections during the controversy that erupted in Cape Town in the wake of the Lambeth Conference. (As a former British colony, the Cape Province had a large Anglican community.) Not one of the 63 South African bishops who attended the conference voted in favor of the resolution on birth control, and when they returned to South Africa they denounced the new policy. The bishops' position sparked a great deal of reaction from the public, positive as well as negative. The controversy also provoked discussion of the extreme destitution that raged in Cape Town as the Depression ravaged the country, and solutions to the crisis. During the debate, several major newspapers cited social welfare agencies that endorsed birth control as a way to ameliorate poverty and to mitigate maternal mortality.

Anxious to sidestep controversy, the MCC – unlike the RWS – studiously avoided notoriety. During its first year, the MCC did not even advertise the existence of the Mothers' Clinic for fear of attracting protesters. Instead, they relied on word of mouth and referrals from other charitable and health agencies to inform women about the clinic. In its first annual report, the MCC explained, "with deliberate avoidance of controversy ... [i]t has been the considered policy of the Committee to concentrate on the teaching of Birth Control to the unemployed and poorer classes of the population rather than to carry on any abstract controversy."[48] Members were also quick to react to publicity that they believed undermined the legitimacy of the MCC and threatened the clinic's existence. Furthermore, when an article appeared in the *Cape Times* in 1933 that was ostensibly on birth control but was really about South African eugenists' desire for a state system of forced sterilization, the MCC responded immediately. Two days later the newspaper published a clarification by the editors explaining that sterilization was a separate issue from birth control, and that it should not be associated with the Mothers' Clinic:

> It should be perfectly obvious that [sterilization] has nothing to do with the world of the birth-control clinic, which is concerned in no way with the controversy about sterilization in any form. The

explanation seems to be necessary in case any prejudice against the work of the clinic should be caused by the mention of the two subjects, as though they were identical, in the article mentioned.[49]

The MCC calmly defended the need for accessible birth control in maternalist terms. This is particularly evident in the annual reports that regularly included profiles of mothers worn out from poverty and frequent childbearing. These profiles were clinical in tone and sensational in content. For example, the 1937 annual report described a woman thus: "Mother aged 29. Six Pregnancies, 5 living children. Father T.B. earns £1 2s. 6d. per week as gardener. Mother suffers from Venereal Disease and has discontinued venereal treatment in order to do charring at 2/6 per day."[50] The 1939 report provided this profile of a woman in need of assistance: "Mother 25 when first visited Clinic in 1932. Did not return or write for 4 years in which time had 3 further children and a mental breakdown. Eight living children. Re-attending clinic. (N.E.) [Non-European]."[51] (Until 1939 the MCC did not identify users' race in profiles, suggesting that class and gender concerns predominated over racial interests among the birth-control activists for most of the decade.) These miniature biographies highlighted women's fecundity as well as the high incidence of maternal and infant mortality and ill health in poor families. They also mentioned cases in which women sought help in overcoming infertility, thereby affirming the MCC's commitment to motherhood.

In response to charges from religious authorities that birth control was enabling "immoral" behavior, the MCC reassured the public that every effort was made to confine instruction to married women only although the organization never specified how this was done.[52] In an attempt to address the fear of "race suicide" Woodrow argued that, since middle-class couples were already using contraceptives, equal access to birth control by *all* classes would eliminate the differential birthrate.[53] In fundraising letters the MCC stressed its intention was to serve only poor women.[54] Scott explained that: "Occasional [sic] well-to-do cases who come in error ... are instructed to visit private practitioners, whose addresses are given them."[55] This policy, commonplace among South African birth-control organizations, was probably also intended to prevent hostility from the medical profession, which would have resented the clinics if they absorbed any portion of their clientele.[56] The MCC was careful to cultivate the support of the medical profession, always speaking highly of the doctors volunteering in its clinics.[57]

Another source of opposition to the greater accessibility of birth control was the fear of "swamping" by blacks. As Table 3.1 shows, in

Table 3.1.   Cape Town municipal area's population growth by race, 1865–1959

Year	White	Coloured and Asian	African	Total
1865	15 118	13 065	274	28 457
1875	18 973	14 093	173	33 239
1891	25 393	25 235	623	51 251
1904	44 203	31 318	2 147	77 668
1911	86 239	80 449	1 569	168 257
1921	111 784	89 259	8 684	209 727
1930	134 680	121 670	est.6 000	est.262 350
1936	152 244	135 621	13 583	301 448
1946	180 805	171 767	31 258	383 830
1959	196 560	307 350	72 711	576 621

Source: John Western, *Outcast Cape Town*, p. 48.

1936 whites were still the majority "race" in Cape Town, but the black population (i.e., Coloureds, Asians, and Africans) grew rapidly in the 1930s. Between 1930 and 1936 the African population in the city more than doubled as rural Africans were wrenched off the land and pulled into the city in search of livelihoods. By 1937, racists like MP Karl Bremer were openly calling for segregated "group areas" in order to prevent further "penetration" of blacks into working-class neighborhoods like Woodstock and Observatory.[58] To those who "deplored and feared" the "high fertility of the natives," Woodrow replied that a high birth rate such as existed amongst Africans was accompanied by a high mortality rate and therefore their *survival* rate was lower than whites. She also placated nervous whites with the remark that whites obviously had admirable "racial strength" or else they would have been "driven out" of South Africa long ago. "The higher [racial] type," she claimed in racist terms, "will always be able to take care of itself against the lower types produced by unlimited procreation."[59] By the mid-1930s, then, the MCC was a confident public advocate of birth control.

From its inception, the MCC campaigned prudently for political support. Maternalist and neo-Malthusian justifications for birth control proved to be highly effective. The MCC regularly informed the medical profession and health and welfare agencies of its activities by distributing up to 2500 copies of its annual reports to members of parliament, senators, doctors, and clergy (irrespective of creed), not just in Cape Town but also in towns and villages throughout the Union. Scott felt that the "close contact of the Clergy in the rural areas with the health and poverty of many of their parishioners would ensure their interest in this effort for the betterment of the race." Moreover, copies of a detailed statement of "Clinic Routine Work" were distributed to doctors, nurses, and others.[60] The MCC also offered to meet with interested groups to discuss its work. Many groups requested presentations, including nurses, midwives, political groups, students, municipal health authorities, women's advocates and community groups, and ordinary women such as a group of Coloured women.[61]

Support for birth control was immediately forthcoming from health and charitable agencies that worked with the poor. More than half of the women who visited the Mothers' Clinic in its first year were referred by municipal clinics, and an additional (unspecified) number were referred by the Tuberculosis Care Committee, the Mayor's Relief Fund, the Peninsula Maternity Hospital, and private doctors. The Board of Aid also began referring women after a 1933 study of recipients of assistance recommended that the board "consider the ways and means of preventing the increase of the families of the very poor," and suggested that "[e]fforts could be made ... to persuade parents to avail themselves of the advice and facilities provided by the Mothers' Clinic."[62] In addition, the Cape Town Charities Commission (1932), which was appointed by the Provincial Administrator in May 1931 to inquire into the causes of "acute destitution" in the city and to assess the capacity of charities to provide poor relief, publicly endorsed birth control. As a result of Scott's presentation, the commission concluded that one of the causes of extreme poverty was "the excessive birth rate amongst the very poor."[63] Among the suggested solutions to the high birthrate was "the knowledge and practice of birth control."[64] This was a major source of gratification for the MCC, which perceived the recommendation as proof of birth control's growing legitimacy.[65] Furthermore, after another presentation by Scott, the Commission of Inquiry Regarding the Cape Coloured Population of the Union (1934–37) also commended the promotion of contraceptives. This commission observed that in many Coloured homes "child-bearing is an annual event" and "the large majority of coloured infants" are born in appalling circumstances; it also noted "the wear and tear" on women who experienced "constant and regular child-bearing under poor conditions." The Commission approved of the efforts of birth-control advocates across South Africa to reach out to the Coloured population and expressed the hope that their work would "continue to progress in the careful and circumspect way in which it has been started and conducted during the past few years."[66]

The portraits of worn-out mothers such as those provided in the profiles that appeared in the MCC's annual reports were effective in winning support from medical authorities. In the mid-1930s, the *SAMJ* published summaries of MCC annual reports with numerous examples of women in dire circumstances.[67] In one piece, the editor, Dr. C.L. Leipoldt, went a step further and urged physicians to support the Mothers' Clinic: "In the circumstances we appeal to all members of the profession who are in sympathy with the objects and ideal of [the Mothers' Clinic] to support it, to encourage it by donations, and to cheer it by taking an actual and practical interest in its work."[68] Endorsements like this were noticed by the press. In 1938, the *Cape Times* published an editorial praising the MCC for its "indispensable work among the poorer people." The editors commented that although "race suicide" was indeed "a social problem of the gravest kind," the unrelenting population growth among poor whites and Coloureds was equally dangerous. They wondered how Cape Town had managed as well as it had until then without the MCC.[69]

The MCC was also extremely effective in garnering financial support from all levels of Government, which reflected the state's rapid and growing appreciation of birth control. In 1933, the MCC requested a grant from the Divisional Council.[70] The Council's Medical Officer of Health, Dr. J.P. de Villiers, visited the Mothers' Clinic, and, as a result of his report, the Council's Health Committee agreed "that very useful work is being undertaken" and decided in favor of a grant to be renewed annually.[71] In 1934 the MCC requested £150 from the city in order to begin paying its doctors. Dr. Shadick Higgins, the Medical Officer of Health of Cape Town, inspected and endorsed the Mothers' Clinic, and the municipal finance committee voted in favor of a grant.[72] In 1935, the Provincial Council made its first grant to the MCC. In 1938 Cape Town's city council, following the instructions of the Union Department of Public Health, was also the first municipality to establish a post-natal clinic where women suffering from mental or physical illness "detrimental to them as mothers" could obtain contraception. Management of this new clinic was entrusted to the MCC.[73] Also in 1938, the Union Government started giving £1000 annually to the National Council for Maternal and Family Welfare, the fledgling national coalition of birth-control organizations. As President of the coalition, Ursula Scott played a major role in securing this federal support.

Despite, or perhaps because of, garnering widespread support, the MCC continued to attract controversy from members of the Catholic Church. For example, within weeks of the municipality's decision to support the Mothers' Clinic members of the Catholic Church protested.[74] However their complaint, in turn, sparked angry responses from women. One indignant woman wrote to the *Cape Times*, "There are two valid arguments for birth control – the health of the mother, and the health of the children. It is obviously inhuman, apart from being foolish, to allow wives to be driven into early graves by too much child bearing. A woman debilitated by many confinements can hardly produce bonny babies. Nor can she properly look after those of her children who have survived infancy."[75] Ultimately, Catholic criticism did not dissuade the city from awarding its grant. To the contrary, lack of widespread criticism regarding the city's support for the MCC likely encouraged city officials to renew the grant annually.[76]

Finally, the MCC succeeded in raising funds through social networks. Sports organizations such as the Western Province Rugby Union, the South Africa Turf Club, and the Milnerton Turf Club annually raised funds for the Mothers' Clinic. Ursula Scott's son, Dr. Geoffrey Scott, suggested in an interview that the success of the fundraising campaign was largely due to the relentless persistence of his mother and her colleagues at pressing their husbands and friends for money.[77] They also held annual rummage sales, which often took place at the Scott family's home. According to Dr. Scott, these were popular events at which dozens of women would jostle for items of clothing collected and donated by the members of the MCC.[78] Well-known public figures also made donations: Charlotte Shaw (wife of George Bernard Shaw) made the first donation to the Mothers' Clinic in January 1932 when on holiday in the Cape with her husband.[79] Table 3.2 illustrates the variety of public as well as private sources of the MCC's funding.

With increasing public and financial support, the MCC was able to expand its services. In 1936 the MCC persuaded the Divisional Council Health Committee to allow it to offer contraceptive services at the VD and TB clinics in Grassy Park, another mixed-race neighborhood. This, Ursula Scott told the Council, would enable the MCC to "reach many more of the poor families than would normally be able to journey to the present Clinic at Main Road, Observatory, for necessary treatment and advice."[80] In 1939 the Divisional Council also made space available to the MCC at Hout Bay. In 1938, the Cape Town city council established contraceptive services under the MCC's management in Maitland. Given the MCC's objectives, Maitland was a natural choice for new contraceptive services. It was a rapidly expanding industrial area in the Cape Flats east of the city center. In the early 1930s increasing numbers of dependent and working-class whites and Coloureds moved to Maitland and also nearby Ysterplaat, and poverty was often acute. Destitute residents in the area were living in shacks and other forms of makeshift shelter, and the *Afrikaans Christelike Vroue Vereniging* (the Cape's

Table 3.2.   Major Sources of funding of the Mothers' Clinic and total income, 1932–39*

	1932	1933	1934	1935	1936	1937	1938–39
Donations	209	94	13	105	90	111	76
Fees from users	51	83	77	79	89	91	126
Cape Town City Council	—	50	50	50	50	50	100
Divisional Council	—	—	25	25	25	25	25
Provincial Council	—	—	—	25	25	25	25
Share of Union Govt Grant	—	—	—	—	—	—	212
Milnerton Turf Club	—	25	—	50	50	50	50
South Africa Turf Club	—	—	—	2	1	1	—
Western Province Rugby Union	—	10	—	5	5	—	5
Proceeds from rummage sale	—	29	—	47	46	47	47
Proceeds from tennis tournament	—	—	—	—	61	—	—
Proceeds from doctors	—	—	—	—	—	14	—
Cape of Good Hope Savings Bank Society	—	—	—	—	—	—	25
Total	262	360	362	420	528	417	754

Note: *Amounts in pounds sterling.
Source: The Mothers' Clinic Committee Annual Reports, 1932–39.

Afrikaner women's welfare society) opened offices in Maitland where poor-white women could find free clothing for their families.[81] By 1939 the MCC was operating four clinics in and around Cape Town.

In sharp contrast to Johannesburg's male-dominated RWS in its early years, the MCC was interested in helping mothers and families. The MCC's maternalist approach quickly tamed the majority of opponents and transformed medicalized contraception from a shameful moral issue into a public health service in Cape Town. As we will see in Chapter 5, the MCC was also far more successful than the RWS in attracting and maintaining users. The factors that account for its success included prudent and effective leadership, the support of an internationally renowned British imperialist and birth-control activist (Marie Stopes), and, most significantly, the universal appeal of maternalism in a conservative society in which the feminist movement was small and fractured by class and race.

III

Soon after the Cape Town Mothers' Clinic was up and running, additional maternalist birth-control organizations emerged around the country, in

Pretoria (1932), Benoni, Port Elizabeth, and Pietermaritzburg (1933), and Durban (1936) (see List of Clinics). In 1935, the various birth-control organizations in South Africa came together to form a national birth-control coalition, the SANCMFW, with the hope of reducing the nation's poverty by helping mothers to have smaller families.[82] Like the MCC, the other maternalist groups were managed by middle-class women, most of whom were English-speaking, and were inspired and emboldened by local and international developments to help "rehabilitate" the family. Also like the Cape Town group, they subscribed to a medicalized approach to birth control, professed to restrict services to extremely poor married women, and served users regardless of their apparent racial category, albeit in segregated sessions. (By 1935, even the RWS reported that arrangements for opening Clinics for Coloured, Natives, and Asians were "well in hand."[83]) Finally, they also turned to Marie Stopes for assistance and contraceptives, and affiliated with her organization, the CBC. The South African organizations placed great value on their connection to the metropolitan feminist. But the relationship between Stopes and the South Africans underwent a dramatic transformation during the course of the decade that speaks to changing relations between metropole and colony during the 1930s. Indeed, the relationship between Stopes and her colonial counterparts had never been unidirectional, with influence flowing solely from London to the British Dominion in Africa. Instead, it was reciprocal, negotiated, and mutually constitutive.

Stopes's response to the subsequent South African groups requesting assistance was, once again, nothing less than extraordinary. Despite the pressing demands on her time from her own clinic, constant public speaking engagements, legal battles, and letters from men and women from Vancouver to Cairo and beyond asking for advice regarding a host of sexual issues, Stopes usually replied promptly to queries from South Africa.[84] She not only answered their particular queries and sent contraceptive supplies, she evinced interest in all aspects of their work. She also assisted them financially by sending unsolicited modest donations, ostensibly as "encouragement" and "a sign of our goodwill and ... desire to help," especially with extending services to rural areas.[85] Perhaps most extraordinary, she managed to supply the South African groups with contraceptives and copies of her newsletter during the Second World War, though her London clinic and home were bombed several times and supplies were scarce.

The South Africans were profoundly grateful for Stopes's interest and assistance. Her pamphlets and newsletters were cherished and her attentions deeply appreciated. A woman from Pretoria thanked Stopes for her "unfailing interest in our clinic. We are encouraged and touched by your generosity."[86] In 1932, on the eve of the launch of the Mothers' Clinic, Scott wrote to Stopes, "It is a great help and encouragement to receive [your] interest and support in opening this clinic ... If that now [sic] the clinic is actually on the verge of materializing, largely owing to the inspiration and practical help received from you ... in the past, you will be glad with us to know it is to be a reality."[87] In honour of Stopes, they named their clinic the Mothers' Clinic after hers of the same name. They also paid their respects personally during their trips to London for holidays, as did women from the Pretoria organization in 1933. Scott wrote, "As you know, I hope, it is a great honour and pleasure to those of us in this country to have an opportunity to meet someone who has done so much for women and their families all over the world as you have done."[88] Clearly, many viewed Stopes as the imperial mother of the birth-control movement in South Africa. The Pietermaritzburg group, for example, thanked Stopes for her financial support, which it called "a much appreciated gift from the Mother Society ... to the small daughter in Natal."[89] The Pretoria group referred to the CBC as the "Mother Organization." Like a child in need of a parent, a loyal fan in Pietermaritzburg wrote in 1932, "we need *you* out in South Africa," and asked if she could "spare a little time to get to the colonies" (emphasis in original).[90]

The relationship between Stopes and the South Africans was mutually constitutive. First, their correspondence was an education on both sides. In their letters, the colonial advocates conveyed conventional images of "poor whites" as lacking in self-control and intelligence that Stopes, who never traveled to South Africa, absorbed uncritically. She also engaged in a correspondence during the 1920s with a man in Johannesburg who ranted about poor whites and their uncontrolled fertility, and the expense of supporting them with welfare.[91] As a result of her correspondence with the South Africans she developed an extremely limited understanding of the region and its people. Unsurprisingly, therefore, she concurred that poor South Africans, black and white, were "not particularly clever."[92] In 1932 she wrote to Dr. Sallie Woodrow of the MCC, "I hope, with you, that the coloured people will come, particularly the half-castes for they are such a social problem." In 1945, she wrote to Woodrow a letter that suggests the two women shared similar eugenic and racist ideas about the efficacy of sterilization for people they deemed too stupid to use contraceptives as well as for blacks generally:

Dear Dr. Woodrow, I am glad to hear from you again and interested in what you say. I have long felt that we had to have birth control knowledge and materials available for everybody in the whole world who has intelligence ... and that sterilization must be used for those who have not sufficient intelligence. Sterilization for the male is extremely simple and is described as an "office operation," merely the severence [sic] of the ducts. It can be done in ten minutes and leaves the man perfectly free to enjoy sex union in the normal way with ejaculation [sic] of spermatic secretions and erection, but it does not fertilize the woman. I should say that the best thing would be to popularize that as far as you can among the blacks who have got, say, two, children, and also among any blacks who ask for it, whether they have children or not ... I am enclosing a little leaflet about a very simple method of the sponge and oil which I wrote for the problem in India, but from what you say of the black women I do not know that one could rely on them using it, simple as it is.[93]

In addition to helping shape her views of South Africa, Stopes's connection to her colonial counterparts affected her self-image, which serves as another example of how British domestic identities were shaped in part through the experience of Empire.[94] Pleased with the imperial maternal metaphor, for example, she began to use it herself when making donations to the South Africans.[95] Indeed, fueling her involvement in the South Africans' affairs was a self-serving desire to be the world's foremost authority on birth control. For this reason she viewed the South African groups as the first of a series of satellites in a worldwide movement that she hoped to lead. In the early 1930s, Stopes blithely admitted to her global ambitions, declaring to a friend "I ought to have a clinic in every country in the world," and she once told Scott that she wished to have a "united chain" of Mothers' Clinics across Africa. Her imperial dreams for birth control were reflected in her firmly pro-imperialist sentiments generally. When asked by a newspaper what she would do if she were to become "dictator" of England, she replied she would "Strengthen and link up the British Empire. Plant complete townlets [sic] in suitable unpopulated spots in Canada, Australia, Africa, etc."[96] For this reason she needed the South Africans as much as they needed her.

In her correspondence Stopes soon revealed her assumption that the South African groups belonged to her and were accountable to "Headquarters," as she called the CBC. For example, she instructed them to use only her "Racial" line of contraceptives rather than new locally manufactured brands, and when they did not comply, she complained. She also did not hesitate to meddle in the South Africans' national coalition. In 1934 she asked Scott to try to convince the Pietermaritzburg group to affiliate with the CBC. "I like to think that all of the South African clinics are in touch with us," she wrote to Scott. Scott, of course, already had her hands full managing her own newly opened Mothers' Clinic and did not greet this request warmly. Moreover, such interference was entirely inappropriate for, as Scott informed Stopes, each group was autonomous and answerable to no one but their local memberships. Scott's protest was to no avail as Stopes continued to attempt to control the SANCMFW. Once Stopes even tried to organize a takeover of the RWS because it would not affiliate with the CBC, writing "I have always felt worried about the position in Johannesburg" and instructing Scott and Woodrow in Cape Town to help establish a birth-control organization in Johannesburg that would affiliate with the CBC.[97]

In essence, Stopes perceived the South African movement as a colonial resource. In practical terms this meant she used them as leverage during her struggles to maintain her authority and reputation within the metropole. By the early 1930s Stopes was losing her place at the head of the British birth-control movement to the National Birth Control Association (NBCA), a coalition of individuals and groups founded in 1930 to establish birth-control clinics throughout Britain and to lobby Government to enhance existing services.[98] Stopes was invited to join the NBCA but was constitutionally unable to share authority. Not surprisingly, she quit after three years, hoping to displace it. During the 1920s and 1930s she also faced competition from Margaret Sanger for dominance on the world stage and again was losing, most visibly in the case of India, a major market for birth control that both women tried to colonize.[99] It was the desire to hold at bay domestic and international rivals that led Stopes to place such tremendous significance on her connection to the South African birth-control movement. She hoped it would help her buttress her position at home and abroad. Thus, when she reported on developments in South Africa in her newsletter *Birth Control News*, she implied that their achievements were her achievements also. She wrote in 1936, "We congratulate the South African clinics affiliated to the CBC on a year of wonderfully gratifying activity," and once wrote to Scott, "I have so much appreciated the work you are doing in South Africa," as though Scott was actually working on her behalf.[100] Then, in 1938, the South Africans rebelled.

At the start of the 1930s the South Africans were content to defer humbly to Stopes, as befitted daughters of the imperial mother of birth control. However as they became experienced and effective advocates for national birth-control services, their confidence increased and, conversely, their deference to Stopes decreased. With its message of strengthening the family and nation through healthy mothers, the SANCMFW was crucial to making birth control respectable in South Africa. Ursula Scott was indefatigable and proved to be an excellent national leader and propagandist for birth control. First, she and J.L. Hardy from the RWS, convinced the Union Interdepartmental Committee on Destitute, Neglected, Maladjusted and Delinquent Children and Young Persons (1934–37), appointed to examine the treatment of dependent and delinquent children and youths, that a cause of delinquency was mothers' exhaustion. They stressed the neglect of children by mothers exhausted by "excessive child-bearing." The Committee wholly accepted their arguments and, in its findings, went on to urge the central state to expand contraceptive services in South Africa. The following excerpts from the Committee's report indicate the success of the SANCMFW in presenting its case:

Family Spacing.

Evidence given before the Committee on the domestic situation in homes where the mothers' health is affected and her activities are impeded by too frequent and excessive child-bearing, indicates material neglect of the existing children as a strong contributory factor towards neglect, uncontrollability and delinquency. This is especially the case where the numbers in the family are in excess of the ability of one parent to support, and both parents are obliged to be absent from home. Evidence was given showing that a relatively high percentage of maladjusted cases come from homes where both parties are obliged to work. Extension of facilities for such married mothers to receive instruction in family spacing might assist towards a practical solution of the problem of the background of physical, mental and economic handicaps which so frequently lead to dependency and maladjustment. It is felt that the State should consider making mothers' clinics part of the maternal service of the country to advise on gynaecological treatment for women otherwise unable to procure it, as also to advise on proper methods of birth control where spacing of children is necessary in the interests of the existing members of the family, and also for such women as are medically unfit to bear children.[101]

Ursula Scott also attended the South African Health Congress, held in Cape Town in 1936, at which she spoke at the Plenary Session on Maternal and Child Welfare and the Congress's Declaration included a statement in favor of contraceptive services.[102] In addition she gave a speech at the National Conference on Social Work (1936) and appealed for the inclusion of birth control in any future social service programs for "Europeans and non-Europeans." Afterwards she noted with satisfaction that eight other speakers representing different groups of social workers had also advocated birth control, as did Dr. H.S. Gear, an Assistant Health Officer in the Department of Public Health, and Dr. P.W. Laidler, Medical Officer of Health for East London.[103] Even Edward Thornton, the Secretary for Public Health and Chief Health Officer for the Union, urged the Conference Organising Committee to send Government a resolution that Mothers' Clinics must become an integral part of public health programs in South Africa.[104] Moreover, no one spoke against birth control, "a significant fact in such a very large and representative conference," Scott noted.[105] In 1937 she also addressed the Inter-Departmental Committee on Poor Relief and Charitable Institutions.[106] She even met with Jan Hofmeyr, the Union Minister for Public Health, who was very sympathetic to the council's "urgent need" for facilities in rural and urban areas in which to conduct its "rehabilitative work."[107] In all of her presentations Scott promoted birth control as a necessary measure for all mothers, regardless of their colour. She argued, for example, at the National Council on Social Work that,

> ... it is most important to remember that the mother is usually the dominant factor in direct relation to the child in its early years. She has often unfortunately, insufficient time to deal adequately with the early experiences, both physical and mental, which are so important in the future development of the child ... The health of the mother definitely affects her parental efficiency. May I suggest as a logical deduction from this, that if that parent had more time to devote to each child, the result would be highly beneficial to the child, to the family, and ultimately to the State.[108]

The maternalist message was continually accepted, and every success was a boost to advocates' confidence. (As Chapter 6 shows, Afrikaner nationalist maternalists, in particular Marie Rothmann, also began advocating birth control in the early 1930s, which helped to ease the state's path towards endorsing birth control for the Afrikaans-speaking poor whites.)

IV

By the end of the decade the South African birth-control movement had matured into a self-assured, financially secure national organization. In short, by 1938, much to Stopes's chagrin, the South Africans no longer required her help. This was demonstrated most dramatically when the SANCMFW decided at its 1938 general meeting to affiliate with Stopes's rival, the NBCA. The South African members agreed that the NBCA was their national counterpart, and Ursula Scott approved of its ongoing "scientific investigation" into new technologies of contraception.[109] Scott pointed out that the NBCA was recognized and respected by the British Ministry of Health and for this reason it would be a valuable association for the South African coalition.[110] Stopes was intensely distressed over the South Africans' decision. She wrote to Scott imploring her not to join the NBCA and declared imperiously, "We do not allow any affiliation of any of our Mothers' Clinics" with the NBCA.[111] A few weeks later she explained that the "last thing in the world" that she wanted was for the NBCA to be able to say "that they had the authentic South African Mothers' Clinics affiliated with them."[112] But Scott held firm, explaining that, as a democratic organization, she could not undo the coalition's decision. Furious, Stopes tried telephoning and cabling Scott in an effort to reverse the decision, but to no avail. Feeling betrayed and victimized, she would never forgive Scott, calling her, ironically, an "intimidating tyrant" years after the incident.[113] Hoping to undermine Scott, Stopes even went so far as to claim that she had established the Cape Town Mothers' Clinic herself.[114] Scott tried to mollify Stopes by reassuring her that she was still greatly admired in South Africa, but was unsuccessful. The relationship had been irreversibly inverted. During the Second World War, it was Stopes who needed material and moral support. She wrote to South Africa complaining that she felt "completed neglected" by the South Africans, an "unexpected grief" during the war, and asked for financial support.[115] The South Africans complied as best they could. The MCC sent donations, as did the Pretoria group to aid in the repair of her clinic and home after they were bombed by the Germans. One of her loyal followers in Pietermaritzburg took pity and sent a parcel of jam, sugar, coffee, and sausages.[116] Despite being upset about the SANCMFW's decision to affiliate with the NBCA, Stopes continued to publish updates about the South Africans' activities in *The Birth Control News*.

In the broader, imperial context, the shifting relationship between Stopes and the South African activists highlights the Anglophone settlers' changing identity in South Africa during the 1930s. The Balfour Declaration on Inter-Imperial Relations (1926), secured by Prime Ministers Hertzog of South Africa and Mackenzie King of Canada, which was enacted into legislation in Britain with the Statute of

Westminster (1931), declared Dominion status and sovereign independence to be synonymous, in effect promoting the self-governing Dominions to the status of Britain's constitutional equals. Moreover, under the rule of the United Party in 1934, brought about by the fusion of the (pro-British) South African Party and the Afrikaner National Party the year before, a broad-based white settler identity was taking root in "South Africanism," a political project shared by Boers and British dedicated to bringing together both groups into a single, white supremacist nation.[117] A prominent proponent of South Africanism was the Afrikaner Jan Hofmeyr, who wrote in the early 1930s that elections fought along white ethnic lines held the seeds of "great evil" and that the future of the country depended on cooperation between English and Afrikaner.[118] South Africanism signified the beginning of a true rapprochement between moderate Afrikaners and English-speakers for the first time since the devastating Anglo-Boer War (1899–1902), and its symbols included a new national flag that was agreed upon by both dominant white groups, the adoption in 1925 of Afrikaans as an official language, and later of the Afrikaans *"Die Stem Van Suid-Afrika"* ("The Voice of South Africa") alongside "God Save the King" as national anthems. As William Beinart observes, during the 1930s "a relatively broad settler nationalism seemed to be flourishing."[119]

The development of South Africanism meant that English-speaking whites began to see themselves simultaneously as culturally British and South African – what G.H. Calpin called "Dominion South Africanism."[120] The solidification of a white settler nationalism and growing independence from imperial rule made it possible for the South African birth-control movement to act against the wishes of Stopes. Stopes never recovered from her sense of having been betrayed by the South Africans and correspondence between the parties eventually slowed to a trickle. Her reputation, already waning in Britain, continued its inexorable decline whereas the SANCMFW was settling nicely into the role of a respected national social welfare organization dedicated to helping mothers.

Stopes's failure highlights the success of the South African birth-control movement by the end of the 1930s. In just a few years, the national coalition of birth-control organizations evolved from a fledgling colonial outpost of mostly maternal feminists to a fully independent, confident social movement. In particular, the MCC emerged as the nation's leading group to advocate for mothers' right to accessible contraceptive services, quickly obtaining widespread support from municipal and divisional levels of Government as well as from Cape Town's elites. Its success was recognized by the election of Ursula Scott, leader of the MCC, as president of the SANCMFW. The MCC set the standard for all South African birth-control organizations, and even the RWS, which attracted maternalists and liberals in Johannesburg during the course of the decade, adopted MCC practices in hopes of reproducing its success. As the next two chapters demonstrate, the MCC's maternalist approach to birth control would prove to be more effective in attracting and maintaining users of the Mothers' Clinic than the RWS's eugenic-inspired Women's Welfare Centre.

4
Women's Resistance to Eugenic Birth Control

> The trouble with birth control was that the wrong people were using it. The people who could provide the best stock were limiting their families … while the people over-breeding and producing an excess of inferior children were the very people, such as drunkards and "poor whites," whom it was practically impossible to induce to use contraceptives.
>
> Anonymous letter to the *Cape Times*, 1930

I

The differences in ideologies between the two wings of the birth-control movement – eugenists and maternalists – became even clearer when their ideas were put into practice. The two main birth-control groups, the Race Welfare Society (RWS) and the Mothers' Clinic Committee (MCC), each opened their first clinic in February 1932. Aside from their timing, the two groups also shared a thoroughly medicalized approach to contraceptive services. However, this chapter is concerned with their differences rather than their commonalities, for they had distinct degrees of success in attracting and maintaining users. As this and the subsequent chapter argue, these successes and failures were determined by the two groups' different motives for opening birth-clinics in the first place.

Full of optimism and confidence in their ability to improve the quality of the white race, members of the RWS opened South Africa's first birth-control clinic on Loveday Street in downtown Johannesburg on February 4, 1932. The services provided by the Women's Welfare Centre (or Centre) were available to white women only. From the start, the Centre was modeled after birth-control clinics operating in Britain.

It consisted of two rooms, a waiting room and an examination room that contained two examination beds divided by a curtain, in which providers employed a medicalized set of procedures.[1] For example, during a woman's initial visit she was interviewed about her reproductive history and a record was kept on file. Afterwards a doctor performed a cervical examination in order to ascertain whether she was suitable for the Dutch cap (diaphragm), the main contraceptive prescribed by the clinic's doctors until the late-1930s. If she was, the woman was given one and shown how to use it in conjunction with three percent lactic acid jelly, which was to be smeared around the rim before insertion; a douche of water "some hours" after intercourse was also recommended.[2] Women of higher parities who were physically unsuited for the diaphragm were prescribed the rubber sponge with lactic acid jelly and also told to douche. During the cervical examination doctors screened women for gynecological problems and those found to have venereal disease were referred to the appropriate hospital or clinic. Even the Centre's name had metropolitan origins: in 1921 the English Malthusian League opened the famous Women's Welfare Centre in Walworth, a working-class neighbourhood in southeast London, and a clinic of the same name was later opened in North Kensington, London.[3]

In attempting to reproduce a London birth-control clinic in Johannesburg, members of the RWS, mostly British by birth or descent, revealed their strong cultural ties to Britain. Indeed they saw themselves as residing in "Greater Britain," the term devised in the late-nineteenth century to describe the colonies of settlement within the Empire.[4] Moreover, they sought to signify themselves as part of a modern, international, and progressive social movement intervening in social problems around the globe. Thus the medical model of a center for distributing contraceptives served a need on the part of the Johannesburg eugenists to be recognized as cosmopolitan imperial subjects.

Whether or not their clinic was acceptable to *users*, however, is a different matter altogether for, much to the RWS's surprise and disappointment, poor white women largely stayed away. This jarring disjuncture between the tidy theory and imperfect practice of eugenic birth control was extremely galling to many. As members of the RWS were very well aware, the failure to attract and maintain a significant number of users was quite unlike what was occurring elsewhere in South Africa, especially in Cape Town where the Mothers' Clinic rapidly attracted a steady stream of poor women. As a result, the organization spent much of the decade lamenting "the necessity for the fuller co-operation of the women of Johannesburg."[5] Poor white women's reluctance to utilize medicalized contraceptive services had a major impact on the RWS, eventually forcing it to alter its approach to clinical services as well as to reorganize its structure. Thus, by choosing to avoid the RWS's clinics, disenfranchised women modified the development of biomedical reproductive health care in Johannesburg.

The RWS carefully chose the location of its clinic in Sauer's Building on Loveday Street for its accessibility to its intended targets, poor white women living in the nearby working-class neighbourhoods. Poor whites and Africans settled in the chain of slums that spread from the western districts across the center of Johannesburg to the districts in the east, especially in Jeppe (also known as Jeppestown) to the southeast and Fordsburg and Vrededorp to the southwest (see Maps 2 and 3),[6] which

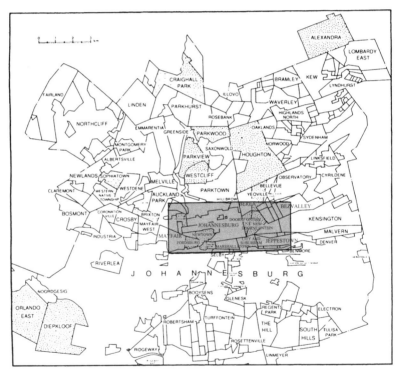

Map 2   Johannesburg suburbs and townships, *c.* 1940. The box indicates the region of the city in which the RWS operated in the 1930s.

Source: B.Bozzoli with the assistance of Mmantho Nkotsoe, *Women of Phokeng: Consciousness, Life Strategy and Migrancy in South Africa, 1900–1983* (London: James Currey, 1991), p. 96.

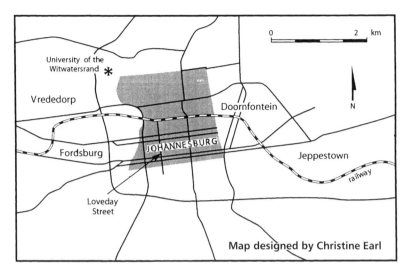

Map 3 Downtown Johannesburg. The map indicates a closer look at the downtown core and adjacent poor and working-class neighborhoods in which the RWS established clinics in the 1930s.

had reputations as the worst slums in Johannesburg.[7] Residents in these locations were a mix of unemployed blacks and whites and newly proletarianized workers who subsisted at an extremely low living standard.[8] Poverty was often acute. In 1933 Johannesburg's City Council found that 1121 white families lived in "unhygienic and overcrowded slum conditions" in areas such as Fordsburg, Jeppe, Doornfontein and Newlands.[9] In the rush to capitalize on people's need for cheap housing, property owners built shacks in their backyards and converted old houses, warehouses, and even stables into tenements in which single rooms were let to whole families. In other cases, people built makeshift homes in crowded slumyards. In the 1920s some of the slumyards in Doornfontein housed over 300 people each; sometimes as many as nine people shared a room.[10] Even worse than the appalling living conditions, in the opinion of municipal authorities, was the fact that slumyards were often racially integrated.[11] In order to alert and attract poor white women living in these neighbourhoods to the Women's Welfare Centre, the RWS circulated pamphlets in both English and Afrikaans and placed advertisements in English and Afrikaans newspapers inviting married women to the clinic's drop-in sessions on two afternoons a week.[12] Officially, services were restricted to married women in order to placate fears that the clinic was contributing to "immorality" by enabling extra-marital sexual activity. However there is no evidence that clinic staff attempted to verify women's marital status.

From the outset the RWS claimed that poor women "urgently needed" its services. However, the RWS's claims contradicted the reality of the clinic's relatively low attendance rates.[13] By 1932, Johannesburg and the surrounding neighbourhoods that sprang up on the Rand because of the mining industry comprised the largest urban center in sub-Saharan Africa, and of the 196 000 white women who lived on the Rand in 1936 (as compared to 107 000 African and 15 000 Coloured women), only a few hundred new visits were made to the Women's Welfare Centre each year.[14] Table 4.1 shows how many women visited the clinic from 1932 to 1941.

The fact that hundreds of women visited the Centre every year certainly was significant, as it testified to white women's desire for, and active attempts to obtain, effective contraceptives in the 1930s. Indeed, the number of visits was impressive even when compared to a leading London birth-control clinic, the North Kensington Women's Welfare Centre, which received visits from 250 women during its first nine months as compared to the Johannesburg Women's Welfare Society that received 263 visits in the first five months of operation (see Table 4.1).[15] But the number of visits women made to the Johannesburg clinic was lower than those to the Mothers' Clinic located in the much smaller city of Cape Town. Moreover, the rate of return visits fluctuated wildly. Had women returned every six months to replenish their supplies of lactic

Table 4.1   Number of visits to the Women's Welfare Centre, 1932–41

Time period	No. of months*	First visits	Revisits	Total
Feb. 2, 1932 to June 30, 1932	5	263	**	263
July 1, 1932 to Dec. 31, 1933	6	587	**	587
Dec. 31 1933 to Dec. 31 1934	12	282	**	282
Dec. 31 1934 to June 30 1936	18	472	1074	1546
June 30 1936 to June 30 1937	12	256	690	946
June 30 1937 to June 30 1938	12	310	887	1197
June 30 1938 to June 30 1939	12	310	1062	1372
June 30 1939 to March 31 1940	9	306	948	1254
March 31 1940 to March 31 1941	12	368	1121	1489
Total				8936

Notes: *These time periods are listed here as reported by the RWS.
** Information not available, therefore total visits from 1932 to the end of 1934 are estimates.
Source: RWS Annual Reports, 1932–41.

acid jelly as instructed and expected, the total number of revisits annually would have steadily risen but instead it varied significantly, sometimes even dropping considerably as shown in Table 4.1. In 1937, in an effort to get at the root of the problem of maintaining users, the RWS reviewed the Women's Welfare Centre's records. Among its findings was the statistic that nearly 50 percent of "lost" cases failed to return after the initial visit.[16]

The RWS, which compared itself to the more successful Cape Town organization, was acutely disappointed by its very modest success at attracting poor and destitute white women of Johannesburg. This directly reflected the RWS's overriding goal of curbing the fertility of putatively degenerate poor whites. The RWS's frustrations were evident not only in comments regarding how few poor whites were attracted to the clinic, but also in its suspicions that it was actually serving the wrong "type" of women. Publicly the RWS provided little in the way of biographical information about the women who utilized the Centre beyond the sole aspect of their identity with which it was preoccupied – their extreme poverty. Frequently it reported that a large proportion of users received contraceptives for free, for this was further evidence it was reaching the much-sought after population of indigents: "Practically all belong to the poorer classes; one third being unable to pay anything and two thirds average only 3/- [three shillings] each."[17] Yet the RWS's frequent claims about users' extreme poverty were deliberately misleading. The group fully realized it was not attracting quintessentially prolific indigent poor white women. In 1937 Edward Mansfield, already uneasy on this score, reviewed the case histories of the Centre's users, and his findings were even more alarming than expected. The type of woman visiting the clinic was changing, he reported, from the "very poor to those in better circumstances."[18] While users came from over 70 townships on the Rand, only 50, from a sample of 256, lived in "definitely poor townships," and of those 50 only 29 lived in the "extremely poor" townships of Alberton, Brixton, Cleveland, Fordsburg, Mayfair, Newlands, Newton, Ophirton, Vrededorp, and Fontainebleau. "There are poor people, doubtless, in every township," Mansfield acknowledged, but the figures raised doubt about whether or not the Centre was meeting the RWS's eugenic goal of helping "irresponsible" poor whites curb their fertility.[19]

In addition to being insufficiently destitute, Mansfield believed that the women utilizing the Women Welfare Centre were also having too few children to be poor whites. The image of the poor white woman that caused the RWS such anxiety was a prolific mother with a large brood of degenerate offspring. But the vast majority of users had relatively few children – just three or four – and some had none at all. The analysis of the records of 213 of the 263 users to visit the Centre during its first six months of operation show that the average age was 29. (Sixty percent of the women were between 18 and 29 years of age, the remaining 40 percent were between age 30 and 47.) On average, each woman had borne only 3.6 children.[20] Statistics based on the subsequent 18 months of activity reveal a similar story. Between February 1932 and August 1933, 700 women attended the Centre and complete records were available for 633.[21] The total number of pregnancies among them was 2530, with the average being four pregnancies per woman. Furthermore, while 26 women (4.1 percent) had experienced between 11 and 15 pregnancies, 29 (4.5 percent) had never been pregnant. The largest number of women, 232 (36.5 percent), had experienced between three and five pregnancies (see Table 4.2). Of the total number of pregnancies, only 2048 (80 percent) resulted in live births. On average, therefore, users had only three children.

The RWS did not publish users' reproductive histories in equal detail in subsequent years, but the information that is available, as shown in Table 4.3, suggests that women with small families continued to comprise the majority of users of the Women's Welfare Centre for the rest of the decade. Note that between 1932 and 1939, the average number of live births per woman dropped steadily from an average of 3.6 to 2.2. Such a small number of children hardly corresponds to the image of the dangerously fertile poor white woman invoked and feared by the RWS.

Table 4.2 Number of pregnancies experienced by 633 out of the 700 women who visited the Women's Welfare Centre, February 1932 to August 1933

Number of pregnancies experienced	Number of women
0	29
1–2	215
3–5	232
6–10	128
11–15	26
16–20	2
21	1
Total	633

Source: I.J. Block, "Observations from the Work of a Birth Control Clinic," *South African Medical Journal*, 8 (1934) 490–2.

Table 4.3 Profile of users of the Women's Welfare Centre, February 2, 1932 to June 30, 1939.

Period	Avg. age	Avg. no. of pregnancies	Avg. no.of live births
Feb. 2, 1932–June 30, 1932	29	*	3.6
July 1, 1932–Dec. 31, 1933	28.5	4	3
Jan. 1, 1934–Dec. 31, 1934	28.25	3.85	2.9
Jan. 1, 1935–June 30, 1936	29	3.5	3
July 1, 1936–June 30, 1937	28	3.3	2.23
July 1, 1937–June 30, 1938	*	*	*
July 1, 1938–June 30, 1939	28.1	3	2.2

Note * Information unavailable.
Source: RWS Annual Reports, 1932–39.

II

So who *were* the women that utilized the Women's Welfare Centre? Contrary to the intention of the RWS, most users were in all likelihood respectable working-class women employed in the city's burgeoning manufacturing sector. After the Government devalued its currency (the South African pound) on December 29, 1932, the South African economy rapidly revived. Going off the gold standard led to a flood of capital investment and the manufacturing industry's output doubled in value between 1933 and 1939.[22] As a result of the thriving manufacturing sector, employment also rose dramatically as jobs were created in textile, food, beverage, clothing, printing and chemical production.[23] These were mainly "white women's jobs." In 1929, 4182 white women worked in Rand industries compared to only 140 Coloured, 169 African and 10 Asiatic women.[24] By 1935, though the population of black women on the Rand was growing, 73 percent of the manufacturing labor force was still white and female.[25]

Women employed in the manufacturing sector were largely the proletarianized daughters of the poor whites who came to Johannesburg from rural areas in the 1920s and 1930s. During the course of interviews with poor whites, the Carnegie Commission of Investigation into the Poor White Problem discovered that of the 110 white Afrikaans-speaking women employed in a Johannesburg shirt factory, 43 had come from rural Transvaal, and 35 were from Cape Province and the Orange Free State; only 30 had been born on the Rand.[26] Commissioners also learned that most impoverished rural families who had moved to urban areas did so in order that their offspring, especially daughters, could find waged work and help the family survive at a time when male unemployment was high.[27] Indeed, between 1926 and 1933, a period of severe unemployment for white men, women's employment in Johannesburg actually rose from 12 000 to 17 000.[28] Poor white men lacked the requisite skills and education to obtain work in the expanding industrial economy and, moreover, they faced competition from cheaper black labor for unskilled work.

During the 1930s wage-earning women often continued working upon marriage or having children, as their families required their wages to survive.[29] Not surprisingly, these working-class women tended to have small families, usually between one and three children.[30] Most had children within the first few years of marriage, working until the seventh or eighth month of pregnancy and returning to work between three and six months after giving birth. Yet even with small families, women lost valuable time on the job and had immense difficulty in locating childcare.[31] The combination of the imperative to work for wages outside the home and the scarcity of childcare led working mothers to take steps to limit their family size. These were the women who, in a pragmatic bid to control their fertility, took advantage of the services on offer at the Women's Welfare Centre, albeit in modest numbers.

Despite knowing otherwise, the RWS continued throughout the 1930s to publicize extreme poverty and high rates of fertility. In doing so it was no doubt attempting to overcome ongoing concern among sections of the public, medical profession, and the state that accessible birth control was causing "race suicide" by encouraging higher rates of contraceptive use among "better" quality middle-class whites. As a leading member of the RWS privately reminded his colleagues in 1937, "Bearing in mind the current apprehension as to unduly falling birth rates, and the close scrutiny of BC [birth control] work that may result, I think we should be particularly careful that the work being done at our Clinic can be justified in detail on eugenic grounds, and is not open to a charge that the Clinic functions blindly without regard to considerations of National Welfare."[32]

Poor women's avoidance of medicalized birth control in Johannesburg was by no means inevitable or predetermined by a "natural" or "inherent" suspicion of reproductive technology or technological interventions on their bodies. This is confirmed by comparing the utilization rates at the Women's Welfare Centre and the clinic in Cape Town, which used the same medical procedures and had greater success at attracting and maintaining users from the same cultural and socio-economic background. Clearly users in urban centres across South Africa embodied what Lock and Kaufert call women's "pragmatic" attitude toward bio-medicine, including new medical technologies: "by force of the circum-stances of their lives," they argue, women have always used whatever technologies are available to them, "if the *apparent* benefits outweigh the costs to themselves, and if technology serves their own ends"[33] (empha-sis in original). Unfortunately, as is all too common for historians trying to reconstruct the experience of disenfranchised people, there are no first-hand accounts, either contemporary or retrospective, of visits made to the Centre in the 1930s, and thus we cannot know for certain women's perception of their experience there. However, a careful read-ing between the lines of the RWS's private and public records and the insights of historians working in other national contexts suggest a com-bination of reasons for the low rate of utilization.

Poor women in Johannesburg, indeed in the country as a whole, faced a series of material, social, and psychological barriers to practicing med-icalized contraception, barriers that undoubtedly made the diaphragm woefully inappropriate for many. Patricia Massey, a doctor who worked at the Cape Town Mothers' Clinic from 1935 to 1938, described the process involved in using another contraceptive that required insertion, the cervical cap: "The caps had to be put in beforehand [before inter-course], but not at the last minute because if you do it perfunctorily it wouldn't work so well, and removed not less than eight hours after intercourse. They had to bring them out and wash them and then dry them and powder them, put them away until the next time in which case they then had to anoint them and insert."[34] Massey believed the success rate of the cervical cap was 87 percent when instructions were followed. But technologies like the diaphragm and cap required a modicum of privacy for insertion and, after utilization, access to water for cleaning and space for storage, steps that were difficult if not impos-sible to carry out in the abysmal, crowded housing conditions of poor families. In slum residential areas many families lived in a single room and had no privacy; it was not uncommon for families to sleep together on the floor without mattresses. Many families also had limited access to water, and sanitary conditions were deplorable. In extreme cases, such as a Doornfontein slumyard in 1924, fifty families shared two squat toilets that were never cleaned by the landlord; the female residents organized themselves to do so.[35]

Lack of transport was another obstacle to women's use of the clinic. Poor families moved frequently in search of cheaper or better accommodation, and moves away from the center of the city would have made a trip to the Women's Welfare Centre either too expensive or time-consuming for women with small children. Unlike the RWS, birth-control providers in London were aware that expensive bus or tram fares could be an insurmountable barrier, and the Cape Town birth-control advocates grappled with the transportation problem in the early 1930s by providing free tram tickets for users.[36] It was not until the late-1930s, when the RWS was taken over by women more sympathetic to users, that the RWS tried to address the issue by providing women who lived too far from central Johannesburg with rides to and from its clinics – at times against their will, as shown below.

Gender oppression was probably also a significant obstacle to women's utilization of birth-control clinics. Certainly many husbands must have cooperated with their wives in using modern contraceptives since it would have been extremely difficult to use a cervical cap, diaphragm or sponge with a pessary without their knowledge. Research on reproductive control in Canada and Britain during the 1930s also challenges the assumption that poor and working-class men were always uncaring about, and often actively opposed to, women's attempts to limit family size during hard economic times, and therefore it is necessary to treat middle-class providers' negative portraits of such men with caution.[37] However some women doubtless did have husbands who opposed, at times violently, their attempts to control their fertility. Dorothea Douglas-Henry, a doctor who worked in Cape Town birth-control clinics (which served women of all 'races') in the 1940s, reported,

> ... women used to talk about their being "used" by their husbands. Women who came to the clinic, white and black, I mean it was a very regular expression – "Oh I'm so tired of being used by my husband every night." That was the attitude, and if the husbands were absolutely and completely against it then very few women would have dared to go to a clinic because in those days, you see, the only thing we had were diaphragms and cervical caps, and they could so easily be found. I mean I know one woman telling me that her husband had insisted that she show him exactly how many of these things that she'd got. You know, one knew of women being beaten up because their husbands found that they had a cap hidden away somewhere they'd never told about.[38]

Opposition to birth control on the part of husbands was also reported by the MCC. For example, in a number of profiles of users published in mid-1930s the MCC noted, "Husband does odd jobs at £1 per week, does not wish wife to practice contraception";[39] "Father, in irregular work as painter, refused to allow his wife to practice contraception";[40] and "Husband destroyed [contraceptive] appliances and Mother had 3 children in 3 successive years, followed by mental breakdown. Returned to Clinic, keeps regular contact and has had no further pregnancies since 1934."[41] While a number of such women must have visited the clinic in secret it is probable that others were unable to do so.[42] No doubt women in Johannesburg faced similar difficulties. At an RWS meeting in 1939 the Centre's nurse reported a case in which a husband wanted her to withhold contraceptives from his wife, the RWS proclaimed that "the wife should have the right to decide."[43]

Another probable obstacle was women's reluctance to touch their genitals. Contemporary and secondary sources from other contexts refer repeatedly to how leery and nervous women were to insert a contraceptive. In Australia, Norman Haire, an internationally renowned medical proponent of birth control, reported in the 1930s that women referred with repugnance to the suggestion that they touch their own bodies.[44] Australian historians also cite evidence of women's negative attitude toward their sexuality and argue that this was an entirely appropriate response by settler women for whom modesty was an essential component of dominant notions of womanliness.[45] In England, a doctor, also writing in the 1930s, corroborates this view with his comment that some women perceived inserting a cap as "unladylike" and "an invitation to sexual intercourse" that went against the normative view that only men should initiate sexual activity.[46] A study of maternal health care in London in the 1930s also argues that women stayed away from birth-control clinics because they did not like the technology on offer.[47] Organizers at the North Kensington Women's Welfare Centre described in 1934 the difficulties women experienced when trying to insert a cervical cap: "women, often flustered, very nervous, shy, entirely new to the idea of Birth Control, and with no physiological knowledge, have to take in and *remember* a number of important instructions. Frequently they forget which way the cap should be inserted; what they should syringe with, and how, and other points" (emphasis in original). Others were simply scared of the internal examination.[48]

The RWS provided little insight into users' experiences and attitudes. However, elsewhere in South Africa birth-control activists were paying a good deal of attention to the perception of users. The Port Elizabeth birth-control organization, for example, formed in 1933, was exceedingly attentive and sensitive to the challenges faced by poor women in day-to-day life and how they shaped their relationship to contraceptive technologies. In the mid-1930s members of the group drew up a questionnaire and visited "lost" users in their homes to elicit their opinions about birth control and the services offered by their clinic. Their report provides a rare glimpse into the range of difficulties South African white women faced:

[A]n effort is made to find out what prevented her return and what difficulties, if any, the patient had experienced. We find that a great deal of patience and tact is necessary to persuade some patients that whatever little time it may take at first to learn how to use an appliance is more than justified by the results of its correct use, and these visits to patients' homes imbue a spirit of trust and confidence which is of paramount importance in our work ... It was found that these visits were of the greatest help both to the patients and to ourselves. Patients speak so much more freely in the privacy of their own homes. We were able to get a very good idea of their reactions to the whole subject of contraception and to the use of particular contraceptives ... From the results of the questionnaire we found that a large proportion of patients definitely dislike using any form of vaginal pessary and that a great number of them had not once used the appliance given them. Others live under conditions which make its use extremely difficult ... [including] the lack of privacy in which so many of them live ... Washable sheaths which are given out under special circumstances proved satisfactory to a few, but unacceptable to a number of husbands and pregnancy had occurred in many women whom we visited who were actually eager to limit their families but unable to find an acceptable contraceptive. It is impossible to lay down hard and fast rules in regard to contraception. Each case must be considered individually and before advising any type of contraceptive, we enquire into the details of the patient's housing problem, her relationship with her husband as to co-operation or otherwise in contraception, and similar relevant matters. Since we realised that a number of patients were being lost through not finding the vaginal pessary acceptable, we have tried to give them an alternative [the condom] ... I want to emphasize that this is not the method of choice at our clinic, but has proved itself a definite standby in cases where the Dutch Cap has failed. Naturally, without co-operation from a husband, or, in the case of a drunken husband, such an alternative to the vaginal pessary does not exist.[49]

Determined to do their best to support women, the Port Elizabeth group's approach was unusually personal and stressed intimate, face-to-face discussion between a doctor and nurse and small groups of women, either at the clinic or else during "afternoon tea talks" in the privacy of a woman's home: "We find that eight is about the best number to whom to speak at a time, as there is then a more personal atmosphere an[d] the women are less reticent to ask questions."[50]

In contrast to such earnest attempts to ameliorate the problems facing women, the RWS exacerbated an already difficult situation through its patriarchal and unsympathetic approach. The leading members of the RWS, who portrayed themselves as "experts" of population health through the discourse of eugenics, and viewed poor whites as deviant, abnormal, and immoral population that required medicalization of their behavior through the intervention of contraceptive technologies. Poor white women were thus ideal "targets of the medical gaze."[51] The construction of poor whites as deviant precluded any serious attempt at understanding users' gender- and class-determined needs. This is most obvious in its decision to employ male doctors, a practice that was unique among South African birth-control organizations and one that continued for a number of years despite the clear preference women showed from the start for female doctors. In its first year of operation, there was an average of 5.5 first time visits to the Women's Welfare Centre on Tuesdays when female doctors were in attendance as compared to an average of 2.5 on Fridays when male doctors were in attendance. Preference for female doctors is not difficult to understand given the intimate nature of the initial encounter when women were required to submit to an internal examination. Given their poverty and consequent lack of experience with biomedicine, most women must have experienced the exam for the first time at the Centre. No doubt many found it embarrassing, difficult, and even painful when performed by a male doctor. The inability of the RWS to understand this difficulty until the mid-1930s reflects the organization's lack of concern for poor women's emotional and mental wellbeing.

Moreover through the early 1930s the RWS and its doctors remained seemingly oblivious to the difficult material conditions under which poor women worked and raised families, and how these conditions hindered attempts to practice medicalized contraception. This insensitivity was evident in the RWS's attitude toward cases where women trying to use a diaphragm became pregnant. According to a report produced after the Centre's first eighteen months of activity, four out of 633 women (less than one percent of all users) voluntarily reported contraceptive failure.[52] But this does not take into account women who experienced contraceptive failure and simply decided not to return; indeed, the RWS admitted that many "lost" cases were probably unreported incidents of contraceptive failure.[53] In 1937, out of a sample of 200 cases examined, four had been "absolute failures," a rate of 2 percent that, though much higher than expected, was still considered quite satisfactory when compared to the rate of failure of 1.3 percent at an unnamed clinic in London. When faced with contraceptive failure, doctors commonly reported that it only occurred in cases where women neglected to use the technology properly. To those who became pregnant while using a diaphragm, "[t]heir mistakes were fully explained and not one was allowed to leave the rooms thinking the method was at fault."[54] According to the RWS, women and not the technology nor the clinic were to blame for unwanted pregnancy. Ignoring all possible reasons as to why the diaphragm was unpopular and inappropriate, the Centre showed little interest in any other kind of contraceptive. After two years of operation (by February 1934) the Centre had prescribed 667 diaphragms, twelve cervical caps and four sponges to 683 first-time users, and by September 1937 the diaphragm was the only contraceptive offered at any of its clinics.[55] In contrast, other birth-control organizations in South Africa provided a range of contraceptive technologies from which to choose. The lack of options, in conjunction with a condescending atmosphere, must account for many women's decision to avoid the Centre. Some of the women who "failed" to return to the Women's Welfare Centre may well have been willing to utilize the new technology or undergo manipulation of their bodies if the culture of the clinic had been more supportive.

Negative experiences at the Centre doubtless had significant consequences regarding visitation rates on the part of potential users. According to the RWS's own records, women's main source of knowledge about the clinic was *other women*: fifty percent of respondents reported learning of the clinic's existence by word of mouth (see Table 4.4). The second most popular source of information was doctors (17 percent) followed by nurses (13 percent). These statistics suggest the crucial importance of women's networks as a source of information about such intimate matters as sex and fertility control. Thus one woman's unpleasant encounter was likely shared with female friends and family members. Women who were unsure about visiting the clinic in the first place, may have avoided it as a result of hearing another's negative impressions. Significantly, the RWS's response to its own findings was yet another symptom of its insensitivity to women's experience. Instead of exploring

Table 4.4   Source of information about birth-control clinics, 1937

Sources	Number
Other users	128
Doctors	43
District and other nurses	34
Clinic nurse	16
Unknown	12
Ladies	10
Press	9
Children's Aid Society	4
Total	256

Source: RWS Executive Committee, October 13, 1937.

the implication of women's networks in such a way as to lead to self-reflection and changes in its procedures, the RWS initially concluded that women should talk less to each other and listen more to elites: too few women, it complained, were learning about the clinics from professionals. To try to ensure that more women did listen, the RWS increased its publicity about the Centre in poor neighborhoods and worked more closely with other social service agencies.[56]

For many destitute and proletarianized white women in Johannesburg, the Women's Welfare Centre clearly did not offer sufficient benefits to overcome their reluctance to visit the clinic. For others the barriers were plainly insurmountable. Disappointed with the RWS, for whatever reason, many couples likely returned to familiar pre-modern, non-medicalized methods of fertility control such as abstinence, coitus interruptus or abortion. Indeed, abortion was common according to the women themselves. Of the 481 "lost pregnancies" (out of a total of 2530 pregnancies) reported by users to the Centre in 1933, 436 were reported as either abortions or miscarriages, which was 17 percent of the total number of pregnancies reported that year.[57] (Another 45 percent of lost pregnancies were stillbirths.)

The RWS was continually baffled by the relatively low level of utilization of the Centre by poor white women and throughout the decade it grappled with how to turn the situation around. Edward Mansfield, a founding member of the RWS, in particular wanted the issue addressed or else, he warned, the organization might be successful in terms of the *number* of users but a failure in terms of *type*. He wished to ensure that the organization maintained its focus on negative eugenics in keeping with the vision initially espoused by H.B. Fantham.

III

Ultimately women's lackluster response to the Women's Welfare Centre had a major impact on the RWS. Beginning in the late 1930s it made a series of changes within the organization and its clinics aimed at overcoming material obstacles as well as women's reluctance to utilize the services. These changes demonstrate that the relationship between users and providers was not one of control from above by providers; instead, and ironically, they suggest that the service providers needed users more than users needed the birth-control clinics. Moreover, the changes effected by the RWS in response to women's refusal to utilize its services demonstrate that women *modified* the medicalization of contraception in Johannesburg, thereby illustrating that medicalization is not simply imposed from above by those with greater social power, it is created jointly through a process of interaction and accommodation between professionals and the targets of their services.[58]

The first significant change was in the delivery of contraceptive services. The RWS finally realized that it was crucial to make the services as accessible as possible, which entailed providing more user-friendly spaces than was possible in a downtown business building. Thus they tried bringing birth control directly to residential neighbourhoods. In 1937, it created a "traveling clinic" consisting of a female doctor and nurse who visited the two densely populated white working-class communities of Jeppe and Vrededorp to hold regular clinic sessions once a week.[59] If the traveling clinic proved successful, the RWS had plans to extend its work into the countryside, considered the potent source of poor whiteism. However, attendance at both clinics was disappointingly low, perhaps a lingering consequence of an unpopular reputation. At one point the Jeppe clinic went for three weeks without a single visit. Nevertheless, the RWS, discouraged though not defeated, resolved to redouble its efforts to find "patients." While the Vrededorp clinic was closed after one year, attendance did improve in Jeppe, as shown in Table 4.5.

In another bid to attract users, the RWS transferred control over clinical procedures from doctors to lay members, much to the resentment and resistance of doctors. From the establishment of the RWS in 1930, doctors had been very active both in opening birth-control clinics and as members of the executive: between 1932 and 1937 they constituted at least half of the elected members.[60] From the start they managed the clinics as they thought best, without the involvement or advice of lay members of the organization. But by March 1937, the RWS was sufficiently concerned about the low number of visits to the Centre to

Table 4.5 Number of visits to the Jeppe birth-control clinic for whites, 1937–41

Time period	First visits	Revisits	Total
June 1937 to June 1938	26	39	65
June 1939 to June 1939	95	85	180
June 1939 to March 1940	88	91	179
March 1940 to March 1941	72	103	175
Total	281	318	599

Sources: RWS Annual Reports for 1938–1941 and Executive Committee Report of November 4, 1938.

demand changes to the clinic's procedures. Edward Mansfield, fresh from a six-month trip to England during which he visited birth-control clinics in Cambridge and London, reported to the RWS that English clinics, just like others in South Africa, offered a choice of contraceptives to women, whereas the RWS only offered the Dutch cap. He found it "difficult to understand why experience here should differ so widely from the experience of other clinics" and wanted to bring its clinical practices in line with others in this regard in hopes it would result in similar success.[61]

But the doctors resisted. By the mid-1930s the Centre's doctors were all women – another important change – who worked free of charge.[62] Evidence suggests that female doctors with family responsibilities were drawn to work for free at the Centre because it afforded an opportunity to continue practicing in their profession outside of the high demands of a private practice.[63] Furthermore, the clinics were a field of medical activity that women could manage free from male interference or competition.The doctors viewed their work at the clinics as a purely medical concern beyond the reach of authority of the lay birth-control activists in the RWS. As a consequence, when the RWS tried to change clinical practices, the doctors fought what they perceived as an incursion onto their territory and tried to reassert their right to absolute control over clinical matters. In a letter to the RWS they stated, "We take this opportunity of pointing out that the methods of contraception taught to patients must lie entirely within the province of the Medical Members."[64] Mansfield responded:

I imagine this paragraph was prompted by questions at the last meeting as to whether a choice of contraceptives should not be given to patients in certain cases. Your views on this were asked for to enable lay members of the Executive to understand why the experience of our clinic seems to be at variance with that of similar institutions which use several kinds of contraceptives and maintain this is necessary, sometimes for physiological and sometimes for psychological reasons. If you could say something on this point it would be useful for I am sure you realise that *lay* members of the Executive are called upon to write annual reports, to attend conferences with other Clinics representatives and with the Government Health Dept.; also to prepare statistics for comparison and discussion with other clinics. There are several cards amongst ou[r] own cases which would suggest to a layman the question whether a choice of contraceptives would not be helpful to the Society's aims (emphasis in original).[65]

The letter merely exacerbated the growing division between medical and non-medical members, and despite the doctors' protest, the RWS decided to implement the same procedures that were in place at birth-control clinics in Cape Town, Pietermaritzburg and Port Elizabeth and offer a range of contraceptives.[66]

Winifred Hoernle was also determined to bring clinical procedures in line with those practiced elsewhere in South Africa. In 1938 she visited the Cape Town clinic to ascertain the reasons for its success.[67] Subsequently, when she tried to implement changes regarding staffing levels and compensation at the Women's Welfare Centre another confrontation with medical staff erupted. Doctors once again emphasized their desire to control the medical aspects of clinical work above all other considerations:

Speaking on behalf of the whole medical committee, she thought she could say this: none of them were [sic] interested in ... They were much more keen that the medical staff should be appointed by the medical committee ... The medical committee felt that a recommendation should come from them ... before such appointments were made.[68]

Nevertheless the RWS overrode the doctors again.[69] With new funds from the Union Department of Public Health in hand, the RWS adopted the system "in vogue at practically all other Birth Control clinics" in both South Africa and England and ran all of its clinics for whites with only two doctors that would now be paid for their labor. This would ensure "that on any given day of the week the patient will meet the same doctor as before," thus making women feel more comfortable and, hopefully, increase the rate of return visits. [70] This decision provoked the doctors working at the Centre to resign *en masse*.[71]

For months after this incident the RWS had difficulty in hiring doctors. According to Hoernle, antipathy toward herself and the rest of the RWS made it difficult to find doctors. Yet the shortage did not curtail services at the Centre, for the nurse on staff was promptly pronounced eminently qualified to fit women with diaphragms. The RWS found this solution to be "perfectly in order as Mrs Davis has done this work for seven years and is fully trained and has excellent qualifications,"[72] That Mrs Davis and other nurses were never considered a permanent solution to the shortage of doctors is testimony to how thoroughly the RWS's vision of birth control, like that of other South African birth-control groups, was medicalized.

Finally, the RWS restructured itself in such a way as to shift the majority of the organization's responsibilities and authority to women. In 1937 the RWS created the Women's Committee to reach out to existing and potential users as well as to social welfare agencies that came into contact with them. Altogether the Women's Committee became responsible for: " ... all Clinics and Clinic extension affairs, medical and lay helpers at the Clinic, contact with other social and Municipal workers who may send clients to the clinic, how to attract the desired and very poor type of patient, clinic fees, publicity methods, follow-up of cases, etc."[73] The Women's Committee was given permission to act independently of the executive in all clinic-related matters. Winifred Hoernle, the catalyst behind the new committee, was chair and she was joined by new recruits as well as by other women who were already volunteering on the executive and in the clinics.[74]

Hoernle was a maternalist who believed the RWS's most important role was to improve the health of poor women and their children. Almost overnight she became the *de facto* leader of the RWS and the central participant in all aspects of the organization. She was an effective and determined leader. By June 1939 there were 32 volunteers on the Women's Committee, four doctors and two nurses. The women volunteers were probably the wives of professional men recruited through the academic social circles to which Hoernle belonged by virtue of her position as a lecturer in the Department of Social Anthropology at the University of the Witwatersrand. After this change in structure the few men still active in the RWS (including Henry Britten, J.L. Hardy, and Mansfield) remained on the executive, which now had a hands-off relationship with the clinics. In effect the men relinquished management and control of the clinics and instead devoted their energy to administrative tasks, campaigning for eugenics (by, for example, advocating legislation in favor of sterilizing the "unfit"), raising funds, and other aspects of public relations. In essence, men took up the governance responsibilities for the organization while women provided the clinical services. The creation of the Women's Committee heralded the transformation of the RWS from a male-dominated to a female-dominated organization.

It is probable that the male eugenists had become disillusioned, or perhaps bored, with birth control. Those who originally established the RWS and its first clinic had been excited by the possibility for social reform and social transformation that eugenic birth control represented. After the clinic was in operation, however, the reality of the task before them became clear and their initial exhilaration cooled. It was already obvious by 1935 that "applied eugenics" in the form of birth control would not cure the social ills of poor whiteism and feeblemindedness. Moreover, delivering contraceptive services was neither simple nor gratifying. Women had to be convinced to practice contraception and exhorted to return for fresh supplies. As direct contact with potential users appeared necessary in order to persuade them to visit the Centre, the men in the RWS must have realized that women would be more effective because their gender enabled them to communicate more successfully regarding the needs and concerns of their poor counterparts. Grassroots, community-based work with poor women likely held little appeal for highly educated male professionals who preferred public speaking, policy development and lobbying Government.[75]

Under Hoernle's guidance the RWS became much more pro-active in reaching out to potential and existing users, and the nature of the new initiatives was personal, involving face-to-face discussion between women about intimate matters. Under the new leadership, the RWS held "talks for mothers" in poor townships. Committees were also formed to make the RWS's services more welcoming and useful. A Reception Committee welcomed women and interviewed them about their reproductive history, and a Follow-up Committee tried to resolve the "lost" cases. Beginning in November 1937, volunteers sent letters to women inquiring about the effectiveness of the contraceptives and stressing the necessity of regular return visits. A self-addressed stamped postcard was enclosed in the letter to encourage them to reply. By November 1938, 525 letters had been sent of which 160 were returned and 65 were answered, results, they assured themselves, that compared favorably with London clinics.[76] Finally a Visiting Committee was established, which made uninvited visits to women in hopes of driving them to the Jeppe birth-control clinic. Volunteers drove to the homes of women who lived outside the city limits and had not returned within six months after attending a clinic. To prepare the women, volunteers sent postcards in advance informing them of the date a driver would arrive to fetch them. Hoernle herself, "together with a band of University Ladies," took the lead in following up on users who "failed" to return.[77]

After six months of driving women from outlying areas to and from its clinics, the RWS claimed publicly that "in this way [we] persuaded many pitiful cases to receive help."[78] In 1939 it provided the following account of the Visiting Committee

> Since the commencement of 1939 patients here [at Jeppe and Vrededorp] have been encouraged to attend [the clinics] by means of fetching them and taking them back to their homes, after treatment, in private motor cars. Many in this district have young families with no help to allow them to leave these children for too long a period. Many have too far to travel and no money to spend on tram-fares. The method has justified itself, as the statistics show. At first, one felt many were coming because they couldn't refuse the car ride and one was dubious about their availing themselves of the help given. Some expressed doubts of the efficacy of the appliances. Lately one has lost that hasty feeling and the women are now coming willingly and ready to avail themselves of the help given. Many are returning for further supplies and express themselves satisfied and grateful. Most important, they are telling their friends of their satisfaction and bringing them with them to the Clinic.[79]

Evidently some women were reluctant to get in the car and be taken to a clinic, yet at least a few acquiesced. Nevertheless, the program was far less successful than was publicly claimed. In the minutes of a private meeting a volunteer reported that, in fact, poor women "too frequently ... were not prepared to come."[80] In the face of women's resistance, the Visiting Committee quietly decided to cease driving to outlying neighbourhoods.

In contrast, networking with other agencies in order to obtain users proved fruitful. For example, the District Nurses Association began requesting the city's Health Visitors to inform their patients about the birth-control clinics, and Social Services, the Rand Aid Society and Children's Aid Society were reporting women "most needing help" to the RWS.[81] Yet many of these women did not choose to visit the Women's Welfare Centre, as the RWS admitted.[82] And much to eugenists' frustration, the "wrong type" of client was still suspected of visiting the Centre. Clearly at a loss for the means to attract indigent white women, in 1939 the leaders of the RWS lamely requested the Centre's nurse "to try to get the poorer women to come."[83]

IV

During the 1930s, thousands of poor and working-class white women utilized the RWS's clinics to obtain inexpensive contraception or gynaecological health care. Clearly these women decided medicalized contraceptive services, and the related technologies, conveyed valuable benefits. The number of return visits are further evidence of the value of the RWS's services. Still, the overwhelming majority of women stayed away. Whether unable, reluctant, or outright resistant, the women of Johannesburg largely avoided the Center, dashing the hopes of eugenists who believed that birth control would solve poor whiteism, feeblemindedness, and other social ills. Through their reluctance to use the clinics, women of all races impeded the expansion of medicalized contraceptive services in Johannesburg during the 1930s.

In 1939 the RWS's Women's Committee changed the name of the downtown birth-control clinic for whites to the Mother's Welfare Clinic. The name change symbolized the influence of the maternalist Hoernle who, along with the women she recruited as volunteers, attempted to refashion the RWS in keeping with the approach of the South African National Council for Maternal and Family Welfare (SANCMFW). Hoernle was more interested in improving maternal and infant health among all races than in eliminating "defective stock," and she looked for direction and inspiration from the MCC, the most successful birth-control organization in South Africa. By December 1939 the Women's Committee was directing the RWS and its clinics.[84] During the Second World War, as the few remaining male members of the RWS were absorbed by the war effort, the RWS became a completely female organization. In March 1944, Henry Britten moved to Pretoria and Winifred Hoernle became chair and shortly thereafter, dozens of women who volunteered at the clinics along with three doctors, two nurses, and six other female volunteers were elected *en masse* to the RWS executive; no men remained.[85] By the end of the Second World War, under Hoernle's guidance, the RWS had recast itself from a eugenist to a maternalist provider of contraceptive services.

5

The Cape Town Mothers' Clinic

This work is ... of such grave importance to the health and
happiness of many poor women and their families.

The Mothers' Clinic Committee[1]

I

On February 15, 1932, the Mothers' Clinic Committee (MCC) opened a
birth-control clinic for poor women of all "races" in Cape Town. Just like
the Race Welfare Society (RWS), the MCC opened its clinic within easy
reach of destitute and working-class women. Also like the RWS, the
Cape Town group implemented clinical procedures established by clinics in London. It modeled their clinic, including its name, after Marie
Stopes's famous Mothers' Clinic, which opened in Holloway, London,
in 1921. But unlike the Women's Welfare Centre in Johannesburg, the
Mothers' Clinic was an immediate success, quickly attracting and maintaining a steady stream of users from a range of racial groups. Its success
was a direct reflection of the MCC's liberal, feminist ideology, as it
perceived women and their needs in a far more sympathetic light than
did the RWS. Through their demonstrated willingness to utilize the
Mothers' Clinic, the poor women of Cape Town played a crucial role in
the expansion of medicalized reproductive health care – not just in their
city but throughout South Africa.

The MCC established the Mothers' Clinic in Observatory, a working-
class district located at one end of the belt of working-class settlement
that stretched from the Cape Town docks inland along the railway line
(see Maps 4 and 5). This was a densely populated and multi-racial residential corridor. As the historian Vivian Bickford-Smith writes, by 1900
this region of the city "was characterized by high density housing and

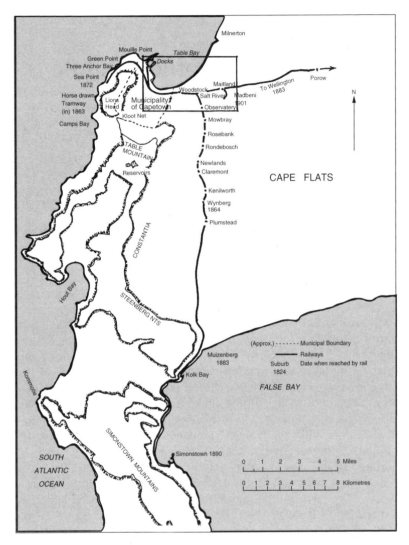

Map 4 The Cape Peninsula, *c.* 1901. The box indicates the city neighborhoods that the Mothers' Clinic served in the 1930s.

Source: V. Bickford-Smith, *Ethnic Pride and Racial Prejudice in Victorian Cape Town* (Johannesburg: Witwatersrand University Press, 1995).

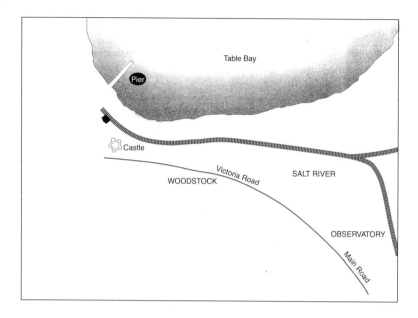

Map 5   A closer look at Woodstock, Salt River, and Observatory, three working-class neighborhoods served by the Mothers' Clinic in the 1930s.

Source: V. Bickford-Smith, E. Van Heyningen and N. Worden, *Cape Town in the Twentieth Century: An Illustrated Social History* (Cape Town: David Philip, 1999), p. 61.

residents were overwhelmingly small shopkeepers, artisans and labourers, with a tiny sprinkling of professionals in the form of an occasional doctor, clergyman or lawyer."[2] Observatory and its neighboring districts of Woodstock and Salt River were popular destinations for the influx of "poor whites" fleeing the Cape countryside in the 1930s. Among the substantial number of Jews who emigrated to South Africa in the first third of the twentieth century, the poorest also settled in Woodstock, Salt River or District Six.[3] These neighborhoods were also home to many Coloureds, who lived mainly in the Cape. In 1930, there were 682 000 Coloureds in the Cape, as compared to a tiny minority of that number in the Transvaal and Orange Free State, and "a large majority" were extremely poor.[4] Those with jobs were generally employed as unskilled laborers. But poverty cut across race and ethnic identities in these neighborhoods, where "socioeconomic statuses of Whites, Coloureds, Indians, a few Chinese, and even sometimes Black Africans were similar."[5] As the economy began growing again after 1933, working-class whites began moving up the socio-economic ladder and to more prosperous parts of the city, and as they left, blacks took their place. Between 1936 and 1960, the white population in this area fell by one-third while the Coloured population increased by almost half.[6]

Observatory was also situated close to the city's expanding, racially integrated industrial manufacturing sector, which employed rising numbers of black and white women in the production of food, beverages, tobacco, paper, and clothing during the 1930s. In 1929, there were 7775 female factory workers in Cape Town: 4964 Coloured and 2778 white.[7] (Only 15 African and 18 Asian women were known to be working in factories at that time.[8]) By 1938, the number of female factories had increased to 13 200, just under half of whom were white.[9] By mid-decade, the clothing industry alone employed about 40 percent of the city's white female workforce.[10] Many of the white women who worked in the factories were members of families of recently urbanized poor whites who had left the Cape countryside in order to find jobs in the city. Indeed, the rural white population in the Cape decreased dramatically in the 1920s. It is estimated that as much as 19 percent of whites born in the province left altogether by 1926. Some moved to the Orange Free State or the Transvaal, while others went to Cape Town.[11] As one elderly white Afrikaans-speaking woman, whose family gave up farming on the Cape *platteland* and moved to Cape Town in 1925, explained to the Carnegie Commission of Investigation on the Poor White Question, "We came to Cape Town in order to work. That's what we came for. Look, many people had already left the farm, people who had their own land and all ... so that their children could work ... And they did not work in shops or offices. In factories."[12] Located alongside the railway line and close to the railway station built in 1878, Observatory was also home to families in which white men worked on the nationalized South African Railways, a major employer of poor whites in the wake of the state's "civilized labour" policy of replacing black with white workers. Among white men residing in Observatory who married in 1932, half reported on their marriage certificates that they worked for the railways as laborers, boilermen, cleaners or drivers.[13]

Observatory's neighboring suburbs of Woodstock and Salt River had the heaviest concentration of the city's white and Coloured "dependants," recipients of assistance from the Cape Town General Board of Aid. In 1933, a sociologist studying 3300 dependents concluded that "the more densely populated and overcrowded areas (for example, District Six, Woodstock, and Salt River) are also those in which the clustering of dependent units, European and Coloured, is the heaviest, the housing and sanitary conditions the worst, and the intermingling of European and Coloured within the same vicinity and buildings the most frequent."[14] Indeed, in the interwar years unemployment was acute in Cape Town: applications from whites alone for work at the Government labor bureau was usually around 10 000, reaching nearly 30 000 in 1933.[15] In short, the Mothers' Clinic Committee situated its birth-control clinic in the heart of working-class and outcast Cape Town.

The Mothers' Clinic was busy from the start. In the first ten-and-a-half months of operation 524 married women visited the clinic in racially segregated sessions; half the women were "non-European" (mainly Coloured women along with some Indian and Malay women) and the other half were white.[16] Indeed, after just one year of operation the unexpectedly large number of users led the MCC to relocate its premises to a more spacious site in Observatory. The clinic also doubled the number of sessions from two to four per week, two each for "European" and "non-European" women.[17] It remained popular throughout the decade. As Table 5.1 shows, 3763 women made 11 308 visits (including first-time and return) to the Mothers' Clinic from February 1932 to March 1939. In contrast, 2835 women made 6769 visits to all five of the RWS's clinics during the same period of time.[18] This is all the more impressive when considering that Cape Town was a much smaller urban center, with a population of 344 200 in 1936, of which 174 000 were whites. The number of whites alone on the Witwatersrand in 1936 was 402 223.[19]

Women visiting the Mothers' Clinic were from a range of racial backgrounds, which reflected both the racial integration that still existed in Observatory and the surrounding communities in the 1930s, and, more importantly, the MCC's liberal approach. The policy of serving women

Table 5.1   Total number of visits to the Mothers' Clinic, 1932–39

Year	First visits	Revisits	Total number of visits
1932	524	n/a	524
1933	756	1269	2025
1934	507	1058	1565
1935	447	1153	1600
1936	523	1356	1879
1937	426	1207	1633
To Mar. 1939	580	1502	2082
Total	3763	7545	11 308

Source: MCC Annual Reports, 1932–39.

Table 5.2 Total number of women who visited the Mothers' Clinic by racial category, 1932–39

Racial category	Number of women	% of Total women
Coloured Women	2092	56
European women	1671	44
Total number of women	3763	100

Source: MCC Annual Reports, 1932–39.

Table 5.3 Total number of women who visited the Mothers' Clinic annually by racial category, 1932–39

Year	No. of new users	European	Non-European
1932	524	262	262
1933	756	379	377
1934	507	228	279
1935	447	221	226
1936	523	204	319
1937	426	166	260
To Mar. 1939	580	211	369

Source: MCC Annual Reports, 1932–39.

of all colors accounts for much of the clinic's popularity. As Table 5.2 shows, just over half of the users (56 percent) that visited the clinic by March 1939 were reportedly "Coloured" (a category that likely masked the presence of women from a variety of racial groups, including Indian, Malay, and African women in addition to Cape Coloured women). Furthermore, as Table 5.3 illustrates, the proportion of "non-European" women visiting the clinic began growing larger than that of whites starting in 1934 and continued to do so for the rest of the decade.

Cutting across racial lines was women's common experience of overwhelming poverty. Of the 524 women to visit the clinic in 1932 almost half (42.7 percent) had husbands who were "totally unemployed while a great many others [were] dependent on casual work." In the following year the proportion was one-third (32.5 percent).[20] In many cases the family income was around 2/- (two shillings) per week, far below a subsistence wage. On the Rand, for example, many white male workers in the 1920s earned the equivalent of farm wages that ranged between 17s 6d and 25s per week, and black wages were comparable, varying between 15s 8d and 23s 9d per week.[21] By comparison the families of

Table 5.4 Occupations by gender as listed in user profiles, Mothers' Clinic, 1932–39

Women's occupation	No. of women	Men's occupations	No. of men
Charwoman	8	Laborer	2
Washerwoman	5	Hawker	2
Domestic servant	4	"Odd jobs"	2
		Storeman	1
		Fisherman	1
		Wood-turner	1
		Ganger	1
		Waiter	1
		Relief-works worker	1
		Railway worker	1
		Gardener	1
		Part-time painter	1
Total	17		15

Source: MCC Annual Reports, 1932–39.

some of the Mothers' Clinic users were clearly destitute and most likely survived on charity.

Throughout the decade the MCC published profiles of women and their husbands who worked in poorly paid, casual occupations. As shown in Table 5.4, users were listed as domestic workers, charwomen, or laundresses, occupations that mirrored their unpaid labor in the home, whereas men held a wide assortment of casual jobs. As one woman who left rural Namaqualand for Cape Town in 1935 remembered, "There wasn't work on the *platteland*. There was also scarcely work in the city ... if you found a job, you grabbed it with both your hands so that you wouldn't lose it."[22]

In addition to casual employment, clinic users also included factory workers, many of whom continued to work outside the home after they married. For these women the additional wage, however low, was essential to their family's survival. Limiting or postponing pregnancy was yet another strategy women employed to reduce the economic burden on the family's already meager income.

The MCC certainly did not introduce the practice of fertility control to the women of Cape Town. In 1932, 42.7 percent of the total number of first-time users reported that they had attempted to prevent conception prior to visiting the Mothers' Clinic (see Table 5.5). Such a large proportion – almost half – indicates that birth control was

Table 5.5   Women who had practiced contraception prior to their first visit to the Mothers' Clinic, 1932–39

Year	No. of women	% of women
1932	224	42.7
1937	200*	46.9
To Mar. 1939	237	40.8

Note: *For 1937, report states "over two hundred women had tried unsuccessfully to prevent conception."
Source: MCC Annual Reports, 1932–39.

a well-entrenched practice. Dr. Patricia Massey, a physician at the Mothers' Clinic from 1935 to 1938, confirmed this point by stating that her interest in providing contraceptive services had been sparked by patients asking her for contraceptives. She recalled that the poor women at the Mothers' Clinic were no different from her middle-class patients in wanting to control their fertility.[23]

Most users had already experienced numerous pregnancies by the time they made their first visit to the Mothers' Clinic. Indeed, for some, childbirth was an annual occurrence. One woman was noted as having had thirteen pregnancies, all of whom survived into childhood. Another woman had, "12 Pregnancies in 11 years. All born alive, all died in infancy."[24] In 1932, 194 of 524 women (37 percent) who visited the clinic had experienced between six and ten pregnancies (see Table 5.6). By March 1939, however, these numbers began to change. By then only 28 percent of first-time users reported having six to ten pregnancies, while conversely, those reporting three to five pregnancies climbed from 31 percent to 37 percent, and those reporting only one to two pregnancies rose from 17 percent to 23 percent. Table 5.7 shows that the average number of pregnancies experienced by women visiting the Mothers' Clinic for the first time dropped steadily from 6.1 in 1932 to 4.87 in 1939. Together Tables 5.6 and 5.7 suggest that during the course of the 1930s women in Cape Town were reducing their family size, possibly a reflection of the growing number of women working for wages as the economy recovered from the Depression and the manufacturing sector expanded. According to the historian Marijke du Toit, many Afrikaans-speaking white women in Cape Town who married in the 1930s had fewer children than their mothers.[25] Unfortunately, the MCC did not provide the age of users in this table and therefore it is impossible to include this factor into an analysis of their reproductive history.

Table 5.6 Number of pregnancies reported by users during first visit to the Mothers' Clinic, statistics listed annually, 1932–39

No. of pregnancies and percentage	1932	1933	1934	1935	1936	1937	1938/39
1–2 pregnancies	89	154	115	107	128	119	132
% of total	16.9	20	23	22	24	28	23
3–5 pregnancies	165	317	194	170	165	167	213
% of total	31.4	42	38	36	32	39	37
6–10 pregnancies	194	216	137	134	177	107	163
% of total	37	29	27	28	34	25	28
11–15 pregnancies	56	61	50	28	26	19	32
% of total	10.6	8	10	6	5	4	6
16–20 pregnancies	11	2	5	*	6	3	2
% of total	2	0.2	1	*	1	0.7	0.3
Total no. of users	524	756	507	477	523	426	580

Note: *This category not included for 1935.

Source: MCC Annual Reports, 1932–39.

Table 5.7 Average number of pregnancies per woman prior to first visit to the Mothers' Clinic, 1932–39

Year	Avg. no. of pregnancies
1932	6.1
1933	5.005
1934	5.49
1935	5.22
1936	5.06
1937	4.67
To Mar. 1939	4.87

Source: MCC Annual Reports, 1932–39.

II

From its inception the Mother's Clinic followed the same clinical procedures practiced in the Women's Welfare Centre in Johannesburg. For example, clinic volunteers interviewed first-time users who were required to reveal personal information such as age, income, and reproductive history, all of which were noted down along with a woman's putative race. Afterwards doctors performed cervical examinations in order to assess which contraceptive would be most appropriate. As the MCC explained in an annual report, during the internal exam doctors also screened women for gynecological and other health problems:

> The routine Gynaecological Examination at the Clinic sometimes reveals abnormalities which may respond to simple treatment. More serious conditions may also be detected at a sufficiently early stage for curative treatment from a specialist. Mothers in poor homes have practically no post natal supervision, and the Committee feels that the clinic is help[ing], to some degree, to remedy this serious position. Cases requiring operative or other treatment have been referred by the Clinic doctors to specialists at Hospitals, VD centres etc., and this valuable branch of the work in relation to the health of the mother cannot be too highly stressed.[26]

Through such routine gynecological exams, doctors found many ailments: in 1932, for example, 105 women (20 percent of the total users that year) were referred to private doctors, hospitals, or municipal clinics to be treated for TB and VD.[27]

Unlike the Women's Welfare Centre, the Mothers' Clinic had a range of contraceptives from which to choose. Cervical caps were the favorite option (just as it was at the Stopes clinic), but, according to Sallie Woodrow, a co-founder of the MCC and its first Medical Officer, they were often useless because "the majority of our patients come so torn and mutilated with excessive child-bearing that they are unable to wear [them] at all."[28] For these women, doctors recommended the diaphragm or rubber sponge. The latter option was especially useful for women who were so poor they were deemed unlikely to return to the clinic to replenish supplies, because the sponge could be effective when used in conjunction with cooking oil. (The MCC purchased caps and sponges from Stopes, who developed her "Racial" line of contraceptives in the 1920s.) Caps and diaphragms were prescribed in conjunction with lactic acid jelly as well as soluble vaginal suppositories (commonly called pessaries), consisting of quinine sulphate and salicylic acid in dollops of cocoa butter, for additional protection. Doctors instructed women to insert vaginal suppositories along with their cap or diaphragm five to ten minutes before intercourse. This allowed time for the suppository to soften but was not so long that it turned to liquid and lost its effectiveness as a barrier. The sponge, which, ideally, was to be soaked in oil prior to usage, was also recommended in tandem with a pessary.[29] For a time the clinic also prescribed the Graafenberg ring (an intrauterine device).

For women who were unable to use any form of technology requiring insertion, doctors prescribed condoms, which were reportedly unpopular with some husbands.[30] Dr. Dorothea Douglas-Henry, who worked in MCC clinics in the early 1940s, recalled "Very, very few men would have considered using condoms. They were very definitely part of the illicit sex scene ... they weren't associated with the marital relationship because as far as men were concerned [regarding sex] they had their rights."[31]

The women of Cape Town faced the same kinds of obstacles as those of Johannesburg when it came to utilizing the new technologies successfully, including miserable housing, insensitive husbands, and plain exhaustion. Sallie Woodrow recalled that the failure rate with the cervical cap and diaphragm was "very high" and cited "basic lack of privacy, uncooperative husbands and the apathy of tired and overburdened mothers" as the greatest barriers.[32]

The first and foremost obstacle was the atrocious housing. Users required a modicum of privacy to insert and remove the devices, and they also needed access to water, powder, and space with which to keep them clean and stored. But workers' and dependants' homes were usually overcrowded and families often lived in one or two rooms. For example, the MCC reported one case where three families with at least five children each lived in a three-roomed house, thus leaving little privacy in which to conduct such intimate practices.[33] A 1933-study of poverty in Cape Town provided graphic descriptions of housing conditions. Among the thousands of dependants studied, "It was ... usual to find one family per room, so that it often happened that anything from fifteen families upwards were housed in the same building under the most uncomfortable conditions."[34] Among 21 percent of "European" and 44 percent of "Non-European" dependants surveyed, five or more persons slept in rooms judged suitable for two. Furthermore, over 20 percent of "Non-European" families had to fetch water from outside their dwelling (usually from the backyard or the end of a passageway), and over half of the "Europeans" (54 percent) and almost all of the "Non-Europeans" (93 percent) reported that they had no bathroom or else shared one with up to sixteen households. Many lavatories were in a "shocking" condition.[35] Only 18 percent of "European" and 6 percent of the "Non-European" dependants had lavatories for the exclusive use of their households. Indeed, when discussing why few white Afrikaans-speaking women could obtain "respectable" work in shops, Marie Rothmann, a leading Afrikaner nationalist, explained that in part this was because "in her overcrowded home (which is often shared by the whole family)" a woman cannot "give herself the bodily care and attention that are necessary for giving her a good personal appearance."[36] Under such deplorable circumstances the cervical cap and diaphragm must have required more effort and attention from women than their material circumstances allowed. Moreover, the technologies required forethought and the ability to recall a list of directions. Woodrow reported that "the patients are told to remove their caps or sponges the afternoon or evening following intercourse and on no account to leave them in more than 24 hours."[37] For women who suffered from blinding exhaustion and the stress that accompanied the struggle of surviving yet another day of poverty, such instructions would have been challenging if not impossible to follow. Other barriers included lack of transport for rural women (see below) and lack of support from husbands. As discussed in Chapter 4, Dr. Dorothea Douglas-Henry reported that, when she worked at the Cape Town clinic in the early 1940s, some women suffered violent opposition at the hands of their husbands who resented their wives' efforts to exert control over their own fertility. Given such serious difficulties, some users may well have simply given up trying to use the new technologies and reverted to pre-medicalized methods of fertility control.

Yet despite the many obstacles facing women who attempted to practice medicalized contraception, women continued to utilize the Mothers' Clinic to a remarkable extent. The MCC's success in attracting and then maintaining users, in spite of such challenges, reflected the organization's intertwined strands of liberal and maternal feminist ideology, for it set out to translate its ideas about birth control into a supportive clinical environment for women of all races.

Members of the MCC and the staff at the Mothers' Clinic tried their best to treat women respectfully and compassionately. As Woodrow told her medical colleagues in the 1930s, the staff at the Mothers' Clinic sought to maintain an "atmosphere of confidence and sympathy."[38] Ursula Scott, the MCC's chair, repeatedly highlighted with pride the clinic's female doctors' gentle, caring approach, noting the "kindly care and patience [the doctors] have exercised,"[39] and their "unfailing interest, kindness, and patience, coupled with their medical efficiency ... [which] have been a great help to the Mothers who visit the centre."[40] Such claims are corroborated by an important independent observer, Marie Rothmann, who testified enthusiastically to the kindness of the clinic staff after she and a number of Afrikaner nationalist women colleagues from the *Afrikaans Christelike Vroue Vereniging* toured the Mothers' Clinic in 1933. In rhapsodic prose she recounted for

Die Burger, an influential Afrikaner nationalist newspaper, what she witnessed there:

> A person is not right in the head if you don't see the clean, simple, well-stocked clinic with its really good women doctors, enthusiastic manager and staff as a haven … What is it that is so beautiful? In the first place the beautiful spirit. Doctors, nurses, staff helpers, all support one idea, to help, to lessen the load of many problems. It feels when you are dealing with them, the doctors, that they are full of love and helpfulness and what mother is there that is unfeeling towards that?[41]

To Rothmann, contraception was the difference between feeling "like a prisoner" and "a free human being," and she rigourously endorsed the Mothers' Clinic.[42]

While for many years the RWS offered only one contraceptive option – the diaphragm – the Mothers' Clinic offered several, which implies awareness of women's varying experience and needs. Furthermore, the clinic, modeled after Stopes's example, must have been a great deal more concerned about women's sexuality than the eugenists at the RWS. Stopes's radical argument in *Married Love* (1918) that women were entitled to sexual satisfaction within marriage greatly explains the book's sensational popularity as well as Stopes's international reputation. Clearly the Cape Town organization embraced this idea, as was discussed in Chapter 3. No less significant, the MCC also assisted women in overcoming infertility, a service that respected and affirmed women's desire to be mothers. Though always a relatively tiny proportion of the clientele (see Table 5.8), the number of such women increased in the last few years of the decade.

The MCC also showed remarkable responsiveness to users by continually inventing new, and revising old, procedures in order to make them more practical, appropriate, and less intimidating. A number of these procedures were taken up by the RWS after Winifred Hoernle visited the Mothers' Clinic in 1938.[43] The plight of isolated rural women, which caused the MCC particular anxiety, is a case in point. Upon opening its doors, news of the Mothers' Clinic's existence traveled quickly and letters requesting advice and supplies arrived from as far north as South West Africa (Namibia).[44] In 1935, for example, a farmer in Transvaal wrote, "Will you kindly send me full information about Birth Control? I shall be glad to know of any *reliable* literature on the subject in English or Dutch that you can recommend" (emphasis in original).[45] Members

Table 5.8 Number of women seeking "advice desiring pregnancy," 1932–39

Year	No. of Women
1932	9
1933	6
1934	6
1935	5
1936	21
1937	11
1938/39	38

Source: The Mothers' Clinic Committee Annual Reports, 1932–39.

were plainly moved by the "pitiful" letters they received from women in outlying districts and they repeatedly discussed the "real demand for help for mothers in isolated areas" who were beyond their reach.[46] The MCC's policy, which reflected its firm commitment to medicalization and respect for the medical profession, advised rural women to consult with a doctor in order to obtain contraceptives. But as the MCC fully realized, this was often impossible because rural women had little if any access to medical attention and even if they did, most rural doctors were ignorant about methods of birth control. In typical pragmatic fashion, the group devised ways to address the urban–rural divide. In 1933, for example, it began training health practitioners who were destined to work in rural areas, including doctors, nurses, midwives, health visitors, senior medical students, social workers, and even District Surgeons.[47] As Ursula Scott reported,

> The Committee feels that this is a most important branch of the work itself. If the women in rural areas are in the future to receive the same education in spacing and limiting their families as the urban women, it is essential that doctors and the nurses working with them in rural areas, should have some practical knowledge of contraceptive technique.[48]

In the early 1930s, the MCC had a policy of providing tram tickets (donated by the City Tramways) to women who lived away from Observatory.[49] Later it devised the practice of mailing contraceptive supplies to users who had visited the clinic once but were unable to return. Starting in the mid-1930s, women "living at too great a distance" from the clinic had their supplies replenished every year by a volunteer.[50] Over 200 parcels were mailed in 1937 and a further 216 by March 1939; in this way the number of women who utilized the MCC's services was significantly larger than indicated in statistics published in annual reports.[51]

The MCC also adjusted clinical procedures in response to women's experience. Upon encountering users' resistance to being examined by male doctors being trained in contraceptive technique, the MCC abandoned the "experiment" of educating men. Scott never expressed frustration with users' objections to male doctors, only a sense of satisfaction with the "definite desire on the part of qualified [male] practitioners" for an opportunity to gain practical experience.[52] Beginning in 1934, the MCC formed a Follow-Up Committee in order to help women remember to return to the clinic to replenish their supplies of lactic acid jelly. The committee sent notices to users to which there was "an encouraging response."[53]

Certainly at times the MCC's compassion was inflected with condescension borne out of the providers' privileged social status. Members of the MCC were highly educated, white, English-speaking women who were members of Cape Town's social elite, and at times they referred with seeming irritation to "the apathetic attitude of a large number of women to the continuous practice of contraceptive methods."[54] Similarly, failures in contraception were attributed to "either the low mentality of some of the women dealt with, or the apathy in carrying out continuously, the detailed printed and verbal instructions they receive."[55] A portrayal of a user in 1932 was unusually blunt: "Patient 39 years; married 24 years; 21 pregnancies; stupid dull European; deaf and very muddled with her irksome life."[56] By contrast users who kept in touch with the clinic every six months for supplies were said to be "definitely co-operating in the successful practice of sound birth-control methods."[57]

Despite the condescension, the relationship between providers and users was never one of social control. Furthermore, providers developed ever-greater respect for users as their experience in the birth-control movement increased. A key reason for this was their direct involvement in service provision. From its inception the MCC balanced governance responsibilities, including fund raising, policy development, and lobbying, with the hands-on management of the clinics. Members acted as doctors in the Mothers' Clinic, they organized annual fund-raising rummage sales for lower-class women, interviewed users in the clinic, responded to their letters from the countryside, and mailed "follow-up" letters and contraceptive supplies. Their wider range of experience educated them about the material reality of users' lives, resulting in a concomitant willingness to adjust procedures to better serve them. In stark contrast, no overlap in governance and administrative activities occurred in the RWS until the late 1930s when Winifred Hoernle attempted to restructure the organization along the lines of the MCC. Up until that time, the RWS separated the spheres of activity in a gendered fashion; the executive was dominated by male professionals who restricted their activities to policy-related issues, whereas the clinics were staffed by women who performed the day-to-day services. In a sense the education process flowed both ways at the Mothers' Clinic: providers showed users how to use new technologies and users offered providers a window on to the world of hardship. By contrast, the gendered division of labor at the RWS allowed its male leadership to maintain an objectified, abstract, almost fantastical perception of "poor whites" as degenerates "tainting" white racial stock. Their social distance from the women who actually used the contraceptive services ultimately made them less effective in meeting their goal of encouraging more poor white women to limit their family size.

By the mid-1930s, the MCC's increased insight into the challenges facing women desiring to control their fertility was evident in the new tone of its annual reports. For example, Scott wrote of how "In spite of lack of privacy for so many of these unfortunate mothers in their crowded homes – often only one room – most of them do carry out the instructions with care."[58] Similarly, when explaining why some women could not return on a regular basis, Scott reported, "Some mothers live in outlying districts, others are in employment or suffering from ill health, and others find it hard to leave a large family of small children."[59] Such statements contextualized users' relationship to the Mothers' Clinic in a way rarely attempted by the RWS. Nor did the RWS evince the same palpable concern for poor women's health. To Scott, cases in which women managed to secure just a few months' respite from another pregnancy were cause for satisfaction because of the "inevitable beneficial result to mother and child."[60]

The MCC also showed understanding and compassion conveyed in highly maternalist terms for why women would attempt to obtain illegal abortions. Indeed, in public comments about why women would find abortion necessary, it seemed as though by the end of the 1930s the MCC broadened its perception of its mandate to include educating the *public* about poor women's needs in addition to teaching *users* about contraceptive methods:

... the Committee feels that the need for sickly and overburdened mothers to receive advice in sound contraceptive methods, as an alternative to self-induced abortion, is amply demonstrated. As the Professor of Midwifery in Aberdeen University has stated – "Where poverty and malnutrition are realities, it is the good mother and not the bad one who dreads the coming of too many children. Weakness and suffering for themselves they can face, but when the weakness means that they cannot care for the children they have, when the new mouth to feed means that the others must be stinted, who can wonder that in these circumstances the mother tries whatever is at hand, to escape?"[61]

In fact, many women visiting the Mothers' Clinic for the first time were clearly hoping to find assistance securing abortions, which, as discussed in Chapter 2, were probably so common in the 1930s as to render legislation against them unenforceable. In 1932 Ursula Scott reported that 135 women out of a total of 525 first-time visitors in that year, a striking 25.7 percent, were *already pregnant* when they arrived at the clinic. She imparted this statistic in terms that suggest women were ignorant of their condition, but it is much more likely that a good many of those women, already mothers, knew very well that they were pregnant and were hoping to find help in procuring a safe abortion. In Johannesburg Dr. I.J. Block of the RWS reported that this occurred at the Women's Welfare Clinic: "Some [women] came under a misconception that something could or would be done for them to terminate the pregnancy."[62] That users openly reported having had abortions suggests that they had not accepted and internalized the relatively new idea that abortion was immoral. Instead, they brushed off admonitions against it. In Johannesburg, women denied help in obtaining an abortion at the Women's Welfare Centre were, in the eyes of Block, brazen enough to return after "having got rid of the pregnancy in spite of advice from the doctors of the advisability of continuing with the pregnancy."[63]

The MCC and the staff at the Mothers' Clinic were very sympathetic in cases where women were desperate for abortions. Scott once noted: "It has been pitiful to see the distress of these unfortunate mothers once more burdened with an unwanted pregnancy."[64] Notwithstanding these sympathetic overtures, the MCC thoroughly disapproved of the practice – at least officially – and made a clear distinction between abortion and "birth control," the latter being defined solely as conception prevention.[65] Its unequivocal opposition was evident in profiles of users such as the following, found in its 1937 annual report:

> 41 [year old woman], 13 Pregnancies, 6 living children, oldest aged 8 years. Father irregular earnings about £2 0s. 0d. per week. Mother in domestic service, earns £3 5s. 0d. per month, pregnant again at first visit to the Clinic. Appliance brought to Clinic given to Mother by employer to produce an abortion. Strongly recommended not to make use of this but to bear her child and return later for contraceptive advice.[66]

Such statements reflected the MCC's efforts to be perceived by the state and medical profession as a legitimate health service provider. Yet, as if to remind the public of the desperation of women facing unwanted pregnancy, the MCC followed the above profile with another in which an abortion ended in tragedy: "37 [year old woman], 12 Pregnancies. Five died under age of two years, 7 living children. Father's earnings £1 5s. 0d. per week. Mother terribly distressed to find she was pregnant again at first visit to Clinic. This mother subsequently tried to procure an abortion on herself and died."[67]

III

While women received access to a service that they valued, they in turn conferred legitimacy on the MCC. The group's success at attracting users quickly established the Cape Town group as the leading birth-control organization in South Africa. As president of the national coalition of birth-control organizations formed in 1935 (SANCMFW), Scott became the leading advocate of birth control in the country. In that capacity she made persuasive presentations, inflected by maternalist and neo-Malthusian ideas, to a variety of national commissions and conferences, usually winning endorsements for "family spacing." As the busiest birth-control organization in South Africa and the leading member of the national coalition, the MCC also impressed the national Department of Public Health (DPH). As the next chapter shows, Scott met with Edward Thornton, the Secretary for Public Health, and Jan Hofmeyr, the Minister for Public Health, and advised the DPH on ways to expand contraceptive services. Ultimately, poor women of Cape Town played a crucial role in the expansion of access to medicalized contraception in South Africa. It was through their participation at the

Mothers' Clinic that the MCC developed its reputation as the most effective birth-control organization in South Africa. In turn, women's high rate of utilization was the result of the MCC's compassionate and encouraging approach to women. The RWS watched the MCC from Johannesburg with envy, and by the end of the decade was applying some of the lessons learned by its colleagues in Cape Town.

6

State Support for Birth Control

> This subject of birth-control has now emerged from the
> darkness of ignorance and quackery into the light of accepted
> clinical practice.
>
> Dr. Hope Trant, 1935[1]

I

In 1931 the Race Welfare Society (RWS) informed the Department of
Public Health (DPH) about its intention to open a birth-control clinic for
the express purpose of curbing the poor white problem.[2] On the one
hand, the Minister of Public Health, D.F. Malan, a *predikant* (minister) in
the Dutch Reformed Church (DRC), opposed the proposal, most likely
for conservative moral reasons. On the other hand, Edward Thornton,
then the Acting Secretary of Public Health, was receptive to the idea.[3] He
did not support the RWS's initial proposal for a free-standing clinic
devoted solely to distributing contraceptives. This was largely because of
the powerful political and religious opposition to birth control and also
in part because "experience elsewhere," he claimed, showed that many
women attended birth-control clinics not because they wanted to control
their fertility but because they needed medical or surgical treatment of
disease or discomfort – a comment that revealed his ignorance of
women's perennial desire to control their reproductive capacity. However
he was keen about the concept of a clinic where women could obtain
medical attention for all their maternal health needs including for contraceptives. In his counterproposal to the RWS, Thornton explained:

> It seems to the Department that there might be a need in
> Johannesburg for the development of an Outpatient Gynaecological

Clinic where mothers needing advice on physical health matters both of nature and nurture, might be assisted. Such an institution under adequate and skilled supervision could receive minor gynaecological cases, deal with some forms of post-natal aftercare, accept responsibility for counseling mothers of subnormal physical [sic] or mentality, give advice on contraceptive methods where medically needed and act as a clearing house for appropriate treatment of one sort or another.[4]

As shown in Chapter 2, the RWS eagerly adopted his proposed model and went on to open the Women's Welfare Centre the following year. Thornton, who became Secretary of Public Health and Chief Health Officer for the Union in 1932, would work steadily until his retirement in 1938 toward entrenching contraceptive services in South Africa. Given the moral stigma besmirching the issue in respectable society, why did the top civil servant in the DPH immediately support birth control?[5]

Thornton's open-minded response was a sign of his determination to expand the DPH's purview, and signaled the major shift occurring in elites' perception of the role of the state in ensuring the health of its citizens and subjects. From unification until the early 1930s, the DPH had been weak and underfunded. Its legislative mandate, laid out in the *Public Health Act* (1919), was mainly to prevent and control outbreaks of infectious disease of epidemic proportions, the direct result of the devastating influenza pandemic that had ravaged South Africa and the rest of the world the previous year. The passage of the act signaled the growing trend of the state to play an interventionist role in society by creating social and economic conditions for ensuring the health and virility of the nation. In areas of social policy as disparate as housing, education, employment, social welfare, and health care, the state instituted a host of measures intended to alleviate the negative impact of urbanization on poor whites and incorporate them "into the 'respectable' white body politic."[6] The increasing demand for state action on white social problems was conveyed by a 1919 housing commission that declared "there was an undeniable duty upon the state to ensure that all members of the community are healthy and useful citizens, and that no section of the community is allowed to sink to such depths of discontent, depravity, or disease, as to become a menace to the well-being of the rest."[7] However, though an aspect of the DPH's mandate was positive, namely to "promote the public health," there had been a lack of political will, and a shortage of funds and staff, to develop preventive and health promotional public health services during the nation's first two decades of existence.

During the upheaval of the Great Depression, elites' perception of the role of the state changed. By the early 1930s, the African population had deteriorated, which threatened the major source of labor for the nation's industrial economy as well as infection of white society. In addition poor whites were "sinking" almost beyond the point of racial redemption, making "white civilization" vulnerable to "swamping" by blacks. Elites became anxious that the nation was in decline and began expecting that the state should do more to improve the public health and welfare.[8] General Smuts summed up the emergent dominant idea that the state should play a far more active, interventionist role in ensuring the public's health when he told the National Conference on Social Work in 1936, "the care of the human material is becoming more and more a primary function of government [and] we shall see that drastic changes will have to be made in the organization of social welfare departments if this work is to be properly and efficiently discharged."[9] As a result, and in concert with the recommendations of the Carnegie Commission of Investigation on the Poor White Question and a host of other Afrikaner and official conferences, by the early 1930s the DPH wanted to expand the dominant vision of a public health strategy to include recognition of the integral importance of social conditions in determining physical health. As Thornton stated, South Africa required a "medico-social" model of public health, by which he meant "the control of social welfare and public health could not remain divorced either centrally or locally."[10] The emerging vision of an expanded, interventionist state at this turbulent period translated into increased funding for public health starting in 1933.

Thornton earnestly believed that improving public health services in South Africa was "urgently required" for all races and particularly for rural inhabitants.[11] Along with a talented team of civil servants, he worked assiduously to expand the state's narrow focus on disease prevention to include a much greater emphasis on health promotion through education and preventive services.[12] Throughout his tenure as the chief civil servant in the DPH he nurtured a culture of innovation in the DPH and, like his predecessor J.A. Mitchell, promoted a medico-social approach to disease that recognized the inter-relatedness of social as well as biomedical dimensions. For example, Thornton and his staff identified poverty and, by extension, malnutrition as principal factors in the origins and spread of diseases such as tuberculosis and syphilis.[13] As Dr. H.S. Gear, an Assistant Health Officer in the Department of Public

Health, explained in a speech to the National Conference on Social Work, "Defects of disease and ill health arise in large part from the play of social and economic factors, the study and treatment of which thus becomes a health function." He went on to say that proper health care requires tackling any "preventable cause of mortality and morbidity," including maternal mortality.[14]

Keen to promote this new vision of an expanded health care system, Thornton welcomed the RWS's proposal to form a birth-control clinic as an opportunity to address two intimately related, and politically pressing, social and health problems of the day. First, he believed birth control was crucial to solving the poor white problem. As he told Jan Hofmeyr, who succeeded Malan as Minister of Public Health, "I believe that one of the big factors required in South Africa to bring the poor white problem within sight of solution is the provision of medical treatment for gynaecological ailments and the education of poor mothers in family spacing."[15] The final report of the Carnegie Commission, released in 1932, had called the DPH's attention to the tendency of poor whites to produce large families, which was considered both a cause and consequence of their dire condition. Moreover, two of its Afrikaner commissioners, Marie Rothmann and E.G. Malherbe, went on to become influential advocates of birth control. Thornton agreed that poor white fertility required immediate attention. In 1935 he publicly endorsed birth control for the first time, and he did so in terms that invoked neo-Malthusian clichés about the need to limit the family size of poor whites to ensure their rehabilitation:

> The practice of birth control, up to the present, has been mainly among those sections of the community which are able to afford the necessary medical advice. This advice has been beyond the reach of the poor, who are often also the sick and diseased, and who would most benefit by the reasonable limitation of the size of their families.
>
> The reports received from country districts all lay stress on the dire poverty, the lack of all the ordinary comforts of life, the overcrowding, and the difficulty of obtaining any medical or nursing help for the women in childbirth. It is not uncommon to find father, mother and three or more children all sleeping in the same bed.
>
> In addition to the more than ordinary dangers and difficulties that women in such circumstances have to face during childbirth, is the impossibility of finding food, clothing and schooling, for one more child. These people, whose social, economic and often physical and mental conditions are of the lowest, are those who should be shown

how to space and limit their families. *More practical good could be accomplished by this teaching than by any other method.*[16] (emphasis added)

The second problem that Thornton believed could be mitigated through the spread of contraceptive services was the high rate of white maternal mortality. By the early 1930s the Government still had not put in place a national program to deal with the maternal health needs of women in outlying areas. For whites in rural districts who were certified as 'indigent' by a magistrate, free medical care was available from state-subsidized District Surgeons who visited periodically. However this service was inadequate as there were too few District Surgeons for the number of indigents in need of attention and their availability was unreliable for women facing labor on isolated farms. In addition, private physicians and unlicensed lay midwives were only available to those women able to locate them in time and scratch together the requisite fee.[17] By 1930 white maternal mortality was on the rise and, in the climate of fear of national decline prevailing in the white community, concern about white maternal mortality rose to crisis proportions and the issue became intensely politicized. That year Deputy Prime Minister D.F. Malan, Minister of Public Health from 1924–33, was asked in Parliament about the Government's inaction on this issue. He countered that the problem was receiving close consideration from the DPH, which indeed it was.[18] In 1932 the Official Year Book of the Union acknowledged that "Infant and maternity welfare ... have, in the past, been neglected, but during the last few years a greatly increased amount of interest has been taken in these and kindred matters."[19]

As Thornton, a trained physician, knew, doctors were convinced that a growing number of women were dying from botched abortions.[20] Though the apparently high incidence of abortion-related deaths did not lead the male-dominated medical profession to consider improving access to safe abortion services, it did increase medical support for birth control as a means to prevent abortion-related deaths and morbidity. As one doctor remarked in the *South African Medical Journal* (*SAMJ*), "Surely it is wiser to prevent conception than to allow thousands of women to die annually as the result of intentional abortion!"[21] Another urged the medical profession to establish birth-control clinics to "help combat the practice of illegal abortions, that cancer that now destroys the health of our women."[22] In 1932 the first full-length article endorsing contraception appeared in the *SAMJ*, and it was a passionate polemic written by Dr. Sallie Woodrow of the MCC who proclaimed, "The tale of self-induced abortions, with its

trail of misery and ill-health, and its probable effect on maternal mortality and morbidity ... is a horrible reality."[23] The DPH knew of her article
as well as another by Dr. I.J. Block of the RWS who advocated contraception in large part because "it will undoubtedly diminish the present high
incidence of abortions with its attendant dangers."[24] In addition to
preventing abortion, Thornton believed birth control would reduce
maternal mortality and morbidity among women too ill or exhausted to
carry a pregnancy to term successfully. In all likelihood Thornton was
influenced by the British Ministry of Health's decision the previous year
to allow the provision of contraceptives for women for whom pregnancy
would be dangerous, for, as we shall see below, he was careful to recommend a policy that was in keeping with imperial policy.

As his reply to the RWS's initial proposal demonstrates, by 1931
Thornton was interested in accessible contraceptive services as a maternal
health measure. Indeed, his response to the RWS broadened the
eugenists' initially narrow approach to birth control as a means to curb
the reproduction of "defective" whites to one facet of a comprehensive
maternal health clinic. In doing so he recast birth control from a tool of
social control to a preventive health service for mothers. Significantly,
his counterproposal demonstrates that although he drew upon the two
co-existing and competing explanations for white poverty in circulation in South Africa in the 1930s – biological determinism and
environmentalism – he privileged the environmentalist approach, just
as the Carnegie Commission had. This was to be expected from a senior
civil servant working for a United Party Government (1934–48) that
was imbued with a spirit of compromise and cooperation between
Anglophone and Afrikaner moderates intent on integrating both white
groups into a bi-cultural white South Africa. Doing so required the social
incorporation of poor whites, not their abandonment, and Thornton
was intent on using the DPH to help do so.

Thornton's perception of contraceptive services as a maternal health
measure was to a significant extent shaped by Afrikaner and English
maternalist organizations that worked hard to make birth control
respectable in their respective ethnic groups. Of particular importance
was the *Afrikaanse Christelike Vroue Vereniging* (Afrikaans Christian
Women's Union, ACVV), an Afrikaner nationalist women's welfare
organization formed in the Cape in 1904, which lobbied the
Government in the early 1930s to promote and subsidize contraceptive
services as one facet of a comprehensive maternal health service for poor
white women. The ACVV was key in raising public and official
awareness about the problem of white maternal mortality. Especially

important was Marie Rothmann, the ACVV's Organizing Secretary, who, as Marijke du Toit explained, played an "absolutely crucial role" in formulating a vision of health care for poor white women.[25] In the late 1920s she, on behalf of the ACVV, lobbied the DPH to open a network of maternity clinics throughout the rural Cape that would be placed under the control of professionally qualified white nurses. The ACVV was fully committed to the racially exclusive notion of the *volk* (Afrikaner people/nation); indeed, its maternal health ideas were intended in part to eliminate the long-standing practice of black women assisting white women in childbirth.[26] As the sole female investigator for the Carnegie Commission, Rothmann, spent much of 1929 meeting rural white Afrikaans-speaking women and systematically researched the conditions under which white women gave birth, which, as she herself noted, had never before been done.[27] Consequently she identified frequent pregnancies and the absence of professional midwifery during pregnancy and childbirth as primary sources of danger to poor white women in rural South Africa.[28] The final report of the Carnegie Commission incorporated Rothmann's recommendation that Government create a nursing organization for rural areas. In seeking increased state intervention, Rothmann was part of an international trend early in the twentieth century of maternalists urging Governments in modernizing states to take responsibility for health and welfare. Women who were involved in charitable works, like Rothmann, gained intimate and extensive knowledge of the social distress of the poor, and by 1930 she knew better than anyone in the country the awful conditions under which rural white women bore and raised children.

In her role as an investigator for the Commission, Rothmann refrained from endorsing birth control. Nevertheless, it was during this time that she developed her ideas on the issue, and soon she was making public endorsements of birth control. In a pamphlet entitled "Irresponsible Parenthood" she called for "scientific, ethical and healthy birth control" for poor whites on eugenic grounds,[29] a stance shared by colleagues in the ACVV. The organization's Afrikaner nationalism, maternalism and strong rural connections led it to focus on uplifting the *volk* by improving the conditions under which the *arm blank* (poor white) *volksmoeder* (mother of the nation) performed her duty to bear and rear children. Under Rothmann's guidance, the ACVV called for a reduction in the excessively large size of poor-white families.[30] In addition to advocating birth control in her pamphlet and other writings, she argued in favor of birth control among the male Afrikaner leadership at major events like the *Volkskongres* (1934), organized in the wake of

Carnegie Commission for the purpose of formulating a national social welfare plan for poor whites. She also lobbied the state to develop midwifery and contraceptive services, as well as sterilization for women deemed "unsuitable" for motherhood.[31] In 1933 she publicly endorsed birth control in an article for the Afrikaner nationalist newspaper *Die Burger* praising the Cape Town Mothers' Clinic, a copy of which was brought to Thornton's attention.[32] Soon other Afrikaner women's welfare organizations endorsed the practice: in 1933 the *Cronje Vroue Veereniging* (the Orange Free State Women's Union) considered opening its own birth-control clinic and in 1937 the Transvaal *Suid-Afrikaanse Vroue Federasie* (the South African Women's Federation) passed a resolution urging the state to extend contraceptive services.

Thornton implemented a number of the suggestions put forward by the ACVV and other Afrikaner women's welfare organizations. In 1934, in response to the widespread concern about white maternal mortality, the DPH created the post of Medical Inspector for Maternal and Child Welfare with a mandate to assess the need for midwifery and nursing services in rural districts, and to suggest ways in which local women's organizations and other interested bodies could work with governments to establish district nursing. In 1935 the DPH introduced a district nursing program and began subsidizing rural midwives.[33] Also in 1935, Thronton publicly recommended for the first time providing access to contraceptive services, arguing they would lessen poverty in the Union through reducing the size of families of poor and ill whites.[34] The following year, he wrote an internal memorandum to the Minister of Public Health, Jan Hofmeyr, suggesting that the DPH extend contraceptive services to rural areas through newly hired nurses.[35] The Government's interest in the ACVV's suggestions for mitigating maternal mortality and morbidity did not go unnoticed. Rothmann and ACVV president Minnie Roome noted with satisfaction the influence they were having on the DPH. Rothmann attributed it to white women's acquisition of the vote, which suggests that the demands of white women could no longer be so easily ignored.[36] As the historian Jonathan Hyslop has noted, after white women acquired the franchise "the various political formations would have to find ways to incorporate women into their political discourses."[37] The DPH did so by absorbing into public policy some of the ACVV's proposals for improving white maternal health.

The Cape Town Mothers' Clinic Committee (MCC) was also in contact with Thornton. Like the ACVV, the women of the MCC impressed upon him and his colleagues in the DPH the crucial importance of access to contraceptive services in improving the health and performance of South Africa's mothers. Throughout the 1930s the MCC regularly sent copies of its annual report to the DPH, which described in graphic detail the alarmingly poor health of clinic users from all racial categories. They also stressed the beneficial effects of "family spacing," a term that, along with "Mothers' Clinic," Thornton subsequently adopted.[38] Thornton was sympathetic to the MCC's liberal, compassionate approach to service provision, an approach that differed drastically from the RWS's intolerance of poor whites and the ACVV's racism toward blacks. Through the MCC's annual reports Thornton was also made aware of the group's success in attracting and maintaining users. In 1933 Ursula Scott met with Thornton to discuss the MCC's activities and to seek financial assistance. She remarked afterwards with evident pleasure that Thornton had appreciated "the necessity for contraceptive work." He also arranged for her to meet with the new Minister of Public Health whom, she later informed Thornton, "seems to feel the necessity for contraceptive work as you do." She thanked Thornton for his "helpful hints" and said of her visit: "[it was] quite a different business to feel that your sympathy and interest were behind me."[39]

Though the ACVV and MCC differed with regards to "race" they were united in endorsing birth control as a maternal health measure, not as a woman's right. Given the contemporary ideology of gender roles in settler society, they had little choice in the way they cast the issue. In the 1930s there was little discursive space available for feminist critiques of the dominant gender construct of women as mothers whose primary roles were biological and social reproduction. In successfully deploying maternalist rhetoric, the ACVV, MCC, South African National Council for Material and Family Welfare (SANCMFW) and other women's organizations were key in legitimizing fertility control, expanding access to birth control, and assisting thousands of poor women in obtaining greater control over their reproductive capacity. Thus, in the gendered process of nation-building in South Africa, women's welfare organizations helped reinforce a normative role for women in society; together they confirmed women's relationship to the state as "mothers" and not as citizens.

II

Once convinced of the value of contraceptive services as a preventive health measure, Thornton and his colleagues set out to make birth control publicly acceptable. They did so in a variety of ways, beginning by nurturing the birth-control movement. Thornton intended for the voluntary sector and local authorities to deliver contraceptive services; rather than provide these services directly, the DPH would provide financial assistance to extra-state groups to provide the services. This was in keeping with the DPH's legislative mandate to promote public health "through the agency of other bodies."[40] Moreover, in trying to coordinate public and private welfare initiatives, Government recognized that private agencies had "greater elasticity" than the state and had greater freedom to experiment and specialize in one or another aspect of social welfare work.[41] Therefore in the field of maternal health services Government looked to private agencies for assistance. When speaking in Parliament about the new district-nursing program, for instance, Jan Hofmeyr, the Minister of Public Health, stated that in order to bring nursing services to rural areas, "we want to work as far as possible through the local bodies and charitable institutions."[42] Working with extra-state agencies was a pragmatic decision practically forced upon the DPH by budgetary considerations, for despite significant increases in the annual health budget in the 1930s, funds were constantly in short supply and so the need to work through private groups continued. The DPH was also following the example of the British Government's hands-off approach to birth control, to which he paid close attention (see below). In Britain, the Family Planning Association was a publicly funded voluntary organization whose responsibility for service provision allowed the Government to play a supporting rather than leading role.[43]

There was also a political reason for choosing to deliver contraceptive services through extra-state agencies. As Thornton explained to the RWS in 1931, it "was doubtful if there is at present a sufficient degree of unanimity in the medical profession or public opinion to warrant the establishment of a clinic for systematic instruction in artificial contraception and its application."[44] (Though he did not say so, he probably also could not accept the RWS's evident contempt for poor whites who were an overwhelmingly Afrikaans-speaking population.) In an internal memorandum written in 1931 to Malan he claimed that his suggestion to revise the RWS's proposed birth-control clinic into an Outpatient Gynaecological Clinic "expresses sound views to which no one can take exception … [and which] conform generally to the official attitude adopted in most countries in the British Commonwealth of Nations."[45] Birth control was sufficiently controversial to warrant a cautious approach to the issue. In 1936 Thornton wrote to Malan's successor, Hofmeyr, strongly supporting "state guided" birth-control clinics but warned of possible dangers: "There is no doubt in my mind that an enormous advance could be made in public health and social welfare if these clinics under State guidance could be multiplied in the urban areas and particularly if they could be extended to the *platteland* [rural areas]," Thornton wrote. He continued, "It has however a political side which might easily raise acute controversy. It would be impossible, I think, for the State to openly advocate a birth control movement as such. It would be at once plunged into religious and other difficulties."[46]

The DPH was actually the catalyst to the formation of a national birth-control coalition. Dr. E.H. Cluver, an Assistant Health Officer for the Union, visited the RWS's Women's Welfare Centre just a few months after it opened in 1932 and expressed his "appreciation of the work being done" and said the DPH would consider the request for financial support. However, he remarked, it would be much easier to obtain funding from the Government if the birth-control clinics in South Africa "were brought under one control."[47] The RWS immediately acted on Cluver's advice, and approached the two other birth-control groups active in South Africa, in Cape Town and Pretoria, with the suggestion to affiliate. Both responded positively. The RWS designed a national structure that would leave each organization autonomous regarding the management of their own clinics while "enabling co-operation where joint action would be of advantage to the Birth Control movement."[48] The following year the five organizations (by then groups had formed in Port Elizabeth and Benoni) also agreed to form a national council in order to exchange views, share experiences, and facilitate combined action at the national level.[49] Delegates and other participants, including doctors, health visitors, and the city's Medical Officer of Health gathered in Johannesburg at the old Carlton Hotel in June 1935. Excepting those representing the RWS, all the delegates were women.[50] The groups chose a name, the South African National Council for Birth Control (SANCBC) and elected Ursula Scott as chair. Their mandate promised "To advocate and promote the provision of facilities for scientific contraception so that married people may space or limit their families and thus mitigate the evils of ill-health and poverty."[51] Delegates embraced the neo-Malthusian belief that "excessive families amongst the poor" accentuated South Africa's "social problem" of poverty.[52] Members agreed that the ultimate objective of the new Council was to convince Government authorities to accept responsibility for contraceptive services by providing them at municipal clinics for both "Europeans" and "non-Europeans."[53]

Though pleased with this development, Thornton was concerned that the Council's name and mandate would continue to provoke moral conservatives. The terms "birth control" and "family limitation" implied, he thought, that the Council was anti-family. At the 1936 national meeting of the Council Thornton told them the name would curtail its development and "hold back the movement from receiving Government support."[54] As Thornton said to Hofmeyr, birth-control clinics were one thing but Mothers' Clinics, "are a very different story."[55] Therefore he urged the Council to change its name to the South African National Council for Maternal and Family Welfare, which implied a commitment to healthy motherhood and stable families, and "would be acceptable to and gain support from religious as well as political bodies."[56] Scott had already found the Council's original name to be a "serious handicap to progress." For example, she informed member organizations that the National Council for Child Welfare refused to allow the SANCBC to affiliate.[57] As a result, the Council, which considered Thornton a great friend of birth control, unanimously agreed to his request. Delegates changed the name and amended the constitution to place more emphasis on maternal and family welfare.[58]

With a more acceptable name in place, Thornton began promoting nationally subsidized contraceptive services. At the National Conference on Social Work held at Johannesburg (1936), Thornton, chair of the Health Session, submitted a ringing endorsement of accessible birth-control clinics:

Mothers' Clinics

This Conference having due regard to the morbidity and mortality associated with child-bearing in South Africa and the accentuation of the social problem created by excessive families amongst the poor:

1. believes that the National Health programme should be strengthened by the establishment throughout the Union of Mothers' Clinics;
2. considers that such clinics should –
    (a) provide or arrange appropriate medical or surgical treatment for all women suffering from gynaecological ailments who would be unable otherwise to secure such treatment;
    (b) instruct married women in family spacing and, in the case of those who are temporarily or permanently unfit to bear children, in the principles of birth control;
    (c) be subsidised by the DPH which should be empowered to make grants-in-aid to local authorities or voluntary organizations

establishing and maintaining such clinics to the satisfaction or the department; and

3. recommends that adequate provision be made on the departmental estimates accordingly.[59]

Next he set out to secure financial assistance for the birth-control movement. Given the political risk involved, he proceeded cautiously. Hofmeyr, leery of the controversy surrounding birth control, had already turned down requests from the MCC and RWS for subsidies in 1933. After receiving these requests for funding, and in light of the ACVV's support for contraceptive services for poor white women, the Minister requested confidential reports from the Cape Town and Johannesburg Medical Officers of Health (MOHs) on the birth-control clinics operating in their respective cities. In particular he wished to know whether the municipal councils made financial contributions to the clinics, and if so, whether they had sparked protest as a result.[60] Dr. T. Shadick Higgins, the MOH for Cape Town, reported that there had indeed been resistance to the Mothers' Clinic from Catholic groups the year before.[61] Hofmeyr subsequently declined the requests for financial aid.

By 1936 however, Thornton was convinced that birth control was attaining respectability. Internationally, the Anglican Church's positive stance on birth control was having an impact domestically, which helped to erode opposition. Though the South African bishops had all refrained from endorsing birth control at the 1930 Lambeth Conference, they stopped short of condemning couples who chose to use contraceptives, a fact that its advocates pointed out to the DPH when lobbying for support.[62] Closer to home and equally important, the DRC also reversed its position on birth control in the mid-1930s, as discussed in Chapter 2.

Afrikaner nationalists were also key to winning acceptance for birth control among Afrikaner elites. When their work for the Commission was complete, both E.G. Malherbe and Rothmann began publicly campaigning for contraceptive services, and their efforts to convince the religious and political leaders of the DRC and *Afrikanerdom* to accept birth control were crucial to enabling the Government to do so too. Given the long-standing tensions in relations between Afrikaners and Anglophones, the DPH could not be perceived to be unsympathetic to the poorest members of the Afrikaner *volk*. During the 1930s extreme Afrikaner nationalism was steadily growing and posing a challenge to the moderate, bi-cultural political movement known as South Africanism. However, when respected Afrikaner nationalists began making linkages between poor whiteism and high fertility and to argue that birth control would *strengthen*, not diminish, the *volk*, then state endorsement of the practice became politically possible. Afrikaners and Anglophones could find common ground in arguments in favor of rehabilitating poor whites. It was only after the DRC offered moral approval of the practice in 1934 that the DPH began publicly endorsing birth control.

The newly renamed South African National Council for Maternal and Family Welfare also proved to be very successful in convincing government commissions, the medical profession and social welfare agencies to accept birth control as a maternal health measure. As chair of the Council, Scott was indefatigable and proved to be a highly effective leader and propagandist who obtained support for birth control from a variety of national conferences and commissions. Her maternalist message proved persuasive, as it conformed nicely to the government's policy of rehabilitating poor whites that was expanded during and after the Depression and included greater efforts to assist juvenile school leavers and neglected children.

The medical profession also softened its opposition. Doctors began arguing that birth control would help stem the tide of illegal abortion and high white maternal mortality. For example, in 1937 Dr. C. Louis-Leipoldt, editor of the *SAMJ*, wrote a sympathetic editorial on the Cape Town Mothers' Clinic.[63] Women doctors such as Betsy Goddefroy and Sallie Woodrow were especially vocal, offering a variety of feminist, eugenist and neo-Malthusian arguments.[64] Women doctors also joined the birth-control movement from the start as volunteer workers in the clinics. Though some, like Woodrow, demonstrated a sense of feminist solidarity with users, most embodied the gendered assumption that maternal and child health was their "natural" niche. As the sociologist Liz Walker shows, very few women doctors were employed in private practice in South Africa in the 1930s. On the one hand masculine discourses of medicine and prejudicial practices excluded them, and on the other hand they could reconcile working in low-status, low-paid public health services with their domestic responsibilities as wives and mothers.[65]

In her 1932 article urging the medical profession to accept birth control, Woodrow drew upon modernist, cosmopolitan rhetoric, calling it a "rational" and "scientific" practice that was finding growing acceptance globally, including in India, Japan, the US, Germany, Holland, Russia, and China.[66] Situating the nascent South African birth-control movement in an international context was effective, given her audience of self-conscious professionals. She drew only one negative response, from a colleague who condemned birth control for undermining the sanctity of motherhood: "Let women make no mistake: their great work is child-bearing and rearing; and, no matter how distasteful it may be, they must stick to their job."[67] As further evidence of the dramatic sea change occurring in the profession regarding birth control, numerous doctors promptly responded by criticizing not Woodrow, but the anonymous author. Interestingly, their letters in defense of birth control contained eugenic, neo-Malthusian or racist justifications – only one expressed sympathy for women.[68] In subsequent years doctors continued to endorse contraception as a means to secure white supremacy or contain the poor white problem.[69] Dr. P.W. Laidler, MOH for East London, was particularly active in promoting eugenic birth control, arguing in the medical press and in other public fora that "family spacing" along with sterilization were essential measures of preventive health, for without them "the intelligent will be swamped by the deficient."[70]

Probably the key reason for the medical profession's waning opposition was its desire to capture the issue from the volunteer sector and place it under its control. Offering assistance with birth control was a means to attract private clients and to expand medical authority. On both points South African doctors were hardly unique, as studies on developments elsewhere, such as the US, have demonstrated.[71] Recognizing that the trend toward using contraceptive technologies was unstoppable, doctors argued that contraceptive services should be led, even absolutely controlled, by the medical profession. While initially they may not have wished to get involved in the matter, increasingly doctors had little choice. As Dr. Impey bluntly put it in 1932, "The subject of birth control is one that has been forced upon the medical profession by the laity, and it is one we can no longer ignore, either for moral, religious, or any other reason."[72] Dr. I.J. Block of the RWS was much more enthusiastic; as he told the Medical Council of South Africa in 1934, birth control was not simply a private matter but also a public health issue and as such "demands the participation and guidance of the medical profession and the recognition of municipalities and governments."[73] Similarly, Dr. Goddefroy told her colleagues in the Northern Transvaal branch of the South African Medical Association that physicians must show active interest "if we want to be what we should be, the leaders of the public in matters of general hygiene and physical well-being."[74] And Dr. C.C.P. Anning argued that doctors must "wholeheartedly support and guide" birth-control clinics.[75]

Thornton publicized these developments that contributed to birth control's evolution into a public health issue purged of the taint of immorality. In the DPH's annual report for 1937 he reported the

SANCMFW's name change and listed the resolutions passed at its 1936 meeting, and he expressed his belief that the nation's health would be strengthened by the establishment of Mothers' Clinics throughout the Union.[76] In the "Public Health" section of the 1936 edition of the *Official Year Book of the Union*, the DPH listed the SANCMFW as "a national body interested in a specific phase of health work."[77] In 1939, the DPH described the SANCMFW as "one of the most important" private welfare organizations in the country.[78]

III

By 1936 Thornton was ready to take advantage of the more amenable political climate and move beyond simply endorsing birth control. That year he remarked to Hofmeyr, "I should like to see a small grant in aid made to the National Council for Maternal and Family Welfare" to be "administered to the satisfaction of the department."[79] He began by writing to the British Ministry of Health requesting any information it had regarding the British Government's policy toward birth-control clinics during the previous decade. In his letter he stated, "We are on the eve of converting the Churches out here and the present time seems opportune to take a step forward."[80] In order to ascertain the level of support among churches for accessible birth-control clinics he suggested to Hofmeyr that he, in conjunction with the Minister of Social Welfare, convene a private meeting of representatives of the SANCMFW and various churches.[81] He observed, "If co-operation of the churches could be secured to a maternal welfare scheme, then I think the Government could go ahead [and subsidize the Council] without fear of political repercussions."[82]

In September 1937 Thornton arranged a conference in Pretoria where he and two representatives of the SANCMFW met with relevant Government officials and representatives of the Anglican and Dutch Reformed Churches. The officials in attendance were the new Minister of Public Health, R. Stuttaford; Hofmeyr, now the Minister for Education, Social Welfare and the Interior; the Anglican Bishop of Pretoria; the Reverend J.R. Albertyn, General Secretary for Poor Relief for the DRC (and investigator for the Carnegie Commission); and a Reverend Du Toit also from the DRC. (The Catholic Church remained staunchly opposed.) The result of the meeting was the unanimous agreement that the DPH allocate the SANCMFW an annual grant of £1000 to extend its work to slums and rural districts.[83] The allocation was approved in the 1938 parliamentary estimates and renewed annually thereafter.

The money greatly assisted the Council to expand access to birth control. Prior to receiving the grant, the SANCMFW's annual budget was a mere £32, made up of affiliation fees paid by members themselves. With new funds from Government it quickly extended services to white women in rural areas, villages and towns. The Council applied for affiliation with the Red Cross, the South African National Council for Mental Hygiene, the South African National Council of Women and the South African National Council for Child Welfare – organizations it hoped would take an interest in promoting birth control in the countryside.[84] The Council also obtained the names of nurses appointed by the Union Government as part of the newly established rural nursing service and sent them details about the urban-based clinics in hopes they would share them with women in rural districts. In 1938 the Council opened an office in Cape Town in part to meet the growing number of requests from around South Africa for advice on how to start birth-control clinics. Inquiries from women and doctors interested in opening clinics arrived from Outdshoorn, Worcester, Wellington, Stellenbosch, Bloemfontein, Nylstroom, Keetmanshoop, Salisbury, Qumbu, Touws River, Somerset West, Milnerton, Boksburg, and Banhoek, and Walvis Bay, South West Africa (Namibia).[85] As President of the SANCMFW, Scott visited many of these locations to offer information, demonstrations and advice. Furthermore, in 1939, the MCC began giving demonstration lectures to district surgeons destined for rural work on behalf of the DPH, and this also brought results: soon requests for parcels of contraceptive supplies arrived from communities as far flung as Vereeniging, King Williamstown, Umtata, Petersburg, Sterkstroom, Van Rhynsdorp, and Balfour.[86]

The SANCMFW consistently guarded against entangling birth control in the kind of moral quagmire that would only serve to provoke moral conservatives and threaten its work. This is most clear in the decision taken, despite genuine concern about rural women's needs, to refrain from automatically sending pamphlets and contraceptives to women writing for help from country districts. It feared the consequences if contraceptives fell into the "wrong hands," meaning either unmarried or middle-class women. Instead it first replied to requests for help with forms asking a series of personal questions for women such as, for example, their age, health status, housing conditions, husbands' occupations, the number of pregnancies they had experienced, and the number of surviving children. Women were also required to have the form signed by a male authority figure (such as a doctor, health officer, child welfare officer, magistrate, or clergyman) who could vouch for their claims to be "suitable" for assistance. This step proved ineffective, as after a year no forms had been returned. Some members of the SANCMFW believed that women were probably too shy to approach male community leaders regarding such intimate and personal matters; others reported that even before the policy of testing women's suitability, women rarely replied to requests for information, even when self-addressed and stamped envelopes were supplied. Even though they realized the policy was a serious obstacle to women in need of assistance, the SANCMFW concluded it had no choice, arguing that the "policy of the Council must be safeguarded."[87]

After securing state funding Thornton took one more important step for birth control before retiring from public service. At the urging of Ursula Scott he set out to encourage local authorities to provide contraceptive services as another means to extend birth control to rural areas. Numerous times in 1937 and 1938 Scott urged the Minister of Public Health and Thornton to request the cooperation of local authorities in "establishing Mothers' Clinics or co-operating in voluntary efforts by subsidies or by making municipal premises and officers available for the work when desired by competent Committees."[88] Then on June 6, 1938, Thornton circulated a letter on behalf of the Minister of Health to all local authorities in the Union that employed full-time MOHs, in which he stressed the importance to the health of women suffering from various ailments of avoiding pregnancy, and asked local authorities to establish contraceptive services.[89] The bulk of the text of the circular came verbatim from a series of British Ministry of Health circulars, once again demonstrating the DPH's desire to act in strict accordance with imperial policy.[90] For example, the following passage in the 1938 circular is drawn directly from Memorandum 153/MCW, the British Ministry of Health's first policy statement on birth control (written in March 1931) that heavily reinforced the medicalization of birth control:

> Such clinics should be available also for women who are in need of medical advice and treatment for gynaecological ailments, though advice on contraceptive methods should only be given to married women who attend the clinics for such medical advice or treatment and in whose cases pregnancy would be detrimental to health ... What is, or not, medically detrimental to health must be decided by the professional judgment of the registered medical practitioner in charge of the clinic.

The response to Thornton's circular was mixed. Some local authorities, such as King William's Town and Germiston, opened a clinic as a direct result of the circular.[91] Bloemfontein and Krugersdorp indicated their intentions to do so.[92] On the other hand, the councils of Grahamstown, Durban and Springs refused to consider establishing birth-control clinics.[93] (The physician in Grahamstown's post-natal clinic indicated she would try regardless.) Unsurprisingly the circular, as well as Thornton himself, elicited prompt criticism from the Catholic press, less for moral reasons and more out of fear of white depopulation.[94] The Cape Town newspaper *Argus*, reporting on the controversy, noted that Catholics were afraid that the DPH's policy of "birth prevention" would "lead inevitably to the extinction of the white race in South Africa."[95] In response to this concern, the Minister of Public Health reiterated that the DPH did not advocate "birth control" in the negative sense of avoiding having children but "family spacing" for the sake of mothers, their children and the state.[96] Significantly, among DRC leaders criticism was thin and short-lived. For example, early in 1939 the Cape DRC's Vigilance Committee Against Social Evils decided against condemning birth-control clinics.[97]

IV

By the mid-1930s, the political elite in South Africa began to consider that the decline in national health and vitality required a comprehensive and accessible state medical service that placed emphasis on preventive health measures. The rural areas were particularly lacking in adequate medical care for both whites and blacks. As a solution to this serious situation, Member of Parliament (MP) Dr. Baumann proposed in 1935 "team-work" among all branches of health services to construct an effective system free to all:

> ... the world teems with proposals for revision of the existing system. These proposals may be crystallized in two words, namely, 'state intervention.' It is universally conceded that the prosperity of any country is greatly impaired by sickness and invalidity on the part of its citizens ... No responsible person doubts or denies that it is necessary to provide every man, women and child with the most skilled medical service available, irrespective of their capacity to pay.[98]

In 1936 MP Dr. Karl Bremer (a key health spokesperson for the opposition "Purified" National Party) wanted the Government to define public health as "the physical development of the population" and "not only protection against contagious diseases," and he wanted the DPH to take the broader view.[99] In subsequent years members of Parliament

Mr. C.M. Van Coller, Dr. Bremer, and Leila Reitz made similar remarks.[100] In 1942, Dr. Henry Gluckman, announced in Parliament that in South Africa the concept of public health had shifted from "the sphere of mere treatment and passive resistance to disease, to the consideration of the active promotion of health."[101]

In 1944 the National Health Services Commission (known as the Gluckman Commission) (1942–44) recommended establishing a surprisingly forward-looking health care system in South Africa that would focus on preventive health measures rather than a curative system centred on the hospital. This was gratifying for DPH staff who had worked hard to expand the state's narrow focus on disease prevention to include a much greater emphasis on public health promotion. However, although the DPH's vision for public health was popular among members of Parliament it failed to win the necessary support of Cabinet, which had no serious intention to address the underlying structural causes of disease and ill-health in the country. Constrained by the unfavorable political environment and their position as civil servants, civil servants were ultimately stymied in their attempts to implement widespread, effective preventive health measures.[102]

Although he and his colleagues in the DPH had limited success in his efforts to promote general preventive health measures, Thornton, along with extra-state advocates, did succeed in entrenching medicalized contraceptive services in South Africa. Birth control was one preventive health measure that found rapid support from the DPH and elites because it was a conservative response to pressing social problems. The birth-control movement and the state saw contraception as a means to stabilize society, not reinvent it. Despite the few flashes of radical demands for social change, such as Sallie Woodrow's claims for women's social liberation and sexual pleasure, the birth-control movement attracted official and elite support for its attempt to maintain the *status quo* in South Africa. The irony is that despite the inherently conservative aims of the birth-control movement and the state, together these two groups did bring about significant and important changes in South Africa: they made controlling fertility respectable and increased women's access to new methods of contraception.

Conclusion

In South Africa, research on the history of contraception has mainly focused on the National Party's population-control policies and practices from the 1960s to the 1980s, such as providing free hormonal contraceptives in the form of "the pill" or Depo Provera injections while simultaneously denying access to health care to the black majority.[1] During this era, political elites committed to the maintenance of the racist social order were fearful of the growth of the black population, a fear that was exacerbated by intensifying concern in the West about population growth in the Third World.[2] Providing free contraceptives to black women was intended to curb black population growth and thereby buttress *apartheid*.[3]

While the National Party's attempts at population control are known, contraception during the pre-*apartheid* era has barely begun to be researched. This book has shown that population-control ideology and accessible contraceptive services emerged in South Africa decades before *apartheid*-era politicians and their allies in the bureaucracy and medical profession tried to implement population control against blacks. Contraceptive services originated in the 1930s when middle-class social reformers, with support from the Department of Public Health (DPH), attempted to regulate the fertility of the dominant social-problem group of the interwar era: the "poor whites." In the aftershock of the Great Depression, white society became anxious that their young nation was in decline and that the white race was degenerating. Social and political elites were preoccupied with the seemingly uncontrolled proliferation of poor whites, who were "sinking" to the level of "the Native" in ever greater numbers and, in the process, blurring the porous line dividing the races. Others were appalled by the rising maternal mortality rate that seemed to threaten the stability of the family, seen to be the cornerstone of the nation. Despite the longstanding fear of "swamping" by blacks that predated Union in 1910, birth-control advocates in the extra-state agencies that established the country's first birth-control clinics, and in the DPH who supported them, were primarily concerned to reach poor-white women with modern contraceptive technologies. In 1938 the DPH began subsidizing the national birth-control coalition with a substantial grant-in-aid, in hopes that accessible birth control would help rehabilitate poor whites.

South African birth-control advocates in the 1930s clustered into two ideological groupings. One group was led by eugenists (mostly male professionals) who wanted to curb the fertility of putatively biologically "unfit" poor whites and the feebleminded. Controlling the growth of this undesirable population group, they believed, would strengthen the white race and thereby reinforce "white civilization." It would also lighten the tax burden of the middle classes, who deeply resented subsidizing the survival of the poor whites through expensive state relief schemes. Eugenists in South Africa were not unique in their aims; since the 1910s eugenists in Britain, from which their mostly Anglophone South African counterparts derived their ideas, and elsewhere in the industrialized world had promoted birth control for the "unfit."

The second, and by far the larger, group of birth-control advocates was made up of maternal feminists. These were women who wished to improve maternal and infant health and welfare in South Africa. Appalled by the high rate of maternal mortality and the dire circumstances in which mothers of *all* races were trying to maintain families during the hard times of the 1930s, the maternal feminists sought to strengthen mothers by enabling them to space or avoid pregnancies, and thus stabilize the family and the nation state. Inspired by the victory of the suffrage movement for white women, and by their metropolitan role model Marie Stopes, they felt entitled to join in public life in the name of healthy mothers. By winning state support for birth control, they reinforced women's relationship to the state as "mothers" first and foremost.

Together, eugenists and maternal feminists led a campaign among a largely receptive public to transform birth control from a tainted moral issue to a respectable public health matter worthy of the state's financial support. Moreover, regardless of their ideological differences, birth-control advocates shared the same gendered assumptions. All aimed their efforts at regulating *women's* reproductive capacity; men's role in reproduction was mostly overlooked. Moreover, few acknowledged, let alone endorsed, women's right to control their reproductive capacity.

Birth-control advocates, such as Sallie Woodrow, who were sincerely interested in supporting women's struggle for reproductive and sexual freedom, found little if any support in their conservative society. A campaign to improve *maternal health*, on the other hand, proved palatable to dominant political interests.

Biological determinist and environmentalist social reformers worked side by side within the birth-control movement to promote contraception among poor whites. Indeed, the line dividing a eugenist from an environmentalist was blurry, as advocates often drew upon both ideological strands in a haphazard, unsystematic fashion. Both interpretative frameworks were legitimate in the early 1930s. By the end of the decade, however, environmentalism had won. The overriding imperative to uphold white supremacy accounts for the failure of hereditarian eugenic ideas within the birth-control movement, indeed in South Africa generally. In the face of fears about black "swamping," a social rather than biological, explanation for white poverty had far more utility. An environmentalist analysis of poor whiteism was efficacious for both Afrikaner nationalists and political moderates intent on building a bi-cultural (Afrikaans and English) South Africa based on black political marginalization. Both emergent Afrikaner nationalism and South Africanism required rehabilitating poor whites rather than abandoning them to a fatalistic biological destiny; neither group's agenda benefited from a biological determinist approach. The environmentalism that dominated the influential Carnegie Commission of Investigation on the Poor White Question, which despite the hereditarian strand in its analysis was far more concerned with economic and other social causes of white poverty, exemplified the limited purchase of a strictly biological determinist interpretation of poor whiteism.

This book traced the origins of South Africa's birth-control movement until the point in time, 1938, when the DPH began providing it with financial support. But that was hardly the end of the story. Birth control, of course, continued to be a controversial issue in South Africa in subsequent decades. What happened in the years that followed the legitimization of birth control? When and how did the state shift its goal from providing contraceptives mainly to poor whites to focusing on limiting the fertility of blacks? What role did the extra-state birth-control movement play in the development or deployment of the state's racist population control agenda? These are some of the many unanswered questions about South Africa's reproductive politics that historians have yet to answer.

The shift in the source of elites' anxiety over unregulated fertility from poor whites to blacks – and the site of their interventionist efforts from poor-white to black wombs – began to occur as early as the 1940s, with the waning of the "poor white problem" and the waxing of the "black problem," namely black nationalism. Already by 1939 the poor–white crisis was "largely over," as relief measures had fallen to 4.1 percent of the national budget from 15.8 percent in 1933.[4] Indeed, poor whites found jobs in significant numbers as early as 1933, when the economy began booming after the departure from the gold standard. Between 1932 and 1937, the Gross National Product rose from £217 million to £370 million per year while at the same time there was little increase in the cost of living; from 1932 to 1939, well over 100 000 whites found employment.[5] By the end of the decade poor whites had all but disappeared as a visible social group and pressing political problem. The outbreak of the Second World War transformed the South African economy, as a result of government investment in a massively expanded industrial sector, especially in steel, chemical, textile, and armaments industries. The growing industrial sector provided ample opportunity for employment.[6]

The elimination of mass white poverty allowed elites to shift the focus of their anxieties to the growing "black problem." During the Second World War, efforts to block African access to the cities collapsed as wartime industrial expansion and the concomitant shortage of skilled workers led to sharp demands for labor and spectacular growth in the employment of Africans: 134 000 African men entered the industrial sector between 1939 and 1946.[7] Moreover, there was an unprecedented level of black political resistance during the war, and it continued afterward. During the early 1940s there was a resurgence of political resistance to white supremacy by mass African organizations, most notably by the militant Non-European Unity Movement (NEUM), founded in 1943.[8] NEUM called for a universal franchise, compulsory education and full equality between whites and blacks. Also during the Second World War, Dr. A.B. Xuma, President of the African National Congress, began to revive the organization by recruiting young professionals to the Congress Youth League (CYL), established in 1944. Leading lights in the CYL such as Walter Sisulu, Oliver Tambo, and Nelson Mandela soon began organizing blacks on a mass level against their political exclusion and exploitation. Together, massive African urbanization, anxiety over black women's supposed promiscuity, and the growing threat of black nationalism led to reintensification of the old fear of "swamping" by blacks. In the years immediately following the Second World War, this fear began to manifest itself in a new discourse of white anxiety about a black "population explosion" that mobilized the white birth-control movement and the state to start problematizing black fertility. Developments in contraceptive technology, namely the production of the oral hormonal contraceptive and later Depo Provera, provided the material basis for the state's effort to reach black women with contraceptives.[9]

The specifics of the process by which white anxiety led the state to try to implement a population control strategy, as well as the state's relationship with the extra-state national birth-control movement in the course of doing so, remains murky and requires further research. In the years following the democratic transition in 1990, the Planned Parenthood Association of South Africa (PPASA), the direct descendant of the South African National Council for Maternal and Family Welfare, played a central role in lobbying the state for progressive reproductive health policies, which was tremendously important given the devastatingly rapid spread of HIV/AIDS at catastrophic rates of infection[10] PPASA recognized sexual and reproductive rights as "the keystone" to gender equity and implemented sexual and reproductive health education and services to black women throughout South Africa. As a leading health organization, PPASA helped establish the Reproductive Rights Alliance that aimed to empower women by teaching income-generation, job-finding and other life skills that are essential to the meaningful acquisition of reproductive health.[11] For reasons such as these, PPASA claimed by the late 1990s to have gained the confidence of local communities, many of which – in a rare reference to its past – "had good reason to be suspicious of family planning."[12] However, the history of the national birth-control movement between the Second World War and the post-*apartheid* era has not been analyzed. Thus an important goal for future research is to understand the roles and relationship between the state and extra-state agencies in the provision of contraceptive services under *apartheid*. Did the two dovetail ideologically, or did each embody a distinct perspective on the interconnections between "race," gender, and fertility?

The social history of birth control in South Africa has also yet to be written. As we have seen in this book, South Africans of all colors and classes were taking steps to control their fertility long before the importation of commercially manufactured contraceptive technologies in the early 20th century. Indeed, by the 1930s, Ellen Hellmann, whilst conducting her sociological study of an African slumyard in Johannesburg, reported that the most frequent request made of her was for contraceptives and "abortive measures."[13] However, we know next to nothing about ordinary people's experiences in regulating their fertility, such as why they would choose to prevent or end pregnancies and the means by which women, with and without male partners, attempted to do so. This book has shown that the arrival of birth-control clinics, deliberately situated in neighborhoods accessible to the poor of all races, attracted thousands of women by the end of the 1930s, mainly white and some Asian and Coloured women. This demonstrates that women desired additional methods of fertility control. But until researchers utilize the methodology of oral history to ascertain past reproductive decision-making and methods of fertility control we will not move beyond the version of history bequeathed to us by officials and middle-class members of the birth-control movement, who placed inordinate emphasis, naturally enough, on their contributions to these developments.[14]

This book has shown that a comprehensive understanding of the meanings attached to birth control, as well as the relevant institutional and political developments, requires taking into account agency both from above *and* below. The medicalization of birth control in the 1930s was not *imposed* from above by people in authority and higher social status as a form of social control. Instead, it was accomplished jointly by advocates of birth control and users. Through their utilization of the birth-control clinics, poor women facilitated and modified the expansion of medicalization, "even as they appropriate[d] it for their own purposes."[15] They legitimized birth control through their participation, which in turn assisted the DPH in endorsing and funding contraceptive services. Moreover, we have seen how the birth-control organizations changed clinical practises in response to users' needs. Clearly the relationship between providers and users was one of mutual dependence though not of equal power. Users needed contraceptive care just as the providers needed users in order to legitimize their actions. Only oral history can give us further insights into the ways in which women perceived birth-control advocates and their services, and the vital role they played in the evolution of medicalization in South Africa.

Notes

Introduction

1. Cited in H. Giliomee, *The Afrikaners: Biography of a People* (London: Hurst and Company, 2003), p. 310.
2. Studies include: M. Edmunds, "Population Dynamics and Migrant Labour in South Africa," in K.L. Michaelson (ed.), *And the Poor Get Children: Radical Perspectives on Population Dynamics* (New York: Monthly Review Press, 1981), pp. 154–79; M. Gray, "Race Ratios: The Politics of Population Control in South Africa," in L. Bondestam and S. Bergstrom (eds), *Poverty and Population Control* (London: Academic Press, 1980), pp. 137–55; B. Brown, " 'Facing the Black Peril': The Politics of Population Control in South Africa," *Journal of Southern African Studies*, 13, 3 (1987), pp. 256–73; B. Klugman, "The Political Economy of Population Control in South Africa," (BA thesis, University of the Witwatersrand, 1980); B. Klugman, "Decision-Making on Contraception Amongst a Sample of Urban African Working Women," (MA thesis, University of the Witwatersrand, 1988); B. Klugman, "Politics of Contraception in South Africa," *Women's Studies International Forum*, 13, 3 (1990), pp. 261–71; B. Klugman, "Population Policy in South Africa: A Critical Perspective," *Development Southern Africa*, 8, 1 (1991), pp. 19–34; E. Boikanyo, M. Gready, B. Klugman, H. Rees, and M. Zaba, "When is Yes, Really Yes? The Experiences of Contraception and Contraceptive Services Amongst Groups of South African Women," *Report of a Study Conducted for the Women's Health Project, Centre for Health Policy* (Johannesburg: Department of Community Health, 1993); and E. Salo, "Birth Control, Contraception and Women's Rights in South Africa: A Cape Town Case Study," unpublished paper (1993).
3. D.T. Goldberg, *Racist Culture: Philosophy and Politics of Meaning* (Oxford, UK and Cambridge, US: Blackwell Press, 1993), p. 81. For a periodization of the South African racial order see P. Maylam, "South Africa's Racial Order: Some Historical Reflections," paper presented at The Burdens of Race? "Whiteness" and "Blackness" in Modern South Africa, a conference organized by History Workshop and the University of the Witwatersrand Institute for Social and Economic Research, University of the Witwatersrand, Johannesburg, July 5–8, 2001.
4. Brown, "Facing the Black Peril"; Salo, "Birth Control, Contraception and Women's Rights in South Africa," Klugman, "Politics of Contraception in South Africa," and Klugman, "Decision-Making on Contraception Amongst a Sample of Urban African Working Women." The state's growing preoccupation with African population growth was evident in the rising studies it commissioned on black fertility rates in the 1970s. See J.M. Lotter and J.L. van Tonder, "Fertility and Family Planning in Thlabane" (Pretoria: HSRC, 1975); J.M. Lotter and J.L. van Tonder, "Fertility and Family Planning Among Blacks in Africa: 1974" (Pretoria: HSRC, 1976); H.J. Groenewald, "Fertility and Family Planning in Atteridgeville: Data for 1969, 1974 and 1975"

(Pretoria: HSRC, 1978); J.M. Lotter and J.L. van Tonder, "Certain Aspects of Human Fertility in Rural Bophuthatswana" (Pretoria: HSRC, 1978); J.J. van Wyk, "Multipurpose Survey Among Blacks in Urban Areas – 1978: Some Practices with a Contraceptive Effect: Abstinence and Breast-feeding" (Pretoria: HSRC, 1979); and R.B. van der Merwe and J.J. van Wyk, "Fertility and Family Planning in Daveyton: Survey Among Men" (Pretoria: HSRC, 1982).

5. Dr. J.H.O. Pretorius, Deputy Director-General: Regulation, Services and Programmes, Ministry of Health. Short overview of the full submission to the Truth and Reconciliation Commission, 1997, p. 7. In author's possession.

6. Brown, "Facing the Black Peril," p. 267.

7. H. Bradford, "Herbs, Knives and Plastic: 150 Years of Abortion in South Africa," in T. Meade and M. Walker (eds), *Science, Medicine and Cultural Imperialism* (London: Macmillan, 1991), pp. 120–47; C. Burns, "Sex Lessons from the Past," *Agenda*, 29 (1996), 79–91. See also L. Newton-Thompson, "Birth Control Clinics in the Western Cape, *c.*1932 to *c.*1974: A History," (BA thesis, University of Cape Town, 1992).

8. This is a vast literature. Significant studies include the following: On Britain: H. Cook, *The Long Sexual Revolution: English Women, Sex, and Contraception* (Oxford: Oxford University Press, 2004); A. McLaren, *Reproductive Rituals: The Perception of Fertility in England from the Sixteenth Century to the Nineteenth Century* (London: Methuen and Co. Ltd., 1984); A. McLaren, *Birth Control in Nineteenth-Century England* (London: Croom Helm, 1978); J. Lewis, *Politics of Motherhood: Child and Maternal Welfare in England, 1900–1939* (London: Croom Helm, 1980); R.A. Soloway, *Birth Control and the Population Question in England, 1877–1930* (Chapel Hill: University of North Carolina, 1982); J. Weeks, *Sex, Politics and Society: The Regulation of Sexuality Since 1800* (New York: Longman, 1981); D. Cohen, "Private Lives in Public Spaces: Marie Stopes, the Mothers' Clinics and the Practice of Contraception," *History Workshop*, 35 (1993), pp. 95–116. On the United States: L. Gordon, *Woman's Body, Woman's Right: Birth Control in America*, 2nd edn (New York: Penguin Books, 1990); L. Ross, "African American Women and Abortion, 1800–1970," in S.M. James and A. Busia (eds), *Theorizing Black Feminisms* (New York: Routledge, 1994), pp. 141–59; J. Rodrique, "The Black Community and the Birth Control Movement," in *Unequal Sisters: A Multicultural Reader in U.S. Women's History* (New York: Routledge, 1990), pp. 333–44; A. Davis, "Racism, Birth Control and Reproductive Rights," in Marlene Gerber Fried (ed.), *From Abortion to Reproductive Freedom: Transforming a Movement* (Boston: South End Press, 1990), pp. 15–26; C.R. McCann, *Birth Control Politics in the United States, 1916–1945* (Ithaca: Cornell University Press, 1994); J.C. Mohr, *Abortion in America: The Origins and Evolution of National Policy, 1800–1900* (New York: Oxford University Press, 1978); R. Petchesky, *Abortion and Woman's Choice: The State, Sexuality, and Reproductive Freedom*, 2nd edn (Boston: Northwestern University Press, 1990); J. Reed, *From Private to Public Virtue: The Birth Control Movement and American Society Since 1830* (New York: Basic Books, 1978); A. Tone, *Devices and Desires: A History of Contraceptives in America* (New York: Hill and Wang, 2001). On the British Dominions: A. McLaren and A. Tigar McLaren, *The Bedroom and the State: The Changing Practices and Politics of Contraception and Abortion in Canada, 1880–1980* (Toronto: McClelland and Stewart, 1986); S. Klausen, "Doctors and Dying Declarations: State Regulation

of Abortion in British Columbia, 1917–1936," *Canadian Bulletin of Medical History/Bulletin Canadien d'Histoire de la Medecine*, 13 (1996), pp. 53–81; B. Brookes, "Reproductive Rights: The Debate over Abortion and Birth Control in the 1930s," in B. Brookes, C. Macdonald, and M. Tennant (eds) *Women in History: Essays on European Women in New Zealand* (Wellington: Allen and Unwin, 1986), pp. 119–36; H. Smyth, *Rocking the Cradle: Contraception, Sex, and Politics in New Zealand* (Wellington: Steele Roberts Ltd., 2000); S. Siedlecky and D. Wyndham, *Populate and Perish: Australian Women's Fight for Birth Control* (Sydney: Allen and Unwin, 1990). Other significant studies: A. Grossmann, *Reforming Sex: The German Movement for Birth Control and Abortion Reform, 1920–1950* (New York: Oxford University Press, 1995); A.B. Ramírez de Arellano and C. Seipp, *Colonialism, Catholicism, and Contraception: A History of Birth Control in Puerto Rico* (Chapel Hill: University of North Carolina Press, 1983).

9. See for example E.H. Burrows, *A History of Medicine in South Africa upto the End of the Nineteenth Century* (Cape Town and Amsterdam: A.A. Balkema, 1958), M. Gelfand, *Tropical Victory: An Account of Medicine in the History of Southern Rhodesia* (Oxford: Juta, 1953); A.P. Cartwright, *Doctors of the Mines. To Mark the 50th Anniversary of the Founding of the Mine Medical Officers Association of South Africa* (Cape Town: Purnell, 1971); P.W. Laidler, *South Africa and Its Medical History, 1652–1898* (Cape Town: C. Struik, 1971).

10. M. Swanson, "The Sanitation Syndrome: Bubonic Plague and the Urban Native Policy in the Cape Colony, 1900–1909," *Journal of African History*, 18, 3 (1977), pp. 387–410; R. Packard, *White Plague, Black Labour: Tuberculosis and the Political Economy of Health and Disease in South Africa* (Berkeley: University of California Press, 1989); S. Marks and N. Andersson, *Health and Apartheid* (Geneva: WHO, 1983); S. Marks and N. Andersson, "Diseases of Apartheid," in John Lonsdale (ed), *South Africa in Question* (London: Cambridge African Studies Centre with James Currey, 1985), pp. 172–99; S. Marks and N. Andersson, "Typhus and Social Control: South Africa, 1917–1950," in R. MacLeod and M. Lewis (eds), *Disease, Medicine and Empire: Perspectives on Western Medicine and the Experience of European Expansion* (London and New York: Routledge, 1988), pp. 257–83; S. Marks and N. Andersson, "Industrialisation, Rural Change and the 1944 National Health Services Commission," in S. Feierman and J. Janzen (eds), *The Social Basis of Health and Healing in Africa* (Berkeley: University of California Press, 1992), pp. 131–61; S. Marks, *Divided Sisterhood: Race, Class and Gender in the South African Nursing Profession* (London: Macmillan Press, 1994); and K. Jochelson, *The Colour of Disease: Syphilis and Racism in South Africa, 1880–1950* (Basingstoke and Oxford: Palgrave in association with St. Antony's College, 2001).

11. On segregation and apartheid see W. Beinart and S. Dubow (eds), *Segregation and Apartheid in Twentieth-Century South Africa* (London: Routledge, 1995); D. Posel, *The Making of Apartheid, 1948–1961: Conflict and Compromise* (Oxford: Clarendon Press, 1991).

12. McLaren and McLaren, *Bedroom and the State*, p. 11.

13. Siedlecky and Wyndham, *Populate and Perish*, p. 135; Smyth, *Rocking the Cradle*, p. 124; McLaren and McLaren, *Bedroom and the State*, p. 9.

14. In 1910, eight years after the British defeated the Boers in the South African War (1899–1902), the British colonies of the Cape and Natal merged with the

Boer republics of the Orange Free State and Transvaal to form the self-governing British Dominion of South Africa.

15. M. Lewis, "The Health of the 'Race' and Infant Health in New South Wales: Perspectives on Medicine and Empire," in MacLeod and Lewis (eds), *Disease, Medicine and Empire*, p. 301.

16. Cited in Giliomee, *The Afrikaners*, pp. 304–5.

17. C. Burns, "Reproductive Labours: The Politics of Women's Health in South Africa, 1900 to 1960" (PhD thesis, Northwestern University, 1995), pp. 226–28.

18. See the collection of essays in R. Morrell (ed.), *White But Poor: Essays on the History of Poor Whites in Southern Africa* (Pretoria: University of South Africa, 1992); C. Bundy, "Vagabond Hollanders and Runaway Englishmen: White Poverty in the Cape Before Poor Whiteism," in W. Beinart, P. Delius and S. Trapido (eds), *Putting a Plough to the Ground: Accumulation and Dispossession in Rural South Africa, 1850–1930* (Johannesburg: Ravan Press, 1986).

19. A.L. Stoler, "Making Empire Respectable: The Politics of Race and Sexual Morality in 20th-Century Colonial Cultures," *American Ethnologist*, 16, 4 (1989), p. 635.

20. Planned Parenthood Association of South Africa, Johannesburg (hereafter PPASA JHB), Minutes of the Second Meeting of the South African National Council for Birth Control, October 6–7, 1936, p. 8. On Reitz's election to Parliament see R. Macnab, *The Story of South Africa House: South Africa in Britain – The Changing Pattern* (Johannesburg: Jonathan Ball Publishers, 1983), p. 127.

21. See D. Roediger, *Wages of Whiteness: Race and the Making of the American Working Class* (London and New York: Verso, 1991).

22. B. Bozzoli and P. Delius, "Radical History and South African History," *History from South Africa: Alternative Visions and Practices* (Philadelphia: Temple University Press, 1991), pp. 3–25.

23. The published collections of conference papers from the History Workshop series held at the University of the Witwatersrand in the 1970s and 1980s offer a comprehensive view of the work of radical social historians. See B. Bozzoli (ed), *Town and Countryside in the Transvaal* (Johannesburg: Ravan Press, 1983); B. Bozzoli (ed), *Class, Community and Conflict: South African Perspectives* (Johannesburg: Ravan Press, 1987); P. Bonner, P. Delius and D. Posel (eds), *Apartheid's Genesis, 1935–1962* (Braamfontein: Ravan Press, 1993).

24. S. Dubow, *Scientific Racism in Modern South Africa* (Cambridge University Press, 1995), p. 5; N. Roos, *From Workplace to War: Class, Race and Gender Amongst White Volunteers, 1939–1953* (PhD thesis, University of North West, 2001); J. Hyslop, "Why Did Apartheid's Supporters Capitulate? 'Whiteness,' Class and Consumption in Urban South Africa, 1985–1995," *Society in Transition*, 31, 1 (2000), pp. 36–44; and J. Hyslop, "The Imperial Working Class Makes Itself 'White': White Labourism in Britain, Australia, and South Africa Before the First World War," *Journal of Historical Sociology*, 12, 3 (1999), pp. 398–421.

25. S. Klausen, "The Birth Control International Information Centre and the Promotion of Contraceptive Services in the Colonial World, 1930–39." Unpublished paper presented at the University of Lethbridge, March 2003.

26. A.L. Stoler and F. Cooper, "Between Metropole and Colony: Rethinking a Research Agenda," in F. Cooper and A.L. Stoler (eds), *Tensions of Empire:*

Colonial Cultures in a Bourgeois World (Berkeley: University of California Press, 1997), p. 4.

27. See especially A. Burton, *Burdens of History: British Feminists, Indian Women, and Imperial Culture, 1865–1915* (Chapel Hill: University of North Carolina Press, 1994); M. Sinha, *Colonial Masculinity: The "Manly Englishman" and the "Effeminate Bengali" in the Late Nineteenth Centur*y (Manchester: Manchester University Press, 1995); A.L. Stoler, *Race and the Education of Desire: Foucault's History of Sexuality and the Colonial Order of Things* (Durham: Duke University Press, 1995); A.L. Stoler, *Carnal Knowledge and Imperial Power: Race and the Intimate in Colonial Rule* (Berkeley: University of California Press, 2002); A. Iriye, *Cultural Internationalism and World Order* (Baltimore, Johns Hopkins University Press, 1997); and the collection of essays in Stoler and Cooper (eds), *Tensions of Empire*.

28. The term "Greater Britain" was coined by Charles Dilke at the end of the nineteenth century. Cited in P.A. Buckner and C. Bridge, "Reinventing the British World," *The Round Table*, 368 (2003), p. 77.

29. See, for example, K. Fisher, " 'She Was Quite Satisfied with the Arrangements I Made': Gender and Birth Control in Britain 1920–1950," *Past and Present*, 169 (2000), pp. 161–93.

30. See M. Lock and P. Kaufert, "Introduction," in M. Lock and P. Kaufert, *Pragmatic Women and Body Politics* (Cambridge: Cambridge University Press, 1998), pp. 1–27, as well as the essays in this excellent collection.

31. See J. Lewis, *Politics of Motherhood* and A. Davin, "Imperialism and Motherhood," in F. Cooper and A.L. Stoler (eds), *Tensions of Empire*, pp. 87–151. These studies focus on national and international policies and politics in the development of maternal and infant health services.

32. For a nuanced analysis of the interconnections between local and the national organizations in the provision of maternal and infant welfare services see L. Marks, *Metropolitan Maternity: Maternal and Infant Welfare Services in Early Twentieth Century London* (Amsterdam: Rodopi, 1996).

33. PPASA JHB, Minutes of the Second Meeting of the South African National Council for Birth Control, October 6–7, 1936, p. 6.

Chapter 1: Fears of National Decline and the Politics of Birth Control

1. *Debates of the House of Assembly*, vol. 23, May 8, 1934, p. 3324.

2. See A. Leathard, *The Fight for Family Planning: The Development of Family Planning Services in Britain 1921–1974* (London: Macmillan, 1980).

3. The DRC comprised three white Afrikaans-speaking churches, the *Nederduits Gereformeerde Kerk*, the *Hervormde Kerk*, and the *Gereformeerde Kerk* (also known as the *Doppers*). See Chapter Two for discussion on the DRC's stance on birth control.

4. *Senate Report from the Select Committee on the Medical, Dental, and Pharmacy Bill* (Pretoria: Government Printer, 1917), pp. 4, 43, 48–49, 51.

5. Comment by Dr. C.T. Anderson, *ibid.*, p. 51. For other comments by doctors see pp. 1–5, 22–27, 36–51, 55–60.

6. *Ibid.*, p. 60.

7. W. Darley-Hartley, "The Traffic in Contra-Ceptives," *South African Medical Record*, 15 (1917), pp. 17–18; William Darley-Hartley, "Legislation Against Contra-ceptives," *South African Medical Record*, 15 (1917), pp. 81–84. For analysis of Darley-Hartley's conservative attitude towards birth control and gender relations see: S. Klausen, " 'For the Sake of the Race': Eugenic Discourses in the *South African Medical Record*, 1903–1926 and the *Journal of the Medical Association of South Africa*, 1927–1931," *Journal of Southern African Studies*, 10, 1 (1997), pp. 27–50.

8. "Minutes of the Meeting of the Northern Transvaal Branch of the Medical Association of South Africa (BMA)," *South African Medical Journal*, 6 (1932), p. 476.

9. Cited in H. Giliomee, *The Afrikaners: Biography of a People* (London: Hurst and Company), pp. 304, 410.

10. *Senate Report from the Select Committee on the Medical, Dental, and Pharmacy Bill*, p. 50.

11. "Minutes of the Meeting of the Northern Transvaal Branch of the Medical Association of South Africa (BMA)," p. 477.

12. H. Bradford, "Herbs, Knives and Plastics: 150 Years of Abortion in Southern Africa," in T. Meade and M. Walker (eds), *Science, Medicine and Cultural Imperialism* (New York: St. Martin's Press, 1991), pp. 120–47; S. Burman and M. Naude, "Bearing a Bastard: The Social Consequences of Illegitimacy in Cape Town, 1896–1939," *Journal of Southern African Studies*, 17, 3 (1991), 373–413.

13. C. Burns, "Sex Lessons from the Past?" *Agenda*, 29 (1996), 79–91.

14. "More Views on Birth Control. A 'Practical Necessity' in Modern Society," *Cape Times*, August 14, 1930.

15. M. Lewis, "The 'Health of the Race' and Infant Health in New South Wales: Perspectives on Medicine and Empire," in R. MacLeod and M. Lewis (eds), *Disease, Medicine and Empire. Perspectives on Western Medicine and the Experience of European Expansion* (London and New York: Routledge, 1988), p. 302.

16. See for example A. Davin, "Imperialism and Motherhood," in F. Cooper and A.L. Stoler (eds), *Tensions of Empire: Colonial Cultures in a Bourgeois World* (Berkeley: University of California Press, 1997), pp. 87–151; B. Semmel, *Imperialism and Social Reform: English Social-Imperial Thought, 1895–1914* (London: Allen and Unwin, 1960); G. Mosse, *Toward the Final Solution. A History of European Racism* (Madison, WI.: University of Wisconsin Press, 1985); N. Stepan, *The Idea of Race in Science: Great Britain 1800–1960* (London: Macmillan, 1982); G.R. Searle, *The Quest for National Efficiency. A Study in British Politics and Political Thought, 1899–1914* (Berkeley: University of California Press, 1971); A. Mayne, " 'The Dreadful Scourge': Responses to Smallpox in Sydney and Melbourne, 1881–82," in *Disease, Medicine, and Empire*, pp. 219–41; and R. Sullivan, "Cholera and Colonialism in the Philippines, 1899–1903," in *Disease, Medicine, and Empire*, pp. 285–300; Richard A. Soloway, *Demography and Degeneration: Eugenics and the Declining Birthrate in Twentieth-Century Britain* (Chapel Hill: University of North Carolina Press, 1990); A. McLaren, *Our Own Master Race: Eugenics in Canada, 1885–1945* (Toronto: McClelland and Stewart Inc., 1990).

17. S. Siedlecky and D. Wyndham, *Populate and Perish: Australian Women's Fight for Birth Control* (Sydney: Allen and Unwin, 1990), pp. 23–4.
18. H. Smyth, *Rocking the Cradle: Contraception, Sex, and Politics in New Zealand* (Wellington: Steele Roberts Ltd., 2000), p. 13.
19. McLaren, *Our Own Master Race*, ch. 3, "Stemming the Flood of Defective Aliens,' pp. 46–67.
20. Cited in Giliomee, *The Afrikaners*, p. 288.
21. *Ibid.*, p. 330.
22. *Ibid.*, p. 353.
23. *Ibid.*, p. 336.
24. M. Swanson, "The Sanitation Syndrome: Bubonic Plague and the Urban Native Policy in the Cape Colony, 1900–1909," *Journal of African History*, 18, 3 (1977), pp. 387–410; K. Jochelson, *The Colour of Disease: Syphilis and Racism in South Africa, 1880–1950* (Basingstoke and Oxford: Palgrave in association with St. Antony's College, 2001).
25. P. Bonner, "1920 Mineworkers Strike: A Preliminary Account," in B. Bozzoli (ed) *Labour, Townships, and Protest: Studies in the Social History of the Witwatersrand* (Johannesburg: Ravan Press, 1979), pp. 273–97; H. Bradford, *A Taste of Freedom: The ICU in Rural South Africa, 1923–1930* (New Haven: Yale University Press, 1987); C. Walker, *Women and Resistance in South Africa*, 2nd edn (Cape Town: David Philip, 1991); R. Hill and G. Pirio, " 'Africa for the Africans': The Garvey Movement in South Africa, 1920–1940," in S. Marks and S. Trapido (eds), *The Politics of Race, Class and Nationalism in Twentieth Century South Africa*, pp. 209–53; C. Bundy, "Land and Liberation: Popular Rural Protest and the National Liberation Movements in South Africa, 1920–1960," in *ibid.*, pp. 254–85; D. Crummey (ed), *Banditry, Rebellion and Social Protest in Africa* (London: J. Currey, 1986); W. Beinart and C. Bundy (eds), *Hidden Struggles in Rural South Africa: Politics and Popular Movements in the Transkei and Eastern Cape, 1890–1930* (Johannesburg: Ravan Press, 1987); P. Bonner, "The Transvaal Native Congress, 1917–1920: The Radicalization of the Black Petty Bourgeoisie on the Rand," in S. Marks and R. Rathbone (eds), *Industrialisation and Social Change in South Africa* (London: Longman, 1982), pp. 270–313; P. Walshe, *The Rise of African Nationalism in South Africa: The ANC, 1915–1952* (Berkeley: University of California Press, 1971); T. Lodge, *Black Politics in South Africa Since 1945* (London: Longman, 1983).
26. Cited in M. Adler, "The Literary, Personal, and Socio-Political Background of William Plomer's *Turbott Wolfe*" (MA thesis, University of Witwatersrand, 1988), p. 228.
27. A. Jeeves, *Migrant Labour in South Africa's Mining Economy: The Struggle for the Gold Mines' Labour Supply, 1890–1920* (Johannesburg: Witwatersrand University Press, 1985); W. Beinart, *The Political Economy of Pondoland, 1860–1930* (Cambridge: Cambridge University Press, 1982); M. Lacey, *Working for Boroko: The Origins of a Coercive Labour System in South Africa* (Johannesburg: Ravan Press, 1981); W. Macmillan, *Complex South Africa* (London: Faber and Faber, 1930); and S. Plaatje, *Native Life in South Africa* (London: P.S. King and Son, 1916).
28. Cited in C. Bundy, *The Rise and Fall of the South African Peasantry* (Berkeley: University of California Press, 1979), p. 1.

29. P. Rich, "Ministering to the White Man's Needs: The Development of Urban Segregation in South Africa, 1913–1923," *African Studies*, 37 (1978), pp. 177–91.
30. Cited in Jochelson, *Colour of Disease*, p. 112.
31. T.R.H. Davenport, *South Africa: A Modern History*. 3rd edn (Bergvlei: Southern Book Publishers, 1987), p. 546.
32. R. Morrell, "The Poor Whites of Middelburg, Transvaal, 1900–1930: Resistance, Accommodation and Class Struggle," in Robert Morrell (ed), *White But Poor: Essays on the History of the Poor Whites in Southern Africa, 1880–1940* (Pretoria: University of South Africa, 1992), p. 2.
33. See the collection of essays in *White But Poor*; T. Keegan, *Racial Transformation in Industrializing South Africa: The Southern Highveld to 1914* (Basingstoke: Macmillan, 1987); R. Davies, *Capital, State and White Labour in South Africa* (Atlantic Highlands, NJ: Humanities Press, 1979); C. Bundy, "Vagabond Hollanders and Runaway Englishmen: White Poverty in the Cape Before Poor Whiteism," in W. Beinart, P. Delius, and S. Trapido (eds), *Putting the Plough to the Ground: Accumulation and Dispossession in Rural South Africa, 1850–1930* (London: James Currey, 1986), pp. 101–28; for an account of land dispossession for Africans and whites in the late nineteenth and early twentieth centuries see W. Beinart and P. Delius, "Introduction," in *Putting a Plough to the Ground*; T. Clynick, "Afrikaner Political Mobilization in the Western Transvaal: Popular Consciousness and the State, 1920–30," (PhD thesis, Queen's University at Kingston, 1996).
34. Church of the Province of South Africa, University of the Witwatersrand, Pim Papers, Johannesburg, File Fa 9/3. Johannesburg Joint Council of Europeans and Natives, Report of the Housing Committee, 1923, 4. Cited in E. Koch, "Doornfontein and its African Working Class, 1914–1935; A Study of Popular Culture in Johannesburg" (MA thesis, University of the Witwatersrand, 1983), p. 42. Thanks to Jon Hyslop for bringing this thesis to my attention.
35. "Reform versus 'Vested' Interests," editorial, *The Star*, November 5, 1917.
36. "Johannesburg's Slums," *Rand Daily Mail*, January 14, 1916.
37. Cited in P. Lewson, *John X. Merriman* (New Haven: Yale University Press, 1982), pp. 80–87, 297–8.
38. P.W. Laidler, "The Organisation of a Health Programme in Urban Areas," *Report of the National Conference on Social Work* (Pretoria: Government Printer, 1936), p. 157.
39. *Cape Times*, July 24, 1929.
40. Cited in J. Bottomley, " 'Almost Bled to Death': The Effects of the Anglo Boer War on Social Transformation in the Orange River Colony," *Historia*, 44, 1 (1999), p. 191.
41. Jochelson, *Colour of Disease*, p. 56.
42. A.L. Stoler, "Making Empire Respectable: The Politics of Race and Sexual Morality in 20th Century Colonial Cultures," *American Ethnologist*, 16, 4 (1989), p. 645.
43. A.L. Stoler, "Tense and Tender Ties: The Politics of Comparison in North American History and (Post) Colonial Studies," *The Journal of American History*, 88, 3 (2001), p. 3.
44. An example of respectable whites' repulsion at the notion of miscegenation was the popular and critical success of Sarah Gertrude Millin's novel *God's*

Stepchildren, published in 1924, which evoked the fear of degeneration caused by inter-race sexuality. See Adler, *Turbot Wolfe*, p. 237.

45. C.W. de Kiewiet, *A History of South Africa – Social and Economic* (Oxford: Clarendon Press, 1941), vol. 2, p. 221.

46. *Carnegie Commission of Investigation on the Poor White Question in South Africa. The Poor White Problem in South Africa. Joint Findings and Recommendations* (Stellenbosch: Pro Ecclesia, 1932), p. xx.

47. Giliomee, *The Afrikaners*, p. 344.

48. D. Berger, "White Poverty and Government Policy in South Africa, 1892–1934," (PhD thesis, Temple University, 1983), p. 11. Thanks to Neil Roos for bringing this thesis to my attention.

49. Davenport, *South Africa*, p. 533.

50. Macmillan, *Complex South Africa*, p. 229.

51. D. O'Meara, *Volkskapitalism: Class, Capital and Ideology in the Development of Afrikaner Nationalism 1934–1948* (Cambridge: Cambridge University Press, 1983), pp. 36–7.

52. D. O'Meara, "Class, Capital and Ideology in the Development of Afrikaner Nationalism 1934–1938" (PhD thesis, School of Oriental and African Studies, 1979), pp. 3–7, cited in Koch, "Doornfontein and its African Working Class," p. 170.

53. Koch, "Doornfontein and its African Working Class," p. 189.

54. Jochelson, *Colour of Disease*, p. 55.

55. Cited in *ibid.*, p. 125.

56. Koch, "Doornfontein and its African Working Class," p. 170.

57. *Ibid.*

58. Statement made by the Johannesburg Housing Utility Company. Cited in S. Parnell, "Slums, Segregation and Poor Whites in Johannesburg," in *White But Poor*, p. 127.

59. Koch, "Doornfontein and its African Working Class," p. 166.

60. *Debates of the House of Assembly*, vol. 23, May 8, 1934, pp. 3327–8.

61. *Debates of the House of Assembly*, vol. 25, January 29, 1935, p. 778.

62. *Ibid.*, vol. 25, January 29, 1935, p. 778.

63. *Ibid.*, vol. 43, February 17, 1942, p. 2238.

64. *Ibid.*, vols. 45 and 46, March 31, 1943, p. 4408.

65. *Report of the Economic and Wage Commission, 1925*; *Report of the Native Economic Commission, 1930–32*; F.W. Fox and D. Back, "A Preliminary Survey of the Agricultural and Nutritional Problems of the Ciskei and Transkeian Territories with Special Reference to their Bearing on the Recruiting of Labourers for the Gold Mining Industry" (Johannesburg: Chamber of Mines, 1938).

66. S. Marks and N. Andersson, "Issues in the Political Economy of Health in Southern Africa," *Journal of Southern African Studies*, 13, 2 (1987), p. 180.

67. Also cited in Jochelson, *Colour of Disease*, p. 112.

68. *Annual Report of the Department of Public Health, Year Ended June 30, 1938* (Pretoria: Government Printer, 1938), pp. 13–17; *Annual Report of the Department of Public Health, Year Ended June 30, 1939* (Pretoria: Government Printer, 1939), pp. 71–2.

69. Cited in Jochelson, *Colour of Disease*, p. 93.

70. As Anna Davin has pointed out, by the beginning in the early twentieth century, British imperialists viewed population as a vital source of power for the colonizing project. Davin, "Imperialism and Motherhood," p. 10.

71. Statement made in Parliament by MP C.M. Van Coller. *Debates of the House of Assembly*, vol. 25, January 29, 1935, p. 1142.
72. The rate of maternal mortality is "the number of maternal deaths occurring in pregnancy, labour or the postnatal period (conventionally defined as the 6 weeks following delivery)" per 1000 live births. I. Loudon, "Some International Features of Maternal Mortality, 1880–1950," in V. Fildes, L. Marks and H. Marland (eds), *Women and Children First: International Maternal and Infant Welfare 1870–1945* (London and New York: Routledge, 1992), pp. 24–5. During the 1930s the DPH included indirect maternal deaths (in relation to pregnancy and childbirth) in its published figures. Other countries included only direct deaths (in relation to childbirth only), important to note when making international comparisons.
73. *Debates of the House of Assembly*, vol. 14, January 24, 1930, p. 77.
74. *Annual Report of the Department of Public Health, Year Ended June 30, 1935*, (Pretoria: Government Printer, 1935), p. 57.
75. Loudon, "Some International Features of Maternal Mortality, 1880–1950," p. 12.
76. *Debates of the House of Assembly*, vol. 14, January 24, 1930, p. 77; *Annual Report of the Department of Public Health*, 1935, pp. 57–9.
77. S. Marks, *Divided Sisterhood: Race, Class, and Gender in the South African Nursing Profession* (New York: St. Martin's Press, 1994), pp. 67–8.
78. C. Burns, "Reproductive Labours: The Politics of Women's Health in South Africa, 1900 to 1960" (PhD thesis, Northwestern University, 1995), p. 79.
79. *Ibid.*, pp. 77, 83, 108.
80. "Minutes of the Meeting of the Cape Town Division of the Cape Western Branch of the Medical Association of South Africa (BMA)," *South African Medical Journal*, 6 (1932), p. 303.
81. M.E. Rothmann, *The Mother and Daughter of the Poor Family. Vol. V. The Poor White Problem in South Africa, Carnegie Commission of Investigation on the Poor White Question in South Africa* (Stellenbosch: Pro Ecclesia, 1932), pp. 185–90.
82. Cited in Jochelson, *Colour of Disease*, p. 63.
83. *Debates of the House of Assembly*, vol. 14, January 24, 1930, p. 77.
84. *Official Year Book of the Union, 1931–32* (Pretoria: Government Printer, 1932), p. 233.
85. L. Thompson, *A History of South Africa* (New Haven: Yale University Press, 1990), p. 243.
86. *Annual Report of the Department of Public Health, Year Ended June 30, 1936*, (Pretoria: Union of South Africa, 1936), p. 16.
87. *Annual Report of the Department of Public Health, Year Ended June 30, 1937*, (Pretoria: Union of South Africa, 1937), p. 29.
88. *Debates of the House of Assembly*, March 19, 1937, pp. 3524–5.
89. *Ibid.*, p. 3547.
90. *Debates of the House of Assembly*, April 1, 1937, p. 4042.
91. *Annual Report of the Department of Public Health*, 1937, p. 72.
92. Berger, "White Poverty and Government Policy in South Africa, 1892–1934," p. 409.
93. *Ibid.*, pp. 410–11.
94. *Annual Report of the Department of Public Health, Year Ended June 30, 1938* (Pretoria: Government Printer, 1938), p. 52.
95. *Debates of the House of Assembly*, vol. 28, February 26, 1937, p. 2468.

96. See *Annual Report of the Department of Public Health, Year Ended June 30, 1938* (Pretoria: Government Printer, 1938), pp. 13–17; *and Annual Report of the Department of Public Health, Year Ended June 30, 1939* (Pretoria: Government Printer, 1939), pp. 71–2.

97. *Debates of the House of Assembly*, vols. 45 and 46, March 31, 1943, p. 4403.

98. J. Iliffe, *The African Poor. A History* (Cambridge: Cambridge University Press, 1987), p. 117; and E. Hellmann, (ed.), *Handbook on Race Relations in South Africa* (Cape Town: Oxford University Press, 1949), p. 13, Table 6.

99. Jenny Robinson writes that the 1936 Empire Exhibition, held in Johannesburg, was an example of South Africans trying to articulate "a sense of national progress." J. Robinson, "Johannesburg's 1936 Empire Exhibition: Interaction, Segregation and Modernity in a South African City," *Journal of Southern African Studies*, 29, 3 (2003), pp. 759–89.

100. R. Macnab, *The Story of South Africa House: South Africa in Britain – The Changing Pattern* (Johannesburg: Jonathan Ball Publishers, 1983), p. 127.

101. *Debates of the House of Assembly*, (January 8 to May 17, 1937), pp. 2471–2.

102. J. Malherbe, "Women's Movements in South Africa," 1937, p. 2. Janie Malherbe collection, File 195, Killie Campbell Archive, Durban.

103. The same point is made by N. Roos, *From Workplace to War: Class, Race, and Gender Amongst White Volunteers, 1939–1953* (PhD thesis, University of North West, 2001), pp. 99–100. See, for example, J.L. Gray, "Sterility and the Falling Birth-Rate," *South African Medical Journal*, 11 (1937), p. 492.

104. See P.W. Laidler, "The Organisation of a Health Programme in Urban Areas," *Report of the National Conference on Social Work*, p. 157; P.W. Laidler, "The Medico-Social Aspects of Population Density," *South African Medical Journal*, 10 (1936), p. 323; P.W. Laidler, "The Practice of Eugenics," *South African Medical Journal*, 8 (1934), pp. 823–34; J.W. Adams, "Some Population Problems of the World," *South African Medical Journal*, 8 (1934), pp. 131–2; *Debates of the House of Assembly*, vol. 25, January 29, 1935, p. 1142.

105. De Kiewiet, *A History of South Africa*, p. 176.

106. Rothmann, *The Mother and Daughter of the Poor Family*, pp. 156–86.

107. *Ibid.*, pp. 196–7.

108. E.G. Malherbe, *Education and the Poor White, Vol. 3. The Poor White Problem in South Africa*, pp. 212–25.

109. *The Poor White Problem in South Africa. Joint Findings and Recommendations*, paragraph 88, pp. xxiv–xxv.

110. Malherbe, *Education and the Poor White*, p. 212.

111. *The Poor White Problem in South Africa. Joint Findings and Recommendations*, paragraph 89, pp. xxiv–xxv.

112. National Archives of South Africa (NASA), Central Archives Depot (SAB), Archives of the Department of Public Health (GES), 2277, 77/38, vol. 1, undated letter from E.G. Dru-Drury to A.W. Murray.

113. NASA, SAB, GES 2277, 77/38, vol. 1, undated letter from J.B. Holtzhausen to A.W. Murray.

114. "S.A. African Bishops on Birth Control. An Authoritative Statement," *Rand Daily Mail*, August 22, 1930.

115. In Johannesburg newspapers: "Bishops and Birth Control. Practice Permissable in Certain Cases," *Rand Daily Mail*, August 15, 1930; "Thought of God Passing Away," *Rand Daily Mail*, August 15, 1930; "The Lambeth

Conference. Thought of God Passing Away. Decision on Birth Control," *Star*, August 15, 1930. In Cape Town newspapers: "Birth Control Sanctioned," *Cape Times*, August 15, 1930; "Bishop's Call to the Church. Historic Decision at the Lambeth Conference," *Cape Times*, August 15, 1930; "Birth Control Clinics. Is Their Establishment Desirable?," *Cape Times*, August 13, 1930; "More Views on Birth Control. A 'Practical Necessity' in Modern Society," *Cape Times*, August 14, 1930; "Creches and Birth-Control Clinics. Need Emphasized by Experienced Health Visitor," *Cape Times*, August 14, 1930; "Birth Control Sanctioned," *Cape Times*, August 15, 1930; "Protecting the Children. Problem of Tubercular Parents," *Cape Times*, August 15, 1930; "Bishops' Call to the Church," *Cape Times*, August 15, 1930; "Birth Control 'War,' " *Cape Times*, August 16, 1930; "Birth Control Concessions," *Cape Times*, August 18, 1930; "Birth Control and Suicide," *Cape Times*, August 20, 1930; "Birth Control Controversy. South African Prelates in Opposition," *Cape Times*, August 21, 1930; "South African Bishops' 'Revolt,' " August 22, 1930; "Church on Birth Control," *Cape Times*, August 29, 1930; "Birth Control Clinics," *Cape Times*, September 2, 1930; "An 'Unholy' Row to Follow Bishops' Decision. Approval of Birth Control," *Cape Argus*, August 15, 1930; "Frank and Decisive Findings. Generally Welcomed," *Cape Argus*, August 15, 1930, "Encyclical Letter and 75 Resolutions," *Cape Argus*, August 15, 1930. In addition, over thirty letters appeared in the *Cape Times* in the month of August 1930.

116. "Protecting the Children. Problem of Tubercular Parents," *Cape Times*, August 15, 1930.
117. *Cape Times*, September 6, 1930.
118. "Birth Control Clinics. Is Their Establishment Desirable?," *Cape Times*, August 13, 1930.
119. *Ibid.*
120. *Ibid.*
121. "Birth Control Clinics Urged. 'A Duty to the Nation.' Support From Well-Known Speakers," *Rand Daily Mail*, April 29, 1931.
122. Letter, *Cape Times*, August 25, 1930.
123. J.L. Gray, "Sterility and the Falling Birth-Rate," *South African Medical Journal*, July 24, 1937, p. 492.
124. Soloway, *Demography and Degeneration*, p. 160.
125. J. Weeks, *Sex, Politics and Society: The Regulation of Sexuality Since 1800* (London and New York: Longman, 1981), p. 44.
126. "More Views on Birth Control. A 'Practical Necessity' in Modern Society," *Cape Times*, August 14, 1930.
127. *Cape Times*, August 20, 1930.
128. *Ibid.*
129. *Ibid.*
130. Letter, *Cape Times*, August 22, 1930.
131. J.R. Albertyn, *The Poor White and Society. Vol. IV. The Poor White Problem in South Africa*.
132. S. Dubow, *Racial Segregation and the Origins of Apartheid in South Africa, 1919–36* (Basingstoke: Macmillan, 1989), p. 4 and S. Dubow, "Afrikaner Nationalism, Apartheid, and the Conceptualisation of 'Race,' " *The Journal of African History*, 33, 2 (1992), 209–37.

133. Cited in W. Beinart, *Twentieth Century South Africa* (Oxford: Oxford University Press, 1994), p. 70.
134. *Ibid.*, p. 71.
135. Cited in R. Hyam, *Elgin and Churchill at the Colonial Office, 1905–1908: The Watershed of the Empire-Commonwealth* (London: Macmillan, 1968), p. 141. At the time Churchill was Parliamentary Under-Secretary of State for the Colonies. See also G.B. Pyrah, *Imperial Policy and South Africa, 1902–1910* (Oxford: Clarendon Press, 1955).
136. S. Dubow, "Scientism, Social Research and the Limits of 'South Africanism': The Case of Ernst Gideon Malherbe," *South African Historical Journal*, 44 (2001), pp. 99–142.
137. Berger, "White Poverty and Government Policy in South Africa, 1892–1934," p. 31.
138. *Ibid.*, pp. 301–2.
139. Stoler, "Making Empire Respectable," p. 644.

Chapter 2: Birth Control and the Poor White Problem

1. H.B. Fantham, "Eugenics," *Child Welfare*, 9,7 (1930), p. 5.
2. N. Stepan, *"The Hour of Eugenics": Race, Gender,* and *Nation in Latin America* (Ithaca: Cornell University Press, 1991), p. 10.
3. The historiography on eugenics is massive and growing. Major studies include F. Dikötter, "Race Culture: Recent Perspectives on the History of Eugenics," *American Historical Review*, 103, 2 (1998), pp. 467–78; F. Dikötter, *Imperfect Conceptions: Medical Knowledge, Birth Defects,* and *Eugenics in China* (New York: Columbia University Press, 1998); N. Stepan, "The Hour of Eugenics"; W. Schneider, *Quality and Quantity: The Quest for Biological Regeneration in Twentieth-Century France* (Cambridge: Cambridge University Press, 1990); M. Adams (ed), *The Wellborn Science: Eugenics in Germany, France, Brazil, and Russia* (New York: Oxford University Press, 1990); R. Soloway, *Demography and Degeneration: Eugenics and the Declining Birthrate in Twentieth-Century Britain* (Chapel Hill: North Carolina University Press, 1990); D. Kevles, *In the Name of the Race: Genetics and the Uses of Human Heredity* (New York: Knopf, 1985); A. McLaren, *Our Own Master Race: Eugenics in Canada, 1885–1945* (Toronto: McClelland and Stewart Inc., 1990); S.J. Gould, *The Mismeasure of Man*, revised edn (New York: W.W. Norton and Company, 1996); G. Jones, *Social Hygiene in 20th Century Britain* (London: Croom Helm, 1986).
4. Schneider, *Quality and Quantity*, p. 4.
5. C. Webster, "Introduction," in C. Webster, (ed.), *Biology, Medicine and Society 1840–1940* (Cambridge: Cambridge University Press, 1981), pp. 1–13.
6. Dikötter, "Race Culture: Recent Perspectives on the History of Eugenics," p. 467.
7. M. Adams, "Toward A Comparative History of Eugenics," in *The Wellborn Science*, pp. 217–26.
8. S. Dubow, *Scientific Racism in Modern South Africa* (Cambridge: Cambridge University Press, 1995); S. Klausen, " 'For the Sake of the Race': Eugenic

Discourses of Feeblemindedness and Motherhood in the *South African Medical Record, 1903–26*," *Journal of Southern African Studies*, 10, 1 (1997), pp. 27–50.

9. "Future of the White in Question," *Star*, February 4 1933.

10. P.W. Laidler, "The Practice of Eugenics," *South African Medical Journal*, 8 (1934), p. 823.

11. A portion of the following discussion about the RWS was published previously in "The Race Welfare Society: Eugenics and Birth Control in Johannesburg, 1930–1939," in Saul Dubow (ed,) *Science and Society in Southern Africa* (Manchester: Manchester University Press, 2000), pp. 164–87.

12. University of the Witwatersrand, Historical Papers Collection, William Cullen Library, Johannesburg (HPW), Race Welfare Society Documents (RWS), June 26, 1930.

13. "Loss to the Rand: Professor Fantham for Canada," *Star*, September 21, 1932; and "Honour for Prof. Fantham – The South Africa Medal," *Star*, June 10, 1931.

14. Fantham and Porter's articles include "Notes on Some Cases of Racial Admixture in South Africa," *South African Journal of Science*, 24 (1927); "Some Further Cases of Physical Inheritance and Racial Admixture Observed in South Africa," *South African Journal of Science*, 27 (1930); "Inheritance of Stature Through Mate-Selection," *Journal of Heredity*, 25 (1935); "Remarks on a "Family" Showing Shortness, Illegitimacy and Simplemindedness," *Eugenical News*, 21 (1936). Articles Fantham authored on his own include: "Heredity in Man: Its Importance both Biologically and Educationally," *South African Journal of Science*, 21 (1924); "Some Factors in Eugenics, Together with Notes on Some South African Cases," *South African Journal of Science*, 22 (1925); "Some Thoughts on the Social Aspects of Eugenics, with Note on Some Further Cases of Human Inheritance Observed in South Africa," *South African Journal of Science*, 23 (1926); "Some Thoughts on Biology and the Race," *South African Journal of Science*, 24 (1927); "How the Lack of a Knowledge of Eugenics Affects One's Pocket," *Transvaal Educational News*, 25 (1928); "Biology and Civilisation," *South African Journal of Science*, 29 (1932); "Glands and Personality," *South African Journal of Science*, 29 (1932); "Biology in Relation to Some Present-Day Problems," *Scientia*, 28 (1934); "Some Further Cases of Physical Inheritance and of Racial Admixture Observed in South Africa," *South African Journal of Science*, 27 (1930).

15. The Eugenics Society of South Africa (ESSA) was as an outgrowth of the Pretoria Eugenic Study Circle (PESC), formed in April 1927, which comprised five scientists and five teachers, including Fantham. Interestingly, seven of the ten original members were Afrikaans-speakers. In 1930 PESC expanded into ESSA. The ESSA was equally distressed over the relatively high birth rates of blacks and poor whites. The group's preoccupation with maintaining white supremacy was summed up by one member, A.J.T. Janse, who wrote, "Only the small percentage of the unfit will secure in South Africa superiority of the white race over the black race; should that percentage become too high, the *white civilisation in South Africa is doomed*" (emphasis in original). From "Eugenics and Its Need in South Africa," ESSA pamphlet, p. 4. See also A.J.T. Janse, "White and Black in South Africa," pamphlet, pp. 3–4. As a study group, the ESSA failed to attract sufficient support and consequently it petered out in November 1931. The RWS succeeded where the

ESSA failed in large part because of its practical program of establishing birth-control clinics. Sources found in the Wellcome Institute for the History of Medicine, Contemporary Archives, London, SA/EUG E.22.

16. M. Malan, *The Quest for Health: The South African Institute for Medical Research* (Johannesburg: Lowry Publishers, 1988), pp. 35, 37.
17. Fantham, "Eugenics," p. 6.
18. *Ibid.*
19. A. Porter, "Eugenics from a Woman's Point of View," *Child Welfare*, 10, 2 (1931), p. 4.
20. G. Jones, "Eugenics and Social Policy Between the Wars," *The Historical Journal*, 25, 3 (1982), p. 722.
21. Fantham, "Eugenics," p. 5.
22. Porter, "Eugenics from a Woman's Point of View," p. 3.
23. Janse, "The Eugenics Society of South Africa."
24. "Henry Britten," in *South Africa's Who's Who*, Ken Donaldson, ed (Cape Town, 1937 and 1944 edns). The Coronation Medal was awarded to leading social welfare reformers, philanthropists, and other social notables on the occasion of the coronation of King George VI on May 12, 1937.
25. Hardy was a partner in the accounting firm Howard Pim and Hardy. Pim was among the first theorists of segregation to outline a plan for a reserve system for Africans, but by 1930 he was a prominent liberal critic of segregation. See S. Dubow, *Racial Segregation and the Origins of Apartheid in South Africa, 1919–36* (Basingstoke: Macmillan, 1989), pp. 23–25.
26. "Mr. J.L. Hardy, O.B.E.," *Rand Daily Mail*, November 26, 1941.
27. HPW, RWS, September 21, 1932.
28. For example, Dr. I.J. Block spoke in favor of birth control at the South African Medical Council's annual general meeting in 1934 and his speech was published as "Observations from the Work of a Birth Control Clinic," *South African Medical Record*, 8 (1934), pp. 490–2.
29. HPW, RWS, September 1, 1931.
30. HPW, RWS, June 30, 1932, Dr. Berry of the executive hosted ten District Surgeons who visited the RWS's first birth-control clinic in 1932. Afterwards, many requested supplies of contraceptives. HPW, RWS, February 25, 1932.
31. "Honour for Prof. Fantham: the South Africa Medal," *Star*, June 10, 1931; RWS, June 29, 1932.
32. HPW, RWS, December 17, 1930 and June 30, 1932.
33. HPW, RWS, August 27, 1931 and September 21, 1932.
34. Public events and the numbers in attendance in 1930: "The Economic Aspects of Birth Control," by Miss Pollack and Dr. Bernstein, 102 people attended; "Ethics of Birth Control," by O. C. Jensen, 74 people attended. In 1931: "Inheritance of Mental Defect," by Dr. A.M. Moll and "The Economic Aspects of Mental Defectiveness," by Miss Pollack, about 70 people attended; "The Social Worker and Eugenics," by Dr. Maria Te Water, 47 people attended; "Why South Africa Needs Birth Control," by George Hills MP, 70 people attended; "Eugenics Versus Disease, Poverty and War," by Dr. Annie Porter and G.H. Shawe, 35 people attended; "Glands and Personality," by H. B. Fantham, 318 people attended; "Points Connected with Heredity in South Africa," by Dr. Porter, 13 people attended. 1932: "Birth Control, Wages and Workers," by George Hills MP, Dr. F. Berry, Dr. A.M. Moll, and Henry Britten,

about 50 people attended; "Biology and Civilization," By H.B. Fantham, 220 people attended. Symposium: May 26, 1931 the RWS and Mental Hygiene Society co-sponsored "The Poor White Question," and about 220 people attended. Dr. Morris Cohen was the Chairman and speakers included Drs Frankel, Malherbe, Te Water and Block, and Mr. Radloff. For reportage of these events see: "Future Welfare of the Race. Serious Problem of the Feeble-Minded. Sterilisation or Segregation?" *Rand Daily Mail*, August 15, 1930; "Improvement of the Race," *Star*, August 15, 1930; "Birth Control a Necessity. Outgrowing World's Food Supply," *Rand Daily Mail*, August 25, 1930; "Birth Control Clinics Urged. 'A Duty to the Nation.' Support from Well-Known Speakers," *Rand Daily Mail*, April 29, 1931; "19 Children on 4/- a Day. Poor Man's Huge Family. Need of Birth Control Clinics Stressed," *Star*, April 29, 1931; "Expert Views on Poor Whites. A Valuable Symposium," *Rand Daily Mail*, May 28, 1931; "Problem of Poor Whiteism. Habits can be Changed. Questions Reviewed from Five Angles," *Star*, May 28, 1931.

35. Cited in D. Berger, "White Poverty and Government Policy in South Africa, 1892–1934," (PhD thesis, Temple University, 1983), p. 274.
36. *Ibid.*, pp. 280–1.
37. *Star*, November 12, 1927.
38. E. Brink, "The Afrikaner Women of the Garment Worker's Union, 1918–1938," (MA thesis, University of the Witwatersrand, 1986), p. 45.
39. S. Parnell, "Slums, Segregation and Poor Whites in Johannesburg, 1920–1934," in Robert Morrell, ed. *White But Poor: Essays on the History of the Poor Whites in Southern Africa, 1880–1940* (Pretoria: University of South Africa, 1992), p. 22.
40. D.O. Meara, *Volkskapitalisme: Class, Capital and Ideology in the Development of Afrikaner Nationalism 1934–1948* (Cambridge: Cambridge University Press, 1983), p. 32.
41. Cited in D. Gaitskell, "Getting Close to the Hearts of Mothers:" Medical Missionaries Among African Women and Children in Johannesburg Between the Wars," in V. Fildes, L. Marks, and H. Marland (eds), *Women and Children First: International Maternal and Infant Welfare 1870–1945* (London and New York: Routledge, 1992), p. 186.
42. E. Koch, "Doornfontein and its African Working Class, 1914–1935; A Study of Popular Culture in Johannesburg" (MA thesis, University of the Witwatersrand, 1983), p. 188.
43. Municipal Magazine, June 1933, 32. Cited in *ibid.*, p. 198.
44. *Ibid.*, p. 171.
45. *Rand Daily Mail*, December 17, 1929.
46. E. Roux, *Time Longer Than Rope: A History of the Black Man's Struggle for Freedom in South Africa* (Madison: University of Wisconsin Press, 1964), p. 272.
47. A. Proctor, "Class Struggle, Segregation and the City: A History of Sophiatown, 1905–40," in Belinda Bozzoli (ed.), *Labour, Townships and Protest: Studies in the Social History of the Witwatersrand* (Johannesburg: Ravan Press, 1979), p. 65.
48. J. Hyslop, "White Working-Class Women and the Invention of Apartheid: "Purified" Afrikaner Nationalist Agitation for Legislation Against "Mixed" Marriages, 1934–9," *Journal of African History*, 36 (1995), p. 62.

49. Fantham, "Eugenics," 7.
50. *Ibid.*, pp. 5–7.
51. Dr. J.W. Adams, "Some Population Problems of the World," *South Africa Medical Journal*, February 24, 1934, pp. 131–2.
52. "Future Welfare of the Race: Serious Problem of the Feeble-Minded. Sterilisation or Segregation?" *Rand Daily Mail*, August 15, 1930.
53. HPW, RWS, December 31, 1934.
54. National Archives of South Africa (NASA), Central Archives Depot (SAB), Archives of the Department of Public Health (GES) 2281, 85/38, vol. 1, RWS fundraising letter, November 29, 1930.
55. Fantham, "Eugenics," 7.
56. Giliomee, *The Afrikaners*, p. 327.
57. "Improvement of the Race," *Star*, August 15, 1930.
58. "19 children on 4/- a day. Poor Man's Huge Family. Need of Birth Control Clinics Stressed," *Star*, April 29, 1931.
59. *Ibid.*
60. HPW, RWS, December 4, 1936.
61. NASA, SAB, GES 2281, 85/38, vol. 1, RWS to the Secretary for Public Health (SPH), May 27, 1931, 2.
62. HPW, RWS, November 9, 1933.
63. *Ibid.*
64. HPW, RWS, June 30, 1936.
65. HPW, RWS, September 21, 1932, Number of cases dealt with at the Clinic, February 2–September 16, 1932.
66. See HPW, RWS, Annual Reports (AR) for 1932, 1933, 1934, 1936, 1937 and 1939.
67. HPW, RWS, AR 1933.
68. Block, "Observations from the Work of a Birth Control Clinic," p. 491.
69. HPW, RWS, Number of cases dealt with at the Clinic February 2–September 16, 1932), September 21, 1932.
70. HPW, RWS, Minutes of the RWS Annual General Meeting, October 13, 1939.
71. HPW, RWS, AR 1939.
72. HPW, RWS, AR 1933.
73. HPW, RWS, August 2, 1932.
74. "Society for Race Welfare. Expansion Claimed in Annual Report," *Star*, October 30, 1936; "Transmission of Disease. Address to Race Welfare Society," *Star*, November 4, 1936; "Survival of Degenerates. Eugenics Combats Race Menace," *Rand Daily Mail*, November 4, 1936; "Practical Clinic Work. The Birth Control Movement," *Star*, August 1, 1937; "Birth Control in City. Race Welfare Meeting," *Star*, November 20, 1937; "Attendance at Race Welfare Clinics Lower," *Rand Daily Mail*, November 20, 1937.
75. HPW, RWS, June 9, 1939.
76. HPW, RWS, October 13, 1939.
77. *Ibid.*
78. HPW, RWS, July 21, 1938.
79. *Ibid.*
80. NASA, SAB, GES 2281, 85/38, vol. 1. Assistant General Secretary of SAAS to SPH, September 16, 1932.

81. "White South Africa in Danger. The Growth of Poverty. Birth Control as a Cure," *Rand Daily Mail*, September 1934; "Gevaar Dat Verstandspeil Van Die Bevolking Daal, *Die Volkstem*, September 1934. See also his presentation to the Goodwill Club, Johannesburg, September 19, 1932, "The Poor White Problem. What Can We do to Solve it? Some General Principles," in Killie Campbell Africana Library, Durban (KC) E.G. Malherbe Collection (EGM), File 477/4, "Notes of Presentation held on Birth Control for the DR Church Synod Behind Locked Doors."

82. E.G.Malherbe, *Never A Dull Moment* (Cape Town: Timmins Pub., 1981), pp. 130–1.

83. KC, EGM, "Notes of Presentation held on Birth Control for the DR Church Synod Behind Locked Doors."

84. Malherbe, *Never A Dull Moment*, p. 131.

85. *Birth Control News*, 13, 2 (1934), p. 26.

86. "Intelligence of the Nation. Size of Family a Factor. Dr. E.G. Malherbe's Address,' *Star*, October 28, 1938; "The C3 Standard," *Star*, October 28, 1938.

87. "Transmission of Disease. Address to Race Welfare Society," *Star*, November 4, 1936.

88. See correspondence of ESSA, Welcome Institute for the History of Medicine, Contemporary Archives, SA/EUG E. 22.

89. Planned Parenthood Association of South Africa (PPASA), Johannesburg Office (JHB), South African National Council for Maternal and Family Welfare Papers (SANCMFW), Minutes of the Second Meeting of the South African National Council for Birth Control, October 6–7, 1936.

90. HPW, RWS, March 11, 1937.

91. PPASA, JHB, SANCMFW, "Minutes of the Postponed General Meeting of the South African National Council for Maternal and Family Welfare," September 27–28, 1938. For a sample of Laidler's eugenic views see: "The Practice of Eugenics"; and "The Medico-social Aspects of Population Density," *South African Medical Journal*, 10 (1936), pp. 317–27.

92. "Birth-Control," *Cape Times*, April 8, 1933.

93. H. Houghton, "Economic Development, 1865–1965," in M. Wilson and L. Thompson (eds), *Oxford History of South Africa*, vol. 2, p. 28. Cited in N. Roos, *From Workplace to War: Class, Race and Gender Amongst White Volunteers, 1939–1953* (PhD thesis, University of North West, 2001), p. 91.

94. Koch, "Doornfontein and its African Working Class, 1914–1935," p. 201.

95. P. Rich, *White Power and the Liberal Conscience: Racial Segregation and South African Liberalism* (Manchester: Manchester University Press, 1984).

96. S. Dubow, "Race, Civilisation and Culture: The Elaboration of Segregationist Discourse in the Interwar Years," in Shula Marks and Stanley Trapido (eds), *The Politics of Race, Class and Nationalism in Twentieth Century South Africa* (London and New York: Longman), pp. 71–94.

97. "Dr. Hoernle dies. A tireless social worker," *Rand Daily Mail*, March 18, 1960; and "Dr. Hoernle dies," *Star*, March 17 1960.

98. E. Hellman, *Rooiyard: A Sociological Study of an Urban Native Slumyard* (London: Oxford University Press, 1948). The study was published a whole fourteen years after its completion.

99. D. Gaitskell, "Housewives, Maids or Mothers: Some Contradictions of Domesticity for Christian Women in Johannesburg, 1903–39," *Journal of African History*, 24 (1983), p. 250; and Gaitskell, "Getting Close to the Hearts of Mothers," p. 199.

100. *Standard Encyclopedia of Southern Africa*, 1st edn. (London: Nasionale Boekhanel Pub. Ltd., 1972), p. 551.

101. Archive of the University of Witwatersrand, J. Laird, "R. F. Alfred Hoernle," p. 286.

102. NASA, SAB, GES 2281, 85/38, vol. 2, "Race Welfare in South Africa," pamphlet, 1940, p. 1.

103. NASA, SAB, GES 2281, 85/38, vol. 2, "The Future of Alexandra Township. An Open Letter to the Citizens of Johannesburg by the Alexandra Health Committee," (Johannesburg: Alexandra Health Committee, 1943), pp. 33–4.

104. HPW, RWS, December 1, 1939.

105. Dubow, *Scientific Racism in Modern South Africa*, Chapter Six, "Mental Testing and the Understanding of the 'Native Mind.'"

106. R.F.A. Hoernle, *Wits University Group Test of Mental Ability, 1925* (Pretoria: Transvaal Education Department, 1926); "Intelligence Tests," *Star*, August 2, 1926; "R.F.A. Hoernle Dead," *Star*, September 21, 1943.

107. HPW, RWS, October 17, 1934 and January 24, 1935.

108. HPW, RWS, August 14, 1935.

109. HPW, RWS, January 20, 1936.

110. HPW, RWS AR 1937.

111. S. Marks, *Divided Sisterhood: Race, Class and Gender in the South African Nursing Profession* (London: Macmillan Press, 1994), p. 11.

112. *Ibid.*, p. 12.

113. Cited in C. Burns, "Reproductive Labours: The Politics of Women's Health in South Africa, 1900 to 1960" (PhD thesis, Northwestern University, 1995), p. 219.

114. L. Marchand, "Obstetrics Amongst South African Natives," *South African Medical Journal*, 7 (1932), p. 329.

115. C.R. McCann, *Birth Control Politics in the United States, 1916–1945* (Ithaca: Cornell University Press, 1994), p. 163.

116. Cited in *ibid.*

117. Prior to the disintegration of African societies it was not uncommon or shameful among certain tribes, such as the Barolong of the western Transvaal, for betrothed women to have one or more children before marriage. To the contrary, doing so proved her fertility, which was highly prized by her new family, and would normally lead to the handing over of *lobola* (bridewealth). In most societies, however, having children before marriage was frowned upon and so youths would be taught forms of sex play that prevented pregnancy from occurring. Regardless of whether having children before marriage was socially acceptable, African societies did not equate sex with sin.

118. HPW, E.J. Krige, "Illegitimacy," paper presented to the conference African Family Life, sponsored by the Christian Council of South Africa and held in Pretoria in June 1940, pp. 21–9.

119. Burns, "Reproductive Labors," p. 65.

120. C. Burns's doctoral dissertation, "Reproductive Labors,' begins to address this gap.

121. HPW, RWS, June 30, 1938.
122. S. Dubow, "Scientism, Social Research and the Limits of "South Africanism": The Case of Ernst Gideon Malherbe," *South African Historical Journal*, 44 (2001), pp. 99–142.
123. C. Bolton, *Poor Whites of the Antebellum South* (Durham: Duke University Press, 1994), p. 5.
124. *Ibid.*, p. 42.
125. *Ibid.*, p. 4. See also C. Berry, *Southern Migrants, Northern Exiles* (Urbana and Chicago: University of Illinois Press, 2000), in particular the introduction, and S. McIlwaine, *The Southern Poor-White from Lubberland to Tobacco Road* (Norman, Ok: University of Oklahoma Press, 1939).
126. J. Smuts, "South African's Human Material," in *Report of the National Conference on Social Work* (Pretoria: Government Printer, 1936), p. 10.
127. *Debates of the House of Assembly*, vol. 23, May 8, 1934, p. 3323.

Chapter 3: Strengthening the Nation's Mothers through Birth Control

1. Planned Parenthood Association of South Africa (PPASA), Cape Town Office (CT) Mothers' Clinic Committee Papers (MCC) Annual Report (AR) 1933.
2. PPASA Johannesburg Office (JHB), South African National Council for Maternal and Family Welfare Papers (SANCMFW) "Summary of Relevant Facts Regarding the Health Activities of the S.A.N. Council of Maternal and Family Welfare," *c.* 1940.
3. PPASA, CT, Elsa (Sallie) Woodrow, "Golden Jubilee," unpublished paper, April 1982.
4. Archives of the Cape Province (KAB) 3/CT 4/1/5/521 E1126/5, "Birth Control Clinics, 1932–36," MCC fundraising letter, 1932.
5. Giliomee, *The Afrikaners: Biography of a People* (London: Hurst and Company, 2003), p. 412.
6. The women gathered at the home of Diana Birch Reynardson, the wife of the ADC to the Governor General. The others present were E. Woodrow, Ursula Scott, Beatrice Newton, Joyce Newton Thompson, Isabel Haddon, and Adele Bell. E. Woodrow. Woodrow, "Golden Jubilee"; see also PPASA CT, S. Woodrow, "The Start of the Family Planning Movement in Cape Town," unpublished document, September 1972.
7. See R. First and A. Scott, *Olive Schreiner* (New York: Schocken Books, 1980) and Cherry Clayton, ed., *Olive Schreiner* (Johannesburg and New York: McGraw Hill, 1983).
8. Interview with Dr. Patricia Massey, Cape Town, April 1997.
9. Interview with Dr. Geoffrey Scott, Cape Town, April 1997.
10. Woodrow, "The Start of the Family Planning Movement in Cape Town."
11. Interview with Dr. Patricia Massey.
12. C. Owen, *The South African Medal Roll of the 1935 Jubilee Medal and the 1937 and 1953 Coronation Medals as Issued to South Africans* (Somerset West: Chimperie Pubs., 1982).
13. WFAVS was formed in Washington in 1974 by the US International Project of the Association for Voluntary Sterilization (IPAVS), an organization established to promote voluntary sterilization throughout the world. IPAVS

sponsored Woodrow to attend the meeting in Washington. Upon her return to South Africa she founded CAVS and was elected chair. In 1976 she attended the Third International Conference on Voluntary Sterilization in Tunis. In 1980 she was key to forming the Association for Voluntary Sterilization of South Africa. Sources: Sallie Woodrow, "Family Planning in South Africa: A Review," *South African Medical Journal*, 50 (1976), pp. 2102–3; PPASA, CT, "Citation at the Presentation of the Salus Medal (Bronze) to Dr. Sallie Woodrow," unpublished document.

14. "Citation at the Presentation of the Salus Medal (Bronze) to Dr. Sallie Woodrow"; L. Newton-Thompson, "Birth Control Clinics in the Western Cape, c1932 to c1974: A History," (BA thesis, University of Cape Town, 1992), p. 15. Newton-Thompson interviewed Woodrow in 1992.

15. The term "The Domestication of Politics" is from P. Baker, "The Domestication of Politics: Women and American Political Society, 1780–1920," in V.L. Ruiz and E. C. Dubois (eds), *Unequal Sisters: A Multi-Cultural Reader in US History*, 2nd edn (New York: Routledge, 1994), pp. 85–110. The second term, "social housekeeping" was found in V. Bickford-Smith, E. van Heyningen, and N. Worden, *Cape Town in the Twentieth Century: An Illustrated Social History* (Cape Town: David Philip, 1999), p. 32. See also S. Koven and S. Michel (eds), *Mothers of a New World: Maternalist Politics and the Origins of Welfare States* (New York: Routledge, 1993); and G. Bock and P. Thane (eds), *Maternity and Gender Policies: Women and the Rise of the European Welfare States, 1880s–1950s* (New York: Routledge, 1991); M. Ladd-Taylor, *Mother-Work: Women, Child Welfare, and the State, 1890–1930* (Chicago: University of Illinois Press, 1994); N. Cott, "What's in a Name? The Limits of 'Social Feminism': or Expanding the Vocabulary of Women's History," *Journal of American History*, 76 (1989), pp. 809–29.

16. P. Scully, "White Maternity and Black Infancy: The Rhetoric of Race in the South African Women's Suffrage Movement, 1895–1930," in C. Fletcher, L.E. Nym Mayhall, and P. Levine (eds), *Women's Suffrage in the British Empire: Citizenship, Nation and Race* (London and New York: Routledge, 2000), p. 68.

17. S. Koven and S. Michel, "Introduction," in Seth Koven and Sonya Michel (eds), *Mothers of a New World*, p. 4.

18. M. Ladd-Taylor, *Mother-Work*, p. 3.

19. *Ibid.*

20. PPASA, CT, MCC AR 1936.

21. PPASA, CT, MCC AR 1935.

22. PPASA, CT, MCC AR 1933.

23. E. Woodrow, "Contraception: Its Justification and Practice," *South African Medical Journal*, 6 (1932), p. 654.

24. PPASA, CT, MCC AR 1932.

25. Newton-Thompson, "Birth Control Clinics in the Western Cape," p. 13.

26. M. Stopes, *Married Love: A New Contribution to the Solution of Sex Difficulties* (London: Putnam, 1918).

27. R. Soloway, *Birth Control and the Population Question in England, 1877–1939* (Chapel Hill: University of North Carolina Press, 1982), p. 212.

28. R. Hall, *Passionate Crusader: The Life of Marie Stopes* (New York: Harcourt Brace Jovanovich, 1977); J. Rose, *Marie Stopes and the Sexual Revolution* (London: Faber and Faber, 1992); Soloway, *Birth Control and the Population Question in*

England; A. Geppert, "Divine Sex, Happy Marriage, Regenerated Nation: Marie Stopes's Marital Manual *Married Love* and the Making of a Best Seller, 1918–1955," *Journal of the History of Sexuality*, 8, 3 (1998), pp. 389–433; J. Lewis, *The Politics of Motherhood: Child and Maternal Welfare in England, 1900–1939* (London: Croom Helm, 1980).

29. Soloway, *Birth Control and the Population Question in England*, p. 220.
30. See Wellcome Trust (WT) Library for the History of Medicine (LHM), Marie Stopes Collection (PP/MCS) letters to Stopes from readers (M. L. General); see a selection of the letters in R. Hall (ed.) *Dear Dr. Stopes: Sex in the 1920s* (London: Deutsch, 1978).
31. University of the Witwatersrand, William Cullen Library, Johannesburg (HPW), FAB329, "Memorandum on a Scheme for the Following up on Miss Higson's Tour in South Africa, 1932–33."
32. "More Views on Birth Control. A 'Practical Necessity' in Modern Society," *Cape Times*, August 14, 1930.
33. WT, LHM, PP/MCS, M.L. General.
34. Out of fear of getting pregnant she almost broke off her engagement with E.G. Malherbe until she learned from Stopes's books how to prevent conception. J. Malherbe, "I Didn't Want a Baby Either," *Eve's Journal*, (September 1939), p. 119. Found in Killie Campbell Africana Library, Durban (KC), J. Malherbe Collection (JM), File 188/2. See also her correspondence with Marie Stopes, JM, File 152.
35. KC, E.G. Malherbe Collection, File 477/4, "Notes of Presentation Held on Birth Control for the DR Church Synod Behind Locked Doors."
36. British Library, Department of Manuscripts, London, UK, Stopes Papers, Add. MS 58582–58583 (BL Stopes Collection), Scott to Stopes, February 10, 1932.
37. Woodrow, "Contraception: Its Justification and Practice," p. 655.
38. *Ibid.*, p. 656.
39. C. Walker, "The Women's Suffrage Movement: The Politics of Gender, Race and Class," in C. Walker (ed.), *Women and Gender in Southern Africa* (Cape Town: David Philip, 1990), pp. 313–45.
40. Woodrow, "Contraception: Its Justification and Practice," p. 654.
41. Pamela Scully argues the same for the South African suffrage movement, which also consisted of "upper-to middle-class, well-educated women who identified with Britain and generally supported the British empire in Africa." Scully, "White Maternity and Black Infancy," p. 71.
42. BL Stopes Collection, Woodrow to Stopes, September 1931.
43. The following discussion about the relationship between Marie Stopes and the South African birth-control movement was first published as: S. Klausen, "The Imperial Mother of Birth Control: Marie Stopes and the South African Birth-Control Movement, 1930–1950," in Greg Blue, Martin Bunton, and Ralph Crozier (eds), *Colonialism and the Modern World* (Armonk, NY: M.E. Sharpe, 2002), pp. 182–99. Reprinted here with permission from M.E. Sharpe.
44. Deborah Cohen argues that, in spite of her eugenic rhetoric, Stopes provided high quality, respectful care of women. D. Cohen, "Private Lives in Public Spaces: Marie Stopes, the Mothers' Clinics and the Practice of Contraception," *History Workshop*, 35 (1993), pp. 95–116.
45. BL Stopes Collection, Woodrow to Stopes, May 13, 1932, and Stopes to Woodrow, June 24, 1932.

46. A.L. Stoler, "Tense and Tender Ties: The Politics of Comparison in North American History and (Post) Colonial Studies," *The Journal of American History*, 88, 3 (2001), p. 12. Stoler applies to the colonial context the insights of Mary P. Ryan regarding gender in nineteenth-century urban America. M.P. Ryan, *Civic Wars: Democracy and Public Life in the American City during the Nineteenth Century* (Berkeley: University of California Press, 1997).
47. Woodrow, "Contraception: Its Justification and Practice," p. 653.
48. PPASA, CT, MCC AR 1932.
49. "Birth-Control," *Cape Times*, April 8, 1933.
50. PPASA, CT, MCC AR 1937.
51. PPASA, CT, MCC AR March 1939.
52. KAB 3/CT 4/1/5/521 E1126/5, "Birth Control Clinics, 1932–36," MCC 1932 fundraising letter, p. 1. Other examples include MCC AR 1932 and 1933.
53. Woodrow, "Contraception: Its Justification and Practice," p. 653.
54. KAB 3/CT 4/1/5/521 E1126/5, "Birth Control Clinics, 1932–36," MCC 1932 fundraising letter, p. 1.
55. PPASA, JHB, SANCMFW, Minutes of the First Meeting of the Council of S.A. Birth Control Clinics, June 21–22, 1935, appendix, Statement of Work at the Mothers' Clinic, p. 3.
56. The Pretoria Mothers' Clinic provided more details than other organizations regarding guidelines used to determine if women were sufficiently poor to warrant free or subsidized services: "Patients treated who cannot afford to consult a private doctor, that is,

    Family of 1 child: Maximum wage £20.0.0 per month
    Family of 2 children: Maximum wage £22.0.0 per month
    Family of 3 or more children: Maximum wage £25.0.0 per month.

    Patients whose husbands are earning more than £25 a month are advised to consult a doctor privately; or bring a note from their doctor asking the clinic doctor to advise and supply suitable contraceptives." PPASA JHB, SANCMFW, Minutes of the First Meeting of the Council of S.A. Birth Control Clinics, June 21–22, 1935, appendix, Pretoria Mothers' Clinic, 35, Court Chambers: St. Andries Street.

57. PPASA, CT, MCC AR 1937.
58. Cited in J. Western, *Outcast Cape Town* (Minneapolis: University of Minnesota Press, 1981), p. 57.
59. Woodrow, "Contraception: Its Justification and Practice," p. 653.
60. PPASA, CT, MCC AR 1939.
61. See PPASA, CT, MCC AR 1935, 1936, 1937.
62. O.J.M. Wagner, "Poverty and Dependency in Cape Town: A Sociological Study of 3300 Dependents receiving assistance from the Cape Town General Board of Aid," (PhD thesis, University of Stellenbosch, 1936), p. 134.
63. KAB 3/CT 4/1/5/793 G523/5, *Report of the Capetown Charities Commission*, 1932, p. 2.
64. *Ibid.*, p. 3.
65. PPASA, CT, MCC AR 1932.
66. PPASA, CT, MCC AR 1937.
67. "The Mothers' Clinic," *South African Medical Journal*, 10 (1936), p. 385; "The Mothers' Clinic," *South African Medical Journal*, 11 (1937), p. 4.

68. Editorial, *South African Medical Journal*, 11 (1937), p. 490.
69. *Cape Times*, May 27, 1938.
70. The Divisional Council system was created in the Cape Colony in 1855. Divisions were divided into six districts, each of which elected one member to the Divisional Council. In 1910 all the Councils were placed under the direct control of the Provincial Administration of the Cape Province. The initial role of the system was to construct and maintain roads and to control district schools. Powers of the Councils were extended by 1917 to include the authority to appoint special committees and health officers, and to donate grants to schools and organizations. M. Potgieter and M. Mannann, "The Historical and Administrative Development of Divisional Councils in General," (Cape Town: Archives of the Cape Province, 1971), pp. 1–3.
71. KAB 4/CT 1/2/1/1/47, "Minutes of Standing Committees," December 15, 1933, p. 529 and December 19, 1933, p. 164.
72. KAB 3/CT 4/1/5/521 E1126/5, "Birth Control Clinics, 1932–36," letter from A. Bell to Cape Town Clerk, September 6, 1935.
73. PPASA, CT, MCC AR 1939.
74. "Birth Control Clinics. Protests Against City Council Grant," *Cape Times*, April 6, 1933.
75. *Cape Times*, August 18, 1933.
76. For evidence of subsequent grants see KAB 3/CT 4/1/5/521 E1126/5, "Birth Control Clinics, 1932–36."
77. Interview with Dr. Geoffrey Scott. Woodrow also reported that this occurred. Newton-Thompson, "Birth Control Clinics in the Western Cape," p. 23.
78. Interview with Dr. Geoffrey Scott.
79. Woodrow, "The Start of the Family Planning Movement in Cape Town."
80. KAB 4/CT 1/2/1/1/53, "Minutes of Standing Committees," August 4, 1936, p. 105.
81. M. du Toit, "Women, Welfare and the Nurturing of Afrikaner Nationalism: A Social History of the Afrikaans Christelike Vroue Vereniging, c. 1870–1939," (PhD thesis, University of Cape Town, 1996), p. 183.
82. PPASA, JHB, SANCMFW, Minutes of the First Meeting of the Council of the S.A. Birth Control Clinics, June 21–22, 1935, appendix, "Constitution of the South African National Council for Birth Control."
83. *Ibid.*, appendix, Women's Welfare Centre.
84. One hundred and fifty-four letters between Stopes and South African birth-control advocates have survived and it is clear from the correspondence that many have not.
85. BL Stopes Collection, Stopes to Philip, January 11, 1935; Stopes to Belonje, February 19, 1936.
86. BL Stopes Collection, Scott to Stopes, October 7, 1937.
87. BL Stopes Collection, Scott to Stopes, January 23, 1932.
88. BL Stopes Collection, Scott to Stopes, March 25, 1935.
89. BL Stopes Collection, Fifth Annual Report of the Pietermaritzburg Mothers' Welfare Society, 1938–1939.
90. BL Stopes Collection, Burgess to Stopes, April 6, 1932.
91. BL Stopes Collection, see the six letters between Stopes and Braidwood between 1924 and 1929.
92. BL Stopes Collection, Stopes to Woodrow, January 11, 1932; see also Stopes to Burgess, October 8, 1928.

93. PPASA, CT, Stopes to Woodrow, February 8, 1945, MCC.
94. See A. Burton, *Burdens of History: British Feminists, Indian Women, and Imperial Culture, 1865–1915* (Chapel Hill: University of North Carolina Press, 1994); M. Sinha, *Colonial Masculinity: The "Manly Englishman" and the "Effeminate Bengali" in the Late Nineteenth Century* (Manchester: Manchester University Press, 1995).
95. BL Stopes Collection, Stopes to Pretoria Mothers' Clinic, July 15, 1938; Stopes to Belonje, July 15, 1938.
96. Rose, *Marie Stopes and the Sexual Revolution*, p. 209.
97. BL Stopes Collection, Stopes to Scott and Woodrow, October 8, 1935.
98. The three organizations were the International Birth Control Centre, the National Birth Control Council and the Society for the Provision of Birth Control Clinics.
99. S. Ahluwalia, "Troubled Histories: Politics of Birth Control in Colonial India, 1920–1947" and I. Chowdhury, "Instructions for the Unconverted: Birth Control, Marie Stopes and Indian Women," papers presented at "Population, Birth Control and Reproductive Health in Late Colonial India," a conference organized by the Centre for the History and Culture of Medicine Programme, School of Oriental and African Studies, London, November 18–19, 1999.
100. "In South Africa: A Very Successful Year," *Birth Control News*, March 1936, p. 78.
101. *Report of the Interdepartmental Committee on Destitute, Neglected, Maladjusted and Delinquent Children and Young Persons, 1934–1937* (Pretoria: Government Printer, 1937), p. 51.
102. PPASA, JHB, SANCMFW, Minutes of the Second Meeting of the South African National Council for Birth Control, October 6–7, 1936, p. 3. On the Congress's Declaration in favor of birth control see P.W. Laidler, "The Organisation of a Health Programme in Urban Areas," *Report of the National Conference on Birth Control* (Pretoria: Government Printer, 1936), p. 152.
103. R.L. Scott, "Birth Control and Family Spacing," *ibid.*, pp. 177–8.
104. E. Thornton, "Health and Social Welfare," *ibid.*, p. 180.
105. PPASA, JHB, SANCMFW, Minutes of the Second Meeting of the South African National Council for Birth Control, October 6–7, 1936, p. 3.
106. PPASA, JHB, SANCMFW, Minutes of the Postponed General Meeting of the South African National Council for Maternal and Family Welfare, September 27–28, 1938, appendix, "President's Report on Council Progress, October 1936–September 1938."
107. *Ibid.*
108. R.L. Scott "Birth Control and Family Spacing," *Report of the National Conference on Social Work*, p. 178.
109. PPASA, JHB, SANCMFW, Report of Discussions at Third General Meeting held at the Martin Melck House, Cape Town, September 27–28, 1938, p. 8.
110. *Ibid.*, pp. 9–10.
111. BL Stopes Collection, Stopes to Scott, June 1, 1938.
112. BL Stopes Collection, Stopes to Scott, July 4, 1938.
113. BL Stopes Collection, Stopes to Burgess, May 19, 1948.
114. *Ibid.*
115. BL Stopes Collection, Stopes to Burgess, April 1, 1943.

116. BL Stopes Collection, Stopes to Burgess, June 16, 1946.
117. J. Lambert, "Keeping English-Speaking South Africans British, 1934–1947," unpublished paper presented at The Burden of Race? "Whiteness" and "Blackness" in Modern South Africa, Conference held at Wits in July 2001; S. Dubow, "Scientism, Social Research and the Limits of 'South Africanism': The Case of Ernst Gideon Malherbe," *South African Historical Journal*, 44 (2001), pp. 99–142.
118. A. Paton, *Hofmeyr* (Cape Town: Oxford University Press, 1965), pp. 110–35.
119. W. Beinart, *Twentieth-Century South Africa* (Oxford: Oxford University Press, 1994), pp. 109–10.
120. G.H. Calpin, *There are no South Africans* (London: Thomas Nelson, 1941), pp. 12–13. Cited in Lambert, "Keeping the English-Speaking South Africans British, 1934–1947," p. 2.

Chapter 4: Women's Resistance to Eugenic Birth Control

1. Intermediate Archives Depot, Johannesburg (IADJ), Archives of the Johannesburg City Health Department (SGJ), Box 35, File 2/25/2, Birth Control, 1931–60, Dr. Milne, Medical Officer of Health (MOH) for Johannesburg, Confidential Report to Edward Thornton, Secretary for Public Health (SPH), on the Race Welfare Society clinic, September 20,1933.
2. University of the Witwatersrand, Historical Papers Collection, William Cullen Library, Johannesburg (HPW), Race Welfare Society Documents (RWS), Dr. Mary Gordon's Medical Report, August 19, 1935.
3. A. Leathard, *The Fight for Family Planning: The Development of Family Planning Services in Britain 1921–1974* (London: Macmillan, 1980).
4. P. A. Buckner and C. Bridge, "Reinventing the British World," *The Round Table*, 368 (2003), p. 77.
5. HPW, RWS, Minutes of the Annual General Meeting (AGM), December 1, 1938 and Annual Report (AR) 1939.
6. E.W.N. Mallows, "Johannesburg: An Outline History," (Self-published, 1982), pp. 5–6.
7. E. Brink, "The Afrikaner Women of the Garment Workers' Union, 1918–1938," (MA thesis, University of the Witwatersrand, 1986), p. 29; S. Parnell, "Public Housing as a Device for White Residential Segregation in Johannesburg," *Urban Geography*, 9 (1988), pp. 584–602.
8. S. Parnell, "Slums, Segregation and Poor Whites in Johannesburg, 1920–1934," in R. Morrell (ed.), *White But Poor: Essays on the History of the Poor Whites in Southern Africa, 1880–1940* (Pretoria: University of South Africa, 1992), p. 121; E. Koch, "Without Visible Means of Subsistence: Slumyard Culture in Johannesburg, 1918–1940," in Belinda Bozzoli (ed.), *Town and Countryside in the Transvaal: Capitalist Penetration and Popular Response* (Johannesburg: Ravan Press, 1983), pp. 151–76.
9. Cited in Brink, "The Afrikaner Women of the Garment Workers' Union," p. 28.
10. S. Kark, "The Economic Factor in the Health of the Bantu in South Africa," *The Leech*, 5, 3 (1934), pp. 11–22.
11. Parnell, "Slums, Segregation and Poor Whites in Johannesburg," p. 123.

12. For example, 5000 copies (2500 in Afrikaans and 2500 in English) of "Letter to Mothers" were produced advertising the Women's Welfare Centre. Cards given to visitors reminding them of their next appointment were also available in Afrikaans and English, HPW RWS, November 18, 1932. Regarding advertisements placed in Afrikaans and English newspapers see HPW RWS, February 16, 1939.
13. HPW, RWS, Minutes of the RWS AGM, December 1, 1938.
14. J. Hyslop, "White Working-Class Women and the Invention of Apartheid: 'Purified' Afrikaner Nationalist Agitation for Legislation Against 'Mixed' Marriages, 1934–9," *Journal of African History*, 36 (1995), pp. 62–3.
15. L. Marks, *Metropolitan Maternity: Maternal and Infant Welfare Services in Early Twentieth Century London* (Amsterdam: Rodopi, 1996), p. 279.
16. HPW, RWS, November 4, 1938.
17. HPW, RWS, Number of cases dealt with at the Clinic, February 2, 1932 to September 16, 1932.
18. HPW, RWS, February 61, 1939.
19. HPW, RWS, October 13, 1937.
20. HPW, RWS, "Number of Cases Dealt with at the Clinic, February 2, 1932 to September 16, 1932," and AR 1932.
21. I.J. Block, "Observations from the Work of a Birth Control Clinic," *South African Medical Journal*, 8 (1934), p. 490. Block, who joined the RWS's executive in 1933, presented the report to the 1933 meeting of the South African Medical Council Conference in Cape Town.
22. N. Mandy, *A City Divided–Johannesburg and Soweto* (Johannesburg: Macmillan South Africa, 1984), pp. 44–47.
23. I. Berger, *Threads of Solidarity. Women in South African Industry 1900–1980* (London: James Currey, 1992).
24. M. E. Rothmann, *The Mother and Daughter of the Poor Family. Vol. 5. The Poor White Problem in South Africa. Carnegie Commission of Investigation on the Poor White Question in South Africa* (Stellenbosch: Pro Ecclesia, 1932), p. 213.
25. Hyslop, "White Working-Class Women and the Invention of Apartheid," pp. 62–3.
26. J.F.W. Grosskopf, *Economic Report. Rural Impoverishment and Rural Exodus. Vol. 1. The Poor White Problem in South Africa*, p. 185.
27. Rothmann, *The Mother and Daughter of the Poor Family*, p. 208.
28. Hyslop, "White Working-Class Women and the Invention of Apartheid," pp. 62–3.
29. In 1932, the Chief Inspector of Factories reported that, "There is a growing tendency for women to remain in or return to factory work after marriage," cited by M. L. Ballinger, "Social and Economic Problems of the Bantu," *Report of the National Conference on Social Work* (Pretoria: Government Printer, 1936), p. 357. See also Brink, "The Afrikaner Women of the Garment Workers' Union," p. 83.
30. Brink, "The Afrikaner Women of the Garment Workers' Union," p. 85.
31. *Ibid.*, pp. 85–9.
32. HPW, RWS, Minutes of a Meeting of the RWS Executive Committee, October 13, 1937.
33. M. Lock and P. Kaufert, "Introduction," in M. Lock and P. Kaufert (eds), *Pragmatic Women and Body Politics* (Cambridge: Cambridge University Press, 1998), p. 2.

34. Interview with Dr. Patricia Massey, Cape Town, April 1997.
35. E. Koch, "Doornfontein and its African Working Class, 1914–1935; A Study of Popular Culture in Johannesburg" (MA thesis, University of the Witwatersrand, 1983), p. 103.
36. Marks, *Metropolitan Maternity*, p. 264.
37. K. Fisher, "She Was Quite Satisfied with the Arrangements I Made': Gender and Birth Control in Britain 1920–1950," *Past and Present*, 169 (2000) 161–93; S. Klausen, "Doctors and Dying Declarations: State Regulation of Abortion in British Columbia, 1917–1936," *Canadian Bulletin of Medical History/Bulletin Canadien d'Histoire de la Medecine*, 13 (1996), pp. 53–81.
38. Interview with Dr. Dorothea Douglas-Henry, Vishhoek, April 1997.
39. Planned Parenthood Association of South Africa (PPASA) Cape Town Office (CT), Mothers' Clinic Committee Documents (MCC) AR 1935.
40. PPASA, CT, MCC AR 1937.
41. PPASA, CT, MCC AR 1936. See also AR for 1935, 1936, 1937.
42. Interview with Dr. Dorothea Douglas-Henry.
43. HPW, RWS, November 21, 1939.
44. N. Haire, *Birth-Control Methods (Contraception, Abortion, Sterilisation)* (London: George Allen and Unwin, 1936), p. 120.
45. H. Cook, "Unseemly and Unwomanly Behavior: Comparing Women's Control of their Fertility in Australia and England from 1890 to 1970," *Journal of Population Research*, 17, 2 (2000), p. 129. Cook's article is a useful overview of primary and secondary sources on this issue.
46. M. Fielding, *Parenthood: Design or Accident? A Manual of Birth Control*, 3rd edn (London: Williams and Norgate, 1934), pp. 105–6.
47. Cited in L. Marks, *Metropolitan Maternity*, p. 283.
48. *Ibid.*, p. 277.
49. PPASA, Johannesburg Office (JHB), South African National Council for Maternal and Family Welfare Papers (SANCMFW), Minutes of the First Meeting of the Council of the S.A. Birth Control Clinics, June 21–22, 1935, pp. 2–3, and appendix, Report from the Port Elizabeth Birth Control Clinics, p. 3.
50. *Ibid.*, appendix, p. 1.
51. Lock and Kaufert, "Introduction," p. 7.
52. Block, "Observations from the Work of a Birth Control Clinic," p. 491.
53. HPW, RWS, November 4, 1938.
54. HPW, RWS, AR 1939. See also AR 1938.
55. HPW, RWS, Handwritten memo, "Total visits for 2 years ending February 1934."
56. The RWS attempted to enlist broader co-operation from social welfare agencies, from church missions to charities. Members visited the Children's Aid Society, the District Nurses Association, the Rand Aid Society, and Municipal Social Services, HPW RWS, September 38, 1938. They also circulated a memorandum to charitable societies, social workers, women's associations, and municipal and district nurses, "explaining the [Race Welfare] Society's work and objects and asking them to co-operate by sending suitable patients to the Clinics." HPW RWS, November 4, 1938.
57. Block, "Observations from the Work of a Birth Control Clinic," p. 490.
58. E.K. Abel and C.H. Browner, "Selective Compliance with Biomedical Authority and the Uses of Experiential Knowledge," in Lock and Kaufert (eds), *Pragmatic Women and Body Politics*, p. 311.

59. A clinic was opened at 24 Delarey Street in Vrededorp, where a chemist offered to renovate his shop into a birth-control clinic, and at the Masonic Hall on Ford Street in Jeppe where Infant Clinics were held.

60. For example, in 1932 the executive included nine doctors and six non-medical members, and in 1935 there were twelve physicians and eight lay members. See HPW, RWS Minutes of AGMs 1932 and 1935.

61. HPW, RWS, March 11, 937.

62. HPW, RWS, January 18, 1938.

63. Two female doctors who worked in Cape Town's birth control clinics in the 1930s stated this was a prominent reason for choosing to work in the clinics. Interviews with Dr. Patricia Massey and Dr. Dorothea Douglas-Henry.

64. HPW, RWS, Copy of Report of August 19, 1937 by Dr. M.G. Gordon, of the Meeting of the Clinic Subcommittee Meeting held after the executive committee Meeting of the March 11, 1937 re Clinics.

65. HPW, RWS, Letter from E. Mansfield, Hon. Treasurer of the Race Welfare Society to Dr. M. G. Gordon, Clinic Subcommittee of the Race Welfare Society, September 13, 1937.

66. HPW, RWS, October 13, 1937.

67. HPW, RWS, January 18, 1938.

68. HPW, RWS, February 25, 1938.

69. HPW, RWS, July 21, 1938.

70. HPW, RWS, November 4, 1938.

71. HPW, RWS, February 61, 1939.

72. *Ibid.*

73. HPW, RWS, October 13, 1937.

74. Women who joined the Women's Committee include Mrs. J. Mitchell Hunter (who was awarded a Coronation Medal in 1937 for her work related to women's welfare), Mrs M.K. Robertson, Mrs Greenwood, Mr. Mitchell Hunter, Mrs Petty, Mrs Chivers, Dr. Spilhaus, and Mrs Thom. HPW RWS, October 16 and November 17, 1937.

75. For example, in 1941 the RWS executive teamed up with the National Council for Mental Hygiene to organize a symposium on voluntary sterilization at the University of the Witwatersrand on October 29, 1941. R.F.A. Hoernle chaired the event. HPW RWS, advertisement of event.

76. HPW, RWS, November 4, 1938.

77. HPW, RWS, June 9, 1939.

78. *Ibid.*

79. HPW, RWS, AR 1939.

80. HPW, RWS, June 9, 1939.

81. *Ibid.*

82. HPW, RWS, November 4, 1938.

83. HPW, RWS, February 16, 1939.

84. HPW, RWS, December 31, 1939.

85. HPW, RWS, December 1, 1939, February 17, 1942 and March 31, 1944.

Chapter 5: The Cape Town Mothers' Clinic

1. Planned Parenthood Association of South Africa (PPASA), Cape Town Office (CT), Mothers' Clinic Committee Documents (Cape Town: MCC, 1935).

2. V. Bickford-Smith, "The Origins and Early History of District Six," in Shamil Jeppie and Crain Soudien (eds), *The Struggle for District Six: Past and Present* (Cape Town: Buchu Book, 1990). p. 37.
3. V. Bickford-Smith, E. van Heyningen, and N. Worden, *Cape Town in the Twentieth Century: An Illustrated Social History* (Cape Town: David Philip, 1999), p. 72.
4. H. Giliomee, *The Afrikaners: Biography of a People* (London: Hurst and Company, 2003), p. 388.
5. J. Western, *Outcast Cape Town* (Minneapolis: University of Minnesota Press, 1981), p. 35.
6. *Ibid.*, pp. 35–6.
7. M.E. Rothmann, *The Mother and Daughter of the Poor Family. Vol. V. The Poor White Problem in South Africa. Carnegie Commission of Investigation on the Poor White Problem* (Stellenbosch: Pro Ecclesia, 1932), p. 216.
8. *Ibid.*
9. M. Nicol, "A History of Garment and Tailoring Workers in Cape Town, 1900–1939" (PhD thesis, University of Cape Town, 1984), pp. 75–7.
10. Bickford-Smith, van Heyningen and Worden, *Cape Town in the Twentieth Century*, p. 65.
11. M. du Toit, "Women, Welfare, and the Nurturing of Afrikaner Nationalism: A Social History of the *Afrikaans Christelike Vroue Vereniging*, c. 1870–1930" (PhD thesis, University of Cape Town, 1996), p. 165.
12. Cited in *ibid.*, p. 165.
13. *Ibid.*, p. 168.
14. O.J.M. Wagner, "Poverty and Dependency in Cape Town. A Sociological Study of 3300 Dependents Receiving Assistance from the Cape Town General Board of Aid" (PhD thesis, University of Stellenbosch, 1936), p. 36.
15. Bickford-Smith, van Heyningen and Worden, *Cape Town in the Twentieth Century*, p. 101.
16. PPASA, CT, MCC AR 1932.
17. The term "non-European" is unlikely to have included African users because there were relatively few Africans in Cape Town in the 1930s. In the April 1939 annual report the term "Native" was used as distinct from "European" and "non-European" categories.
18. PPASA, CT, MCC AR 1932 to 1939. The records for the first few years of the RWS's Women's Welfare Centre and clinics for black women are incomplete. It is possible that a few hundred additional women visited RWS clinics between 1932 and 1939, but that would not significantly alter the comparison between the RWS and the MCC.
19. Jochelson, *Colour of Disease*, p. 55.
20. PPASA, CT, MCC AR 1932.
21. Parnell, "Slums, Segregation and Poor Whites in Johannesburg, 1920–1934," in R. Morrel (ed.), *White But Poor: Essays on the History of the Poor Whites in Southern Africa*, 1880–1940 (Pretoria: University of South Africa, 1992), p. 117.
22. Cited in Du Toit, "Women, Welfare, and the Nurturing of Afrikaner Nationalism," pp. 178–9.
23. Interview with Patricia Massey, Cape Town, April 1997.
24. PPASA, CT, MCC AR 1933.
25. Du Toit, "Women, Welfare and the Nurturing of Afrikaner Nationalism."

26. PPASA, CT, MCC AR 1936.
27. PPASA, CT, MCC AR 1932.
28. Woodrow, "Contraception: Its Justification and Practice," p. 656.
29. PPASA, Johannesburg Office (JHB), South African National Council for Maternal and Family Welfare Papers (SANCMFW), Minutes of the First Meeting of the Council of S.A. Birth Control Clinics, June 21–22, 1935, appendix, Statement of Work at the Mothers' Clinic, June 1935.
30. *Ibid.*
31. Interview with Dr. Dorothea Douglas-Henry, Vishhoek, April 1997.
32. E. Woodrow, "Family Planning in South Africa: A Review," *South African Medical Journal*, 50 (1976), p. 2102.
33. PPASA, CT, MCC AR 1932.
34. Wagner, "Poverty and Dependency in Cape Town," p. 82.
35. *Ibid.*, pp. 86–91.
36. Rothmann, *The Mother and Daughter of the Poor Family*, pp. 208–9.
37. Woodrow, "Contraception: Its Justification and Practice," p. 657.
38. *Ibid.*, p. 655.
39. PPASA, CT, MCC AR 1935.
40. PPASA, CT, MCC AR 1936.
41. *Die Burger*, August 3, 1933.
42. *Ibid.*
43. University of the Witwatersrand, Historical Papers Collection, William Cullen Library, Johannesburg (HPW), Race Welfare Society Documents (RWS), Minutes of the Executive Committee meeting, January 18, 1938.
44. PPASA, CT, MCC AR 1933.
45. KAB 3/CT 4/1/5/521 E1126/m, "Birth Control Clinics, 1932–36," Letter dated December 12, 1935.
46. PPASA, CT, MCC AR 1933.
47. PPASA, CT, MCC AR 1933 to 1937, and 1939.
48. PPASA, CT, MCC AR 1935.
49. Woodrow, "The Start of the Family Planning Movement in Cape Town."
50. PPASA, CT, MCC AR 1935.
51. PPASA, CT, MCC AR 1937 and 1939.
52. PPASA, CT, MCC AR 1936.
53. PPASA, CT, MCC AR 1933.
54. PPASA, CT, MCC AR 1932.
55. PPASA, CT, MCC AR 1933.
56. PPASA, CT, MCC, Extract from the Medical Officers' Six Months' Report, 1932, p. 4.
57. PPASA, CT, MCC AR 1934.
58. PPASA, CT, MCC AR 1935.
59. PPASA, CT, MCC AR 1936.
60. PPASA, CT, MCC AR 1933.
61. PPASA, CT, MCC AR 1939.
62. Block, "Observations from the Work of a Birth Control Clinic," p. 491.
63. *Ibid.*
64. PPASA, CT, MCC AR 1934.
65. For example, PPASA, CT, MCC AR 1939.
66. PPASA, CT, MCC AR 1937.
67. *Ibid.*

Chapter 6: State Support for Birth Control

1. H. Trant "Modern Contraceptive Methods," *South African Medical Journal*, 9 (1935), p. 407.
2. National Archives of South Africa (NASA), Central Archives Depot (SAB), Archives of the Department of Public Health (GES) 2281 85/38, vol. 1, RWS to Secretary for Public Health (SPH), February 17, 1931.
3. Edward Thornton (1878–?) was born in England. Soon after qualifying in medicine he traveled to South Africa in 1899 to work at the Imperial Yeomanry Hospitals during the South African War. After the war, and after a brief stint of medical service in India, he joined the Cape Colony Health Department in 1903 as a Medical Officer for plague. During the First World War he was appointed Commanding Officer of the South African Military Hospital at Richmond, Surrey, and there he remained until 1920. While there he was appointed to the staff of the Queen Alexandra Hospital for limbless soldiers and, at the request of the South African Government, made a study of artificial limbs and orthopaedic appliances for wounded ex-servicemen. He also chaired a War Office committee formed to study vocational problems facing injured soldiers. In 1919 he was appointed a Knight of the British Empire in recognition of his innovative work in the rehabilitation of disabled soldiers. That same year, with his work in England winding down, he wrote to J.A. Mitchell, South Africa's first Secretary of Public Health, asking whether there was an opening in the newly established DPH, and Mitchell appointed him Senior Assistant Health Officer in 1920. In addition to this post, Thornton became Medical Director for the South African Defense Department from 1920 to 1934, and in 1932 he succeeded Dr. Charles Porter, Medical Officer of Health for Johannesburg, as Honorary Professor of Public Health at the University of the Witwatersrand. He retired in 1938. NASA, SAB, GES 3065, Colonel Sir Edward Newbury Thornton, K.B.E., M.R.C.S., England, L.R.C.P., D.P.H.
4. NASA, SAB, GES 2281 85/38, vol. 1, Proposed Birth Control Clinic, March 11, 1931.
5. The following analysis of the Department of Public Health's approach to birth control was first published as: S. Klausen, " 'Poor Whiteism,' White Maternal Mortality, and the Promotion of 'Public Health': The Department of Public Health's Support for Contraceptive Services in South Africa, 1930–38," *South African Historical Journal*, 45 (2001), pp. 53–78. Reprinted here with the permission of the *South African Historical Journal*.
6. K. Jochelson, *The Colour of Disease: Syphilis and Racism in South Africa, 1880–1950* (Basingstoke and Oxford: Palgrave in association with St. Antony's College, 2001), p. 81.
7. Cited in *ibid*.
8. On the need to improve Africans' health for the sake of the health of whites P.W. Laidler wrote in 1936: "The need to safeguard the health of the European section of the community from the diseases rife among the natives, intestinal parasitism, venereal disease, typhus and tuberculosis, which need is insurance, not negrophilism, has not yet penetrated into the selfish brain of the average man who remains blinded by prejudice. The native is South Africa's biggest business – producers and sellers all agree on that. Independence and physical fitness are disappearing, slowly perhaps, but nevertheless surely."

P. W. Laidler, "The Organisation of a Health Programme in Urban Areas," in *Report of the National Conference on Social Work* (Pretoria: Government Printer, 1936), p. 150, found in Killie Campbell Africana Library, E.G. Malherbe Collection, File 509, National Conference on Social Work.

9. J. Smuts, "South African's Human Material," in *ibid.*, p. 12. See also B.W. McKendrick (ed.), *Introduction to Social Work in South Africa* (Pretoria: Haum Tertiary, 1990).

10. E. Thornton, "Health and Social Welfare," *Report of the National Conference on Social Work*, p. 179.

11. E. Thornton, "Some Problems of Preventive Medicine," *South African Medical Journal*, 8 (1934), pp. 743–7.

12. On efforts to expand public health care in the 1930s, see N. Andersson and Shula Marks, "Industrialization, Rural Health, and the 1944 National Health Services Commission in South Africa" in S. Feierman and J.M. Janzen (eds), *The Social Basis of Health and Healing in Africa* (Berkeley: University of California Press, 1992), pp. 131–61; S. Marks, "Doctors and the State: George Gale and South Africa's Experiment in Social Medicine," in S. Dubow (ed.), *Science and Society* (Manchester: Manchester University Press, 2000), pp. 188–211; S. Marks, "South Africa's Early Experiment in Social Medicine: Its Pioneers and Politics," *American Journal of Public Health*, 87 (1997), pp. 452–9; H. Phillips, "The 1945 Gluckman Report and the Establishment of South Africa's Health Centres," *American Journal of Public Health*, 83 (1993), pp. 1037–9.

13. A. Jeeves, "Public Health in the Era of South Africa's Syphilis Epidemic of the 1930s and 1940s," *South African Historical Journal* 45 (2001), pp. 79–102.

14. H.S. Gear, "South African Public Health Services," *Report of the National Conference on Social Work*, p. 145.

15. NASA, SAB, GES 2281 85/38, vol. 1, SPH to the Minister of Public Health (MPH), December 12, 1936.

16. *Annual Report of the Department of Public Health, Year Ended June 30, 1935* (Pretoria: Government Printer,1935), p. 62.

17. M.E. Rothmann, *The Mother and Daughter of the Poor Family. Vol. 5. The Poor White Problem in South Africa. Carnegie Commission of Investigation on the Poor White Question in South Africa* (Stellenbosch: Pro Ecclesia, 1932), pp. 177–91.

18. *Debates of the House of Assembly*, January 24, 1930, p. 77.

19. *Official Year Book of the Union, 1931–32* (Pretoria: Government Printer, 1932), p. 233.

20. See, for example, "Minutes of the Meeting of the Cape Town Division of the Cape Western Branch of the Medical Association of South Africa (BMA)," *South African Medical Journal*, 6 (1932), p. 303.

21. *Ibid.*

22. B. Goddefroy, "Medical and Ethical Aspects of Abortion," *South African Medical Journal*, 6 (1932), p. 476. She called for the decriminalization of abortion and the provision of free abortion services.

23. Woodrow, "Contraception: Its Justification and Practice," *South African Medical Journal*, 6 (1932), p. 655.

24. I. J. Block, "The Work of a Birth Control Clinic," *South African Medical Journal*, 8 (1934), p. 492. Both Woodrow and Block's articles are found in NASA, SAB, GES 2281 85/38, vol. 1.

25. Du Toit, "Women, Welfare and the Nurturing of Afrikaner Nationalism: A Social History of the *Afrikaans Christelike Vroue Vereniging*, c. 1870–1930" (PhD thesis, University of Cape Town, 1996), p. 14.
26. *Ibid.*, p. 291.
27. Cited in *ibid.*, p. 282.
28. *Ibid.*, p. 284. See also NASA GES 2281 85/38, vol. 1, SPH to MPH, December 12, 1936.
29. *Ibid.*, p. 278.
30. *Ibid.*, p. 277.
31. *Ibid.*, p. 280.
32. *Die Burger*, August 3, 1933. A copy is located in NASA, SAB, GES 2281 85/38, vol. I.
33. *Annual Report of the Department of Public Health, Year Ended June 30, 1935*, p.59.
34. *Ibid.*, p. 62.
35. NASA, SAB, GES 2281 85/38, vol. I. From SPH to the MPH, December 12, 1936.
36. Du Toit, "Women, Welfare and the Nurturing of Afrikaner Nationalism," p. 293. Janie Malherbe, a founder of the Pretoria birth-control clinic, was also conscious in 1937 that women's organizations made a tangible impact on the state by convincing Government to expand social welfare services. Killie Campbell Archive, Durban, J. Malherbe Papers, File 195, Women's Movements in South Africa, pp. 3–4.
37. J. Hyslop, "White Working-Class Women and the Invention of Apartheid: 'Purified' Afrikaner Nationalist Agitation for Legislation Against 'Mixed' Marriages, 1934–39," *Journal of African History*, 36 (1995), p. 61.
38. See NASA, SAB, GES, 2281 85/38, vol. 1.
39. NASA, SAB, GES 2281 85/38, vol. 1. MCC to SPH, June 10, 1933.
40. Thornton, "Some Problems of Preventive Medicine," p. 743.
41. F. Brummer, "Public and Private Social Work in South Africa," *Report of the National Conference on Social Work*, p. 28. Brummer was a Social Research Officer in the Union Department of Education.
42. *Debates of the House of Assembly*, March 1, 1935, p. 2397.
43. A. Leathard, *The Fight for Family Planning: The Development of Family Planning Services in Britain 1921–1974* (London: Macmillan, 1980).
44. NASA, GES, 2281 85/38, vol. 1 SPH to RWS, March 11, 1931.
45. NASA GES 2281 85/38, vol. 1, SPH to MPH, February 27, 1931.
46. NASA GES 2281 85/38, vol. 1, SPH to MPH, December 12, 1936.
47. University of the Witwatersrand, Historical Papers Collection, William Cullen Library, Johannesburg (HPW), Race Welfare Society Documents (RWS), August 2, 1932.
48. HPW, RWS, August 28, 1933.
49. HPW, RWS, October 7, 1934 and January 24, 1935.
50. The delegates were the following: From Port Elizabeth: B. Belonje, Dr. R. Schauder, and R.B. Lawrie. Cape Town: U. Scott, E. Haddon, and Mrs Parker. Pretoria: J. Berrington and Mrs Malan. Johannesburg: H. Britten, R.F.A. Hoernle, M. Reid, Dr. F.D. Berry, Dr. M.S. Gordon, and J.L. Hardy. Benoni: S. Kermack, Miss Forsyth, and Mrs Shepherd.

Additional participants: Dr. Getz, Dr. Sash, Dr. Neros, Dr. Mendelssohn, Mrs French-Lloyd, Miss Morisse (Johannesburg Senior Health Visitor), Dr. Milne (Johannesburg's Medical Officer of Health), Mrs Levine (Johannesburg Mental Hygiene Society), E. Mansfield (RWS), Mrs Tonkin (Government Inspector of Factories, Port Elizabeth), and Mrs Hind (Port Elizabeth). Planned Parenthood Association of South Africa (PPASA), Johannesburg Office (JHB), South African National Council for Maternal and Family Welfare Papers (SANCMFW), Minutes of the First Meeting of the Council of the S.A. Birth Control Clinics, June 21–22, 1935.

51. *Ibid.*, appendix, "Constitution of the South African National Council for Birth Control."
52. *Ibid.*, p. 4.
53. *Ibid.*, p. 3.
54. PPASA, JHB, SANCMFW, Minutes of the Second Meeting of the SANCMFW, October 6–7, 1936, p. 6.
55. NASA, SAB, GES 2281 85/38, vol. 1. SPH to MPH December 12, 1936.
56. PPASA JHB, SANCMFW, Minutes of the Second Meeting of the SANCMFW, October 6–7, 1936, p. 6.
57. *Ibid.*, p. 3.
58. NASA, SAB, GES 2281 85/38 vol. 1. Constitution of the South African National Council for Maternal and Family Welfare, amended May 7, 1938.
59. PPASA JBH, SANCMFW, Minutes of the First Meeting of the SANCMFW, October 6–7, 1936, p. 7.
60. NASA, SAB, GES 2281 85/38, vol. 1, SPH to Dr. H.J. Milne, Medical Officer of Health (MOH) for Johannesburg, and T. Shadick Higgins, MOH for Cape Town, September 11, 1933.
61. NASA, SAB, GES 2281 85/38, vol. 1. Higgins to MPH, September 15, 1933.
62. NASA, SAB GES 2281 85/38, vol. 1, Letter dated May 27, 1931, p. 1.
63. "The Mothers' Clinic," *South African Medical Journal*, 11 (1937), p. 490.
64. See Goddefroy, "Medical and Ethical Aspects of Abortion," and Woodrow, "Contraception: Its Justification and Practice."
65. L. Walker, "The Colour of White: Race, Gender and South African Medical Women," unpublished paper presented at "The Burden of Race? 'Whiteness' and 'Blackness' in Modern South Africa," Conference held at the University of the Witwatersrand, July 2001.
66. Woodrow, "Contraception: Its Justification and Practice."
67. Letter by "MB, ChB," *South African Medical Journal*, 6 (1932), p. 713.
68. Letters to the *South African Medical Journal* 6 (1932), pp. 750–2, pp. 784–6, p. 823; and 7 (1933), p. 26.
69. J.W. Adams, "Some Population Problems of the World," *South African Medical Journal*, 8 (1934), pp. 131–2; Block, "Some Observations from the Work of a Birth Control Clinic"; P.W. Laidler, "The Practice of Eugenics," *South African Medical Journal*, 8 (1934), pp. 823–34; and P.W. Laidler, "The Medico-Social Aspect of Population Density," *South African Medical Journal*, 10 (1936), pp. 317–27.
70. P.W. Laidler, "The Organisation of a Health Programme in Urban Areas," *Report of the National Conference on Social Work*, p. 155.

71. For example, E. Watkins, *On the Pill: A Social History of Oral Contraceptives, 1950–1970* (Baltimore: Johns Hopkins University Press, 1998).

72. "Minutes of the Meeting of the Cape Town Division of the Cape Western Branch of the Medical Association of South Africa (BMA)," p. 303.

73. Block, "Some Observations from the Work of a Birth Control Clinic," p. 492.

74. "Minutes of the Meeting of the Northern Transvaal Branch of the Medical Association of South Africa (BMA)," *South African Medical Journal*, 6 (1932), p. 476.

75. C.C.P. Anning, "Sterility and the Falling Birth-Rate: The Public Health Aspect," *South African Medical Journal*, 11 (1937), p. 497. See also H. Trant, "Modern Contraceptive Methods," *South African Medical Journal*, 9 (1935), pp. 407–14.

76. *Annual Report of the Department of Public Health, Year Ended June 30, 1937* (Pretoria: Government Printer, 1937), p. 76.

77. *Official Year Book of the Union, 1935–6* (Pretoria: Government Printer, 1936), p. 242.

78. *Official Year Book of the Union, 1938–9* (Pretoria: Government Printer, 1939), p. 200.

79. NASA, SAB, GES 2281 85/38, vol. 1, SPH to MPH, December 12, 1936.

80. NASA, SAB, GES 2281 85/38, vol. 1, SPH to the British Ministry of Health, February 12, 1936.

81. NASA, SAB, GES 2281 85/38, vol. 1, SPH to MPH, September 7, 1937.

82. NASA, SAB, GES 2281 85/38, vol. 1, SPH to MPH, December 12, 1936.

83. NASA, SAB, GES 2281 85/38, vol. 1, SPH to the Minister of Finance, November 20, 1937; SPH to the Secretary for Finance, September 18, 1937, and SPH to MOH for Port Elizabeth, April 19, 1938.

84. PPASA, JHB, SANCMFW, Minutes of the Postponed General Meeting of the South African National Council for Maternal and Family Welfare, September 27–8, 1938, p. 2.

85. NASA, KAB 3/STB, 4/1/80, 7/12, 1940 to 1946, "Minutes of the Meeting of the Committee of the Central Bureau," November 17, 1938 and February 23, 1939.

86. PPASA, JHB, SANCMFW, Minutes of the Second Meeting of the Central Bureau Committee, February 23, 1939.

87. PPASA, JHB, SANCMFW, Minutes of the First Meeting of the Council of the S.A. Birth Control Clinics, June 21–2, 1935, p. 2; Report of Discussions at Third General Meeting Held at the Martin Melck House, Cape Town, on Tuesday and Wednesday, September 27–8, 1938, p. 13; Minutes of the Meeting of the Executive Committee, September 28, 1938; Minutes of the Meeting of the Executive Committee, March 3, 1939; and Minutes of the Executive Committee, March 3, 1939.

88. NASA, SAB, GES 2281 85/38, vol. 1, SANCMFW to MPH, April 27, 1937, SANCMFW to MPH, May 22, 1938 and SANCMFW to SPH, May 26, 1938.

89. NASA, SAB, GES 2281 85/38, vol. 1, Mothers' Clinics circular, June 6, 1938.

90. The June 6, 1938 circular included paragraph 4 of Memorandum 153/MCW, the British Ministry of Health's first policy statement on birth control of March 1931, and Circular 1408, dated May 31, 1934. Copies of the British policies are in NASA, SAB, GES 2281 85/38, vol. 1.

91. NASA, SAB, GES 2281 85/38, vol. 1, Town Clerk of the Borough of King Williams' Town to the SPH, July 12, 1938; Town Clerk of Germiston to SPH, March 22, 1939.

92. NASA, SAB, GES 2281 85/38, vol. 1, Town Clerk of Bloemfontein to SPH, July 19, 1938; Town Clerk of Krugersdorp to SPH, March 25, 1939.

93. NASA, SAB, GES 2281 85/38, vol. 1, Town Clerk of Durban to SPH, July 14, 1938; Town Clerk of Grahamstown to SPH, August 8, 1938; Town Clerk of Springs to SPH, April 17, 1939.

94. The Catholic newspaper *Southern Cross* criticized Thornton and the 1938 circular. The editorial opposed birth control out of concern over "race suicide" and referred to Britain's declining birth-rate and the urgent necessity of peopling the Empire. "The Choice," *Southern Cross*, July 20, 1938.

95. "Birth Control Clinics. Sir Edward Thornton's Appeal. Catholic Journal's Criticism," *Cape Argus*, July 21, 1938.

96. *Southern Cross*, August 5, 1938.

97. *Cape Times*, February 23, 1939.

98. *Debates of the House of Assembly*, vol. 25, February 5, 1935, p. 1128.

99. *Ibid.*, vol. 27, June 3, 1936, p. 4985.

100. *Ibid.*, vol. 25, February 5, 1935, p. 1139; *ibid.*, vol. 27, June 3, 1936, p. 4985; *ibid.*, vol. 29, February 26, 1937, p. 2471.

101. *Ibid.*, vol. 43, February 17, 1942, p. 2195.

102. For discussion of the failure to implement the recommendations of the National Health Services Commission (1942–44), see Andersson and Marks, "Industrialisation, Rural Change and the 1944 National Health Services Commission," in S. Feierman and J. Janzen (eds), *The Social Basis of Health and Healing in Africa* (Berkeley: University of California Press, 1992), pp. 131–61; A. Jeeves, "Public Health in the Era of South Africa's Syphilis Epidemic of the 1930s and 1940s," *South African Historical Journal*, 45 (2001), pp. 79–102; and H. Phillips, "The 1945 Gluckman Report and the Establishment of South Africa's Health Centres," *American Journal of Public Health*, 83 (1993), pp. 1037–9.

Conclusion

1. See the Introduction.

2. B. Klugman, "The Political Economy of Population Control in South Africa," (BA thesis, University of the Witwatersrand, 1980), p. 6.

3. On the development and implement of *apartheid*, see D. O'Meara, *Forty Lost Years: The Apartheid State and the Politics of the National Party, 1948–1994* (Randburg and Athens: Ravan Press, 1996), and D. Posel, *The Making of Apartheid, 1948–1961: Conflict and Compromise* (Oxford: Clarendon Press, 1991).

4. H. Giliomee, *The Afrikaners: Biography of a People* (London: Hurst and Company, 2003), p. 345.

5. H. Houghton, "Economic Development, 1865–1965," in M. Wilson and L. Thompson (eds), *Oxford History of South Africa*, Vol. 2 (Oxford: Clarendon Press, 1969–71), p. 28.

6. O'Meara, *Forty Lost Years*, p. 21.

7. D. O'Meara, *Volkskapitalisme: Class, Capital and Ideology in the Development of Afrikaner Nationalism 1934–1948* (Cambridge: Cambridge University Press, 1983), p. 24.

8. Giliomee, *The Afrikaners*, p. 452.

9. C. Burns also makes this point in "Reproductive Labors: The Politics of Women's Health in South Africa, 1900 to 1960" (PhD thesis, Northwestern University, 1995), p. 389.

10. R.W. Johnson, "AIDS Hits Home in South Africa," *National Post*, May 15, 1999, p. B10. Using 1998-test-data from pre-natal clinics (the only reliable indicators of infection rates), Johnson reports that the rate of HIV infection in KwaZulu Natal was 32.5 percent. He estimates that life expectancy at birth in KwaZulu Natal has declined from 62 years in 1998 to 28 in 1999, a devastating statistic.

11. Planned Parenthood Association of South Africa (hereafter PPASA), Johannesburg Office (JHB), *Annual Report of the Planned Parenthood Association of South Africa* (Johannesburg: PPASA, 1998); PPASA, JHB, *Repro News*, 1, 1 (1997), p. 5.

12. Comment made by a representative of the British Overseas Development Agency, one of the PPASA's overseas sponsors. PPASA, *Annual Report*.

13. E. Hellmann, *Rooiyard: A Sociology Survey of an Urban Native Slum Yard* (Oxford: Oxford University Press, 1948), p. 61. Hellmann's research was conducted in the mid-1930s.

14. For an example of the use of oral history methodology to uncover "ordinary" people's experiences in reproductive decision-making see K. Fisher, " 'She Was Quite Satisfied with the Arrangements I Made': Gender and Birth Control in Britain 1920–1950," *Past and Present*, 169 (2000) 161–93. For an excellent example of a contribution to social history in the South African context see B. Bozzoli with M. Nkotsoe, *Women of Phokeng: Consciousness, Life Strategy, and Migrancy in South Africa, 1900–83* (Portsmouth, NH: Heinemann, 1991).

15. E.K. Abel and C.H. Browner, "Selective Compliance with Biomedical Authority and the Uses of Experiential Knowledge," in M. Lock and P. Kaufert (eds), *Pragmatic Women and Body Politics* (Cambridge: Cambridge University Press, 1998), p. 321.

Bibliography

Manuscript sources

Official archive sources

South African National Archives, Pretoria (NASA), Central Archive Depot (SAB) Archives of the Department of Public Health (GES)
2281 85/38, vols. 1 and 2.
3065, Colonel Sir Edward Newbury Thornton, K.B.E., M.R.C.S., England, L.R.C.P., D.P.H.
Cape Archive Depot (KAB)
3/CT 1/1/1/87 Cape Town City Council
3/CT 1/1/9/1/5–8 Cape Town City Council
3/CT 1/4/7/5/1/1–3 Cape Town Health and Hospital Committee
3/CT 4/1/5/521 E1126/5 Birth Control Clinics 1932–36
3/CT Box 206 Mothers Clinics – Family Planning 1959–71
4/CT 1/1/1/40–8 Divisional Council
"The Historical and Administrative Development of Divisional Councils in General," Compiled by M. Potgieter and M. Mannann, 1971.
Intermediate Archives Depot, Johannesburg (IADJ), Archives of the Johannesburg City Health Department (SGJ)
Box 35, File 2/25/2, Birth Control, 1931–60.

Unofficial archive sources

Killie Campbell Africana Library, Durban (KC)
E. G. Malherbe Collection
File 477/4, "Notes of presentation held on Birth Control for the DR Church Synod behind locked doors."
File 509, *Report of the National Conference on Social Work* (Pretoria: Government Printer, 1936).
J. Malherbe Collection
File 152, Correspondence with Marie Stopes.
File 188/2, *Eve's Journal*, September 1939.
File 195, "Women's Movements in South Africa."
Planned Parenthood Association of South Africa (PPASA), Johannesburg Office (JHB).
SANCMFW, South African National Council for Maternal and Family Welfare Papers, 1935–48.
Planned Parenthood Association of South Africa (PPASA), Cape Town Office (CT).
MCC, Mothers' Clinic Committee Documents, 1930–45.
Historical Papers, University of the Witwatersrand, Johannesburg (HPW).
RWS, Race Welfare Society Documents, 1930–44.
A 881: J.H. Pim Papers.
A 1419 17: Ellen Hellmann Papers.

AD 843: South Africa Institute of Race Relations Records.

AD 843: South Africa Institute of Race Relations, Rheinallt Jones Papers.

AD 843: South Africa Institute of Race Relations, J.L. Hardy Papers.

Report of the conference on African Family Life, sponsored by the Christian Council of South Africa and held in Pretoria in June 1940.

Archives of the University of the Witwatersrand.

Notes on R.F.A. Hoernle.

Wellcome Trust (WT), Library for the History and Understanding of Medicine, London, Western Manuscripts and Archives (LHM).

SA/EUG E. 22, Eugenics Society of South Africa.

PP/MCS, Marie. C. Stopes Collection.

British Library, Department of Manuscripts, London, UK (BL).

Add. MS 58582–58583, Marie Stopes Papers.

Printed primary sources

Official Publications

Annual Report of the Department of Public Health, for the Year Ended 30, June 1935 (Pretoria: Government Printer, 1935).

Annual Report of the Department of Public Health, for the Year Ended 30 June 1936 (Pretoria: Government Printer, 1936).

Annual Report of the Department of Public Health, for the Year Ended 30 June 1937 (Pretoria: Government Printer, 1937).

Annual Report of the Department of Public Health, Year Ended 30 June 1938 (Pretoria: Government Printer, 1938).

Annual Report of the Department of Public Health, Year Ended 30 June 1939 (Pretoria: Government Printer, 1939).

Groenewald, H. J. "Fertility and Family Planning in Atteridgeville: Data for 1969, 1974 and 1975" (Pretoria: Human Sciences Research Council (HSRC), 1978).

House of Assembly Debates (Selected Years)

Hansard Vol. 14 to 46, 1930 to 1943.

Hoernle, R.F.A. *Wits University Group Test of Mental Ability, 1925* (Pretoria: Transvaal Education Department, 1925).

Lotter, J.M. and J.L. van Tonder. "Certain Aspects of Human Fertility in Rural Bophuthatswana." (Pretoria: HSRC, 1978).

——. "Fertility and Family Planning among Blacks in Africa: 1974." (Pretoria: HSRC, 1976).

——. "Fertility and Family Planning in Thlabane." (Pretoria: HSRC, 1975).

Official Year Book of the Union, 1931–2 (Pretoria: Government Printer, 1932).

Official Year Book of the Union 1935–6 (Pretoria: Government Printer, 1936).

Official Year Book of the Union, 1938–9 (Pretoria: Government Printer, 1939).

Pretorius, J.H.O. Deputy Director-General: Regulation, Services and Programmes, Ministry of Health. "Short Overview of the Full Submission to the Truth and Reconciliation Commission," 1997, in author's possession.

Report of the Cape Town Charities Commission, 1932 (Cape Town: Town Clerks Dept., 1932).

Report of the Interdepartmental Committee on Destitute, Neglected, Maladjusted and Delinquent Children and Young Persons, 1934–37 (Pretoria: Government Printer, 1937).

Report of the Commission of Inquiry Regarding the Cape Coloured Population of the Union (Pretoria: Government Printer, 1937).

Report of the Economic and Wage Commission, 1925 (Pretoria: Government Printer, 1925).

Report of the National Conference on Social Work (Pretoria: Government Printer, 1936).

Report of the Native Economic Commission, 1930–32 (Pretoria: Government Printer, 1932).

Senate Report from the Select Committee on the Medical, Dental and Pharmacy Bill (Pretoria: Government Printer, 1917).

Van der Merwe, R.B. and J.J. van Wyk, "Fertility and Family Planning in Daveyton: Survey Among Men." (Pretoria: HSRC, 1982).

Van Wyk, J.J. "Multipurpose Survey Among Blacks in Urban Areas – 1978: Some Practices with a Contraceptive Effect: Abstinence and Breast-feeding." (Pretoria: HSRC, 1979).

Newspapers and periodicals

Birth Control News (London: Society for Constructive Birth Control and Racial Progress).

Cape Argus.

Cape Times.

Die Burger.

Municipal Magazine.

Rand Daily Mail.

Southern Cross.

Star.

Secondary sources

Books, articles, pamphlets, newsletters, book chapters and unpublished papers

Abel, E.K. and C.H. Browner "Selective Compliance with Biomedical Authority and the Uses of Experiential Knowledge," in M. Lock and P. Kaufert (eds), *Pragmatic Women and Body Politics* (Cambridge: Cambridge University Press, 1998), pp. 310–26.

Adam, H. and H. Giliomee. *Ethnic Power Mobilized: Can South Africa Change?* (New Haven: Yale University Press, 1979).

Adams, J.W. "Some Population Problems of the World." *South Africa Medical Journal*, 8 (1934), pp. 131–2.

Adams, M. "Toward A Comparative History of Eugenics," in Mark Adam (ed.), *The Wellborn Science: Eugenics in Germany, France, Brazil, and Russia* (New York: Oxford University Press, 1990), pp. 217–26.

Adams, M. (ed.), *The Wellborn Science: Eugenics in Germany, France, Brazil, and Russia* (New York: Oxford University Press, 1990).

Ahluwalia, S. "Troubled Histories: Politics of Birth Control in Colonial India, 1920–1947." Unpublished paper presented at "Population, Birth Control and Reproductive Health in Late Colonial India," a conference organized by the Centre for the History and Culture of Medicine Programme, School of Oriental and African Studies, London, November 18–19, 1999.

Albertyn, J.R. *The Poor White and Society. Vol. V. The Poor White Problem in South Africa. Carnegie Commission of Investigation on the Poor White Question in South Africa* (Stellenbosch: Pro Ecclesia, 1932).

Allen, G. "Genetics, Eugenics and Society: Internalists and Externalists in Contemporary History of Science." *Social Studies of Science* 6 (1976), pp. 105–22.

Andersson, N. and S. Marks. "Diseases of Apartheid," in John Lonsdale (ed.), *South Africa in Question* (London: Cambridge African Studies Centre with James Currey, 1985), pp. 172–99.

——. *Health and Apartheid* (Geneva: World Health Organisation, 1983).

——. "Industrialization, Rural Health, and the 1944 National Health Services Commission in South Africa," in S. Feierman and J.M. Janzen (eds), *The Social Basis of Health and Healing in Africa* (Berkeley: University of California Press, 1992), pp. 131–61.

——. "Typhus and Social Control: South Africa, 1917–1950," in R. MacLeod and M. Lewis (eds), *Disease, Medicine and Empire: Perspectives on Western Medicine and the Experience of European Expansion* (London and New York: Routledge, 1988), pp. 257–83.

Anning, C.C.P "Sterility and the Falling Birth-Rate: The Public Health Aspect." *South African Medical Journal*, 11 (1937), pp. 493–7.

Anthias, F. and N. Yuval-Davis. "Introduction" in F. Anthias and N. Yuval-Davis (eds), *Woman-Nation-State* (London: Macmillan Press, 1989).

Arndt, S. "African Gender Trouble and African Womanism: An Interview with Chikwenye Ogunyemi and Wanjira Muthoni." *Signs: Journal of Women in Culture and Society*, 25, 3 (2000), pp. 709–26.

Badenhorst, L.T. "South Africa," in B. Berelson (ed.), *Population Policy in Developed Countries* (New York: McGraw Hill, 1974), pp. 385–402.

Baker, P. "The Domestication of Politics: Women and American Political Society, 1780–1920," in V.L. Ruiz and E.C. Dubois (eds), *Unequal Sisters: A Multi-Cultural Reader in US History*, 2nd edn (New York: Routledge, 1994), pp. 85–110.

Beinart, W. *The Political Economy of Pondoland, 1860–1930* (Cambridge: Cambridge University Press, 1982).

——. *Twentieth Century South Africa* (Oxford: Oxford University Press, 1994).

Beinart, W. and C. Bundy (eds), *Hidden Struggles in Rural South Africa: Politics and Popular Movements in the Transkei and Eastern Cape, 1890–1930* (Johannesburg: Ravan Press, 1987).

Beinart, W. and S. Dubow (eds), *Segregation and Apartheid in Twentieth Century South Africa* (New York: Routledge, 1995).

Beinart, W.P. Delius and S. Trapido (eds), *Putting the Plough to the Ground: Accumulation and Dispossession in Rural South Africa, 1850–1930* (London: James Currey, 1986).

Berger, I. *Threads of Solidarity. Women in South African Industry 1900–1980* (London: James Curry, 1992).

Bernstein, H. "Has Planned Parenthood a Place in the Population Explosion." *Public Health* (December 1968), pp. 531–41.

Berkman, J. *Olive Schreiner: Feminism on the Frontier* (St. Alban's, Vt: Eden Press Women's Publication, 1979).

Berry, C. *Southern Migrants, Northern Exiles* (Urbana and Chicago: University of Illinois Press, 2000).

Bickford-Smith, V. "The Origins and Early History of District Six to 1910." *CABO*, 4, 2 (1987), pp. 19–25.

Bickford-Smith, V., E. van Heyningen and N. Worden. *Cape Town in the Twentieth Century: An Illustrated Social History* (Cape Town: David Philip, 1999).

Block, I.J. "Some Observations from the Work of a Birth Control Clinic." *South African Medical Journal*, 8 (1934), pp. 490–2.

Boikanyo, E., M. Gready, B. Klugman, H. Rees and M. Zaba. "When is Yes, Really Yes? The Experiences of Contraception and Contraceptive Services Amongst Groups of South African Women." Report of a study conducted for the Women's Health Project, Centre for Health Policy, Department of Community Health, Johannesburg, 1993.

Bolton, C. *Poor Whites of the Antebellum South* (Durham: Duke University Press, 1994).

Bonner, P. "Desirable or Undesirable Basotho Women?' Liquor, Prostitution and the Migration of Basotho Women to the Rand, 1920–45," in C. Walker (ed.), *Women and Gender in Southern Africa to 1945* (London and Cape Town: James Currey, 1990), pp. 221–50.

——. "The Politics of Black Squatter Movements on the Rand, 1944–52," *Radical History Review*, 46, 7 (1990), pp. 89–116.

——. "The Transvaal Native Congress, 1917–20: The Radicalization of the Black Petty Bourgeoisie on the Rand," in S. Marks and R. Rathbone (eds), *Industrialisation and Social Change in South Africa* (London: Longman, 1982).

——. "The 1920 Black Mineworkers' Strike: A Preliminary Account," in B. Bozzoli (ed.), *Labour, Townships, and Protest: Studies in the Social History of the Witwatersrand* (Johannesburg: Ravan Press, 1979), pp. 273–97.

Bonner, P., P. Delius and D. Posel (eds), *Apartheid's Genesis, 1935–62* (Braamfontein: Ravan Press, 1993).

Bozzoli, B. "Marxism, Feminism and South African Studies," *Journal of Southern African Studies*, 9, 2 (1983), pp. 139–71.

Bozzoli, B. (ed.), *Class, Community and Conflict: South African Perspectives* (Johannesburg: Ravan Press, 1987).

Bozzoli, B. and P. Delius, "Radical History and South African History," *History from South Africa: Alternative Visions and Practices* (Philadelphia: Temple University Press, 1991), pp. 3–25.

Bozzoli, B. with M. Nkotsoe. *Women of Phokeng: Consciousness, Life Strategy, and Migrancy in South Africa, 1900–83* (Portsmouth, N.H.: Heinemann, 1991).

Bottomley, J. " 'Almost Bled to Death': The Effects of the Anglo Boer War on Social Transformation in the Orange River Colony," *Historia*, 44, 1 (1999), pp. 183–209.

Boyer, P. *Urban Masses and Moral Order in America, 1820–1920* (Cambridge, MA.: Harvard University Press, 1978).

Bradford, H. *A Taste of Freedom: The ICU in Rural South Africa, 1923–30* (New Haven: Yale University Press, 1987).

——. "Herbs, Knives and Plastic: 150 Years of Abortion in South Africa." in T. Meade and M. Walker (eds), *Science, Medicine and Colonial Imperialism* (London: Macmillan, 1991) pp. 120–47.

Brink, E. "Maar 'n klomp 'factory' meide": Afrikaner Family and Community on the Witwatersrand During the 1920s," in B. Bozzoli (ed.), *Class, Community and Conflict* (Johannesburg: Ravan Press, 1987), pp. 177–208.

——. "Man-Made Women: Gender, Class and the Ideology of the *Volksmoeder*," in C. Walker (ed.), *Women and Gender in Southern Africa* (Cape Town: David Philip, 1990), pp. 273–92.

Brookes, B. "Reproductive Rights: The Debate over Abortion and Birth Control in the 1930s," in B. Brookes, C. Macdonald, and M. Tennant (eds), *Women in History: Essays on European Women in New Zealand* (Wellington: Allen and Unwin, 1986), pp. 119–36.

Brown, B. " 'Facing the Black Peril': The Politics of Population Control in South Africa." *Journal of Southern African Studies*, 13, 3 (1987) pp. 256–73.

Buckner, P.A. and C. Bridge. "Reinventing the British World," *The Round Table*, 368 (2003), pp. 77–88.

Bundy, C. *The Rise and Fall of the South African Peasantry* (Berkeley: University of Califorvnia Press, 1979).

Bundy, C. "Vagabond Hollanders and Runaway Englishmen: White Poverty in the Cape Before Poor Whiteism," in W. Beinart, P. Delius and S. Trapido (eds), *Putting a Plough to the Ground: Accumulation and Dispossession in Rural South Africa, 1850–1930* (Johannesburg: Ravan Press, 1986), pp. 101–28.

——. "Land and Liberation: Popular Rural Protest and the National Liberation Movements in South Africa, 1920–60," in Shula Marks and Stanley Trapido (eds), *The Politics of Race, Class and Nationalism in Twentieth Century South Africa* (London: Longman, 1987), pp. 254–85.

Burman, S. and M. Naude, "Bearing a Bastard: The Social Consequences of Illegitimacy in Cape Town, 1896–1939," *Journal of Southern African Studies* 17, 3 (1991), pp. 373–413.

Burns, C. "Sex Lessons from the Past," *Agenda*, 29 (1996), pp. 79–91.

Burrows, E.H. *A History of Medicine in South Africa up the End of the Nineteenth Century* (Cape Town and Amsterdam: A.A. Balkema, 1958).

Burton, A. *Burdens of History: British Feminists, Indian Women, and Imperial Culture, 1865–1915* (Chapel Hill: University of North Carolina Press, 1994).

Calpin, G.H. *There are no South Africans* (London: Thomas Nelson, 1941).

Carnegie Commission of Investigation on the Poor White Question in South Africa. The Poor White Problem in South Africa. Joint Findings and Recommendations (Stellenbosch: Pro Ecclesia, 1932).

Cartwright, A.P. *Doctors to the Mines. To Mark the 50th Anniversary of the Founding of the Mine Medical Officers Association of South Africa* (Cape Town: Purnell, 1971).

Chowdhury, I. "Instructions for the Unconverted: Birth Control, Marie Stopes and Indian Women." Unpublished paper presented at "Population, Birth Control and Reproductive Health in Late Colonial India," a conference organized by the Centre for the History and Culture of Medicine Programme, School of Oriental and African Studies (London, November 18–19, 1999).

Clayton, C. (ed.), *Olive Schreiner* (Johannesburg and New York: McGraw Hill, 1983).

Cohen, D. "Private Lives in Public Spaces: Marie Stopes, the Mothers' Clinics and the Practice of Contraception," *History Workshop*, 35 (1993) pp. 95–116.

Cook, H. *The Long Sexual Revolution: English Women, Sex, and Contraception* (Oxford: Oxford University Press, 2004).

——. "Unseemly and Unwomanly Behavior: Comparing Women's Control of their Fertility in Australia and England from 1890 to 1970," *Journal of Population Research*, 17, 2 (2000), pp. 125–41.

Cott, N. "What's in a Name? The Limits of 'Social Feminism': or Expanding the Vocabulary of Women's History," *Journal of American History*, 76, 3 (1989), pp. 809–29.

Crummey, D. (ed.), *Banditry, Rebellion and Social Protest in Africa* (London: James Currey, 1986).

Darley-Hartley, W. "Legislation Against Contra-ceptives," *South African Medical Record*, 15 (1917) pp. 81–4.

———. "The Traffic in Contra-Ceptives." *South African Medical Record*, 15 (1917), pp. 17–18.

Davenport, T.R.H. *South Africa: A Modern History*, 3rd edn (Bergvlei: Southern Book Publishers, 1987).

Davies, R. *Capital, State and White Labour in South Africa* (Atlantic Highlands, NJ: Humanities Press, 1979).

Davin, A. "Imperialism and Motherhood," in F. Cooper and A.L. Stoler (eds), *Tensions of Empire: Colonial Cultures in a Bourgeois World* (Berkeley: University of California Press, 1997), pp. 87–151.

Davis, A. "Racism, Birth Control and Reproductive Rights," in M. Gerber Fried (ed.), *From Abortion to Reproductive Freedom: Transforming a Movement* (Boston: South End Press, 1990), pp. 15–26.

Beinart, W., P. Delius and S. Trapido (eds), *Putting the Plough to the Ground: Accumulation and Dispossession in Rural South Africa, 1850–1930* (London: James Currey, 1986).

Dikötter, F. *Imperfect Conceptions: Medical Knowledge, Birth Defects, and Eugenics in China* (New York: Columbia University Press, 1998).

———. "Race Culture: Recent Perspectives on the History of Eugenics." *American Historical Review*, 103, 2 (1998), pp. 467–78.

Dixon-Mueller, R. *Population Policy and Women's Rights* (London: Praeger, 1993).

Dolan, B. (ed.), *Medicine, Malthus and Morality: Malthusianism after 1798*, (Amsterdam: Rodopi, 2000).

Donaldson, Ken (ed.), *South African Who's Who* (Cape Town and Johannesburg: K. Donaldson, 1937).

Dubow, S. "Afrikaner Nationalism, Apartheid and the Conceptualisation of 'Race'," *Journal of African History*, 33 (1992), pp. 209–37.

———. *Racial Segregation and the Origins of Apartheid in South Africa, 1919–36* (Basingstoke: Macmillan Press Ltd., 1989).

———. *Scientific Racism in Modern South Africa* (Cambridge: Cambridge University Press, 1995).

———. "Scientism, Social Research and the Limits of 'South Africanism': The Case of Ernst Gideon Malherbe," *South African Historical Journal*, 44 (2001), pp. 99–142.

Du Toit, A. "No Chosen People: The Myth of the Calvinist Origins of Afrikaner Nationalism and Racial Ideology," *American Historical Review*, 88, 4 (1983), pp. 920–52.

Du Toit, A. and H. Giliomee. *Afrikaner Political Thought: Analysis and Documents* (Cape Town: David Philip, 1983).

Edmunds, M. "Population Dynamics and Migrant Labour in South Africa," in K.L. Michaelson (ed.), *And the Poor Get Children: Radical Perspectives on Population Dynamics* (New York: Monthly Review Press, 1981), pp. 154–79.

Fantham, H.B. "Race Admixture in South Africa," *Encyclopedia Sexualis*, 21 (1936).

———. "Biology in Relation to Some Present-Day Problems," *Scientia*, 28 (1934).

———. "Glands and Personality," *South African Journal of Science*, 29 (1932).

———. "Biology and Civilisation," *South African Journal of Science*, 29 (1932).

———. "Eugenics," *Child Welfare*, 9, 7 (1930), pp. 3–7.

——. "Some Thoughts on Biology and the Race," *South African Journal of Science*, 24 (1927).

——. "Some Thoughts on the Social Aspects of Eugenics, with Note on Some Further Cases of Human Inheritance Observed in South Africa," *South African Journal of Science*, 23 (1926).

——. "Some Factors in Eugenics, Together with Notes on Some South African Cases," *South African Journal of Science*, 22 (1925).

——. "Heredity in Man: Its Importance both Biologically and Educationally," *South African Journal of Science*, 21 (1924).

——. "How the Lack of a Knowledge of Eugenics Affects One's Pocket," *Transvaal Educational News*, 25 (1928).

——. "Some Further Cases of Physical Inheritance and of Racial Admixture Observed in South Africa," *South African Journal of Science*, 27 (1930).

Fantham, H.B. and A. Porter. "Notes on some Cases of Racial Admixture in South Africa," *South African Journal of Science*, 24 (1927).

——. "Some Further Cases of Physical Inheritance and Racial Admixture observed in South Africa," *South African Journal of Science*, 27 (1930).

——. "Inheritance of Stature through Mate-Selection," *Journal of Heredity*, 25 (1935).

——. "Remarks on a 'Family' Showing Shortness, Illegitimacy and Simplemindedness," *Eugenical News*, 21 (1936).

Fielding, M. *Parenthood: Design or Accident? A Manual of Birth Control*, 3rd edn (London: Williams and Norgate, 1934).

Fields, B. "Ideology and Race in American History," in J. Morgan Kousser and J.M. McPherson (eds), *Region, Race and Reconstruction* (New York: Oxford University Press, 1982).

First, R. and A. Scott. *Olive Schreiner* (New York: Schocken Books, 1980).

Fisher, K. 'She Was Quite Satisfied with the Arrangements I Made': Gender and Birth Control in Britain 1920–50," *Past and Present*, 169 (2000), pp. 161–93.

Fox, F.W. and D. Back. "A preliminary survey of the agricultural and nutritional problems of the Ciskei and Transkeian territories with special reference to their bearing on the recruiting of labourers for the gold mining industry" (Johannesburg: Chamber of Mines, 1938).

Freund, B. "The Poor Whites: A Social Force and a Social Problem in South African History," in R. Morrell (ed.), *White But Poor: Essays on the History of the Poor Whites in Southern Africa, 1880–1940* (Pretoria: University of South Africa, 1992).

Furlong, P. *Between Crown and Swastika: The Impact of the Radical Right on the Afrikaner Nationalist Movement in the Fascist Era* (Middletown, Cape Town: Wesleyan University Press, 1991).

"The Future of Alexandra Township. An Open Letter to the Citizens of Johannesburg by the Alexandra Health Committee" (Johannesburg: Alexandra Health Committee, 1943).

Gaitskell, D. " 'Getting Close to the Hearts of Mothers': Medical Missionaries Among African Women and Children in Johannesburg Between the Wars," in V. Fildes, L. Marks and H. Marland (eds), *Women and Children First: International Maternal and Infant Welfare 1870–1945* (London and New York: Routledge, 1992).

——. "Housewives, Maids or Mothers: Some Contradictions of Domesticity for Christian Women in Johannesburg, 1903–39," *Journal of African History*, 24 (1983), pp. 241–56.

——. "Introduction," *Journal of Southern African Studies*, 10, 1 (1983), pp. 1–16.

Gaitskell, D. and E. Unterhalter. "Mothers of the Nation: A Comparative Analysis of Nation, Race and Motherhood in Afrikaner Nationalism and the African National Congress," in N. Yuval-Davis and F. Anthias (eds), *Mother-Nation-State* (London: Macmillan, 1989).

Gandal, K. *The Virtues of the Vicious: Jacob Riis, Stephen Crane and he Spectacle of the Slum,* (New York: Oxford University Press, 1997).

Gelfand, M. *Tropical Victory: An Account of Medicine in the History of Southern Rhodesia* (Oxford: Juta, 1953).

Geppert, A. "Divine Sex, Happy Marriage, Regenerated Nation: Marie Stopes's Marital Manual *Married Love,* and the Making of a Best Seller, 1918–1955," *Journal of the History of Sexuality,* 8, 3 (1998) pp. 389–433.

Giliomee, H. *The Afrikaners: Biography of a People* (London: Hurst and Company, 2003).

——. "Constructing Afrikaner Nationalism," *Journal of Asian and African Studies,* 18 (1983), pp. 83–98.

Ginsburg, F. *Conceiving the New World Order: The Global Politics of Reproduction* and R. Rapp (eds), (Berkeley: University of California Press, 1995).

Glick, T. "Cultural Issues in the Reception of Relativity," in T. Glick (ed.), *The Comparative Reception of Relativity* (Leiden: D. Reidel, 1987).

Goddefroy, B. "Medical and Ethical Aspects of Abortion," *South African Medical Journal,* 6 (1932), pp. 471–7.

Goldberg, D. *Racist Culture: Philosophy and Politics of Meaning* (Oxford, UK and Cambridge, US: Blackwell Press, 1993).

Gordon, L. *Woman's Body, Woman's Right: Birth Control in America,* 2nd edn (New York: Penguin Books, 1990).

Gould, S.J. *The Mismeasure of Man,* Revised edn (New York: W.W. Norton and Company, 1996).

Gray, J.L. "Sterility and the Falling Birth-rate," *South African Medical Journal,* 11 (1937), pp. 491–3.

Gray, M. "Race Ratios: The Politics of Population Control in South Africa," in L. Bondestam and S. Bergstrom (eds), *Poverty and Population Control* (London: Academic Press, 1980), pp. 137–55.

Greenberg, S. *Legitimating the Illegitimate: State, Markets and Resistance in South Africa* (Berkeley: University of Berkeley Press, 1987).

——. *Race and State in Capitalist Development: Comparative Perspectives* (New Haven: Yale University Press, 1980).

Greenhalgh, S. "Anthropology Theorizes Reproduction: Integrating Practice, Political Economic, and Feminist Perspectives," in S. Greenhalgh (ed.), *Situating Fertility: Anthropology and Demographic Inquiry* (Cambridge: Cambridge University Press, 1995).

Grey White, D. *Arn't I a Woman? Female Slaves in the Plantation South* (New York: Norton, 1985).

Grosskopf, J.W.F. *Economic Report. Rural Impoverishment and Rural Exodus. Vol. 1. The Poor White Problem in South Africa. Carnegie Commission of Investigation on the Poor White Question in South Africa* (Stellenbosch: Pro Ecclesia, 1932).

Grossmann, A. *Reforming Sex: The German Movement for Birth Control and Abortion Reform, 1920–50* (New York: Oxford University Press, 1995).

Guy, J. "Analysing Pre-Capitalist Societies in Southern Africa," *Journal of Southern African Studies,* 14, 1 (1987), pp. 18–37.

Haire, N. *Birth-control Methods (Contraception, Abortion, Sterilisation)* (London: George Allen and Unwin, 1936).

Hall, R. *Passionate Crusader: The Life of Marie Stopes* (New York: Harcourt Brace Jovanovich, 1977).

Hall R (ed.), *Dear Dr. Stopes: Sex in the 1920* (London: Deutsch, 1978).

Harrington, P. "Women in South Africa: The Historiography in English." *The International Journal of African Historical Studies*, 26, 2 (1993), pp. 241–69.

Hartmann, B. *Reproductive Rights and Wrongs: The Global Politics of Population Control and Contraceptive Choice* (New York: Harper and Row, 1987).

Hellmann, E. *Rooiyard: A Sociological Survey of an Urban Native Slum Yard* (Oxford: Oxford University Press, 1948).

Hellmann, E. (ed.), *Handbook on Race Relations in South Africa* (Cape Town: Oxford University Press, 1949).

Herirtage Illustrated Dictionary of the English Language (Boston: Houghton Mifflin Co., 1973).

Hill, R. and G. Pirio. " 'Africa for the Africans': The Garvey Movement in South Africa, 1920–40," in S. Marks and S. Trapido (eds), *The Politics of Race, Class and Nationalism in Twentieth Century South Africa* (London: Longman, 1987), pp. 209–53.

Hobhouse, E. *The Brunt of the War and Where it Fell* (London: Methuen, 1902).

Hofmeyr, I. "Building a Nation from Words: Afrikaans Language, Literature and Ethnic Identity," in S. Marks and S. Trapido (eds), *The Politics of Race, Class and Nationalism in Twentieth Century South Africa* (London: Longman, 1987).

Houghton, H. "Economic Development, 1865–1965," in M. Wilson and L. Thompson (eds), *Oxford History of South Africa*, Vol. 2 (Oxford: Clarendon Press, 1969–71).

Hyam, R. *Elgin and Churchill at the Colonial Office, 1905–08: The Watershed of the Empire-Commonwealth* (London: Macmillan, 1968).

Hyslop, J. "The Imperial Working Class Makes Itself 'White': White Labourism in Britain, Australia, and South Africa Before the First World War," *Journal of Historical Sociology*, 12, 3 (1999), pp. 398–421.

——. Why Did Apartheid's Supporters Capitulate? 'Whiteness', Class and Consumption in Urban South Africa, 1985–95," *Society in Transition*, 31, 1 (2000), pp. 36–44.

——. "White Working-Class Women and the Invention of Apartheid: 'Purified' Afrikaner Nationalist Agitation for Legislation Against 'Mixed' Marriages, 1934–9," *Journal of African History*, 36 (1995), pp. 57–81.

Iliffe, J. *The African Poor. A History* (Cambridge: Cambridge University Press, 1987).

Iriye, A. *Cultural Internationalism and World Order* (Baltimore, Johns Hopkins University Press, 1997).

Jeeves, A. "*Migrant Labour in South Africa's Mining Economy: The Struggle for the Gold Mines" Labour Supply, 1890–1920* (Johannesburg: Witwatersrand University Press, 1985).

——. "Public Health in the Era of South Africa's Syphilis Epidemic of the 1930s and 1940s," *South African Historical Journal*, 45 (2001), pp. 79–102.

Jochelson, K. *The Colour of Disease: Syphilis and Racism in South Africa, 1880–1950* (Basingstoke and Oxford: Palgrave in association with St. Antony's College, 2001).

Johnstone, F. *Class, Race and Gold: A Study of Class Relations and Racial Discrimination in South Africa* (London: Routledge and Kegan Paul, 1976).

Jones, G. "Eugenics and Social Policy Between the Wars," *The Historical Journal*, 25, 3 (1982), pp. 717–28.

Jones, G.S. *Outcast London: A Study in the Relationship between Classes in Victorian Society* (Harmondsworth: Penguin, 1984).

Kark, S. "The Economic Factor in the Health of the Bantu in South Africa," *The Leech*, 5, 3 (1934), pp. 11–22.

Keegan, T. *Racial Transformation in Industrializing South Africa: The Southern Highveld to 1914* (Basingstoke: Macmillan, 1987).

Kevles, D. *In the Name of the Race: Genetics and the Uses of Human Heredity* (New York: Knopf, 1985).

Kiewiet, C.W. de. *A History of South Africa Social and Economic* (Oxford: Clarendon Press, 1941).

Klausen, S. "The Birth Control International Information Centre and the Promotion of Contraceptive Services in the Colonial World, 1930–39." Unpublished paper presented at the University of Lethbridge, March 2003.

——. "Doctors and Dying Declarations: State Regulation of Abortion in British Columbia, 1917–36," *Canadian Bulletin of Medical History/Bulletin Canadien d'Histoire de la Medecine*, 13 (1996), pp. 53–81.

——. " 'For the Sake of the Race': Eugenic Discourses of Feeblemindedness and Motherhood in the South African Medical Record, 1903–26," *Journal of Southern African Studies*, 23, 1 (1997), pp. 27–50.

——. "The Imperial Mother of Birth Control: Marie Stopes and the South African Birth-Control Movement, 1930–50." in G. Blue, M. Bunton and R. Crozier (eds), *Colonialism and the Modern World* (Armonk, NY: M.E. Sharpe, 2002).

Klugman, B. "Population Policy in South Africa: A critical perspective," *Development Southern Africa*, 8, 1 (1991)?

——. "Politics of Contraception in South Africa," *Women's Studies International Forum*, 13, 3 (1990), pp. 19–34.

Koch, E. " 'Without Visible Means of Subsistence': Slumyard Culture in Johannesburg, 1918–40," in B. Bozzoli (ed.), *Town and Countryside in the Transvaal: Capitalist Penetration and Popular Response* (Johannesburg: Ravan Press, 1983).

Koven, S. and S. Michel. "Introduction," in S. Koven and S. Michel (eds), *Mothers of a New World: Maternalist Politics and the Origins of Welfare States* (New York: Routledge, 1993).

Lacey, M. *Working for Boroko: The Origins of a Coercive Labour System in South Africa* (Johannesburg: Ravan Press, 1981).

Ladd-Taylor, M. *Mother-Work: Women, Child Welfare, and the State, 1890–1930* (Chicago: University of Illinois Press, 1994).

Laidler, P.W. "The Medico-Social Aspects of Population Density," *South Africa Medical Journal*, 10 (1936), pp. 317–27.

——. "The Practice of Eugenics," *South African Medical Journal*, 8 (1934), pp. 823–35.

——. *South Africa and Its Medical History, 1652–1898* (Cape Town: C. Struik, 1971).

Lambert, J. "Keeping English-Speaking South Africans British, 1934–47," Unpublished paper presented at "The Burden of Race? 'Whiteness' and 'Blackness' in Modern South Africa," Conference held at Wits in July 2001.

Leathard, A. *The Fight for Family Planning: The Development of Family Planning Services in Britain, 1921–74* (London: Macmillan, 1980).

Legassick, M. "Race, Industrialization and Social Change in South Africa," *African Affairs*, 75, 299 (1976), pp. 224–39.

Legassick, M. and H. Wolpe. "The Bantustans and Capital Accumulation in South Africa." *Review of African Political Economy*, 7 (1976), pp. 87–107.

Leipoldt, C.L. "Medical Inspection of Schools in Relation to Social Efficiency," *South African Journal of Science*, 12 (1915), pp. 530–1.

———. "The Mothers' Clinic." *South African Medical Journal* (July 24, 1937), p. 490.

Lewis, J. *Politics of Motherhood: Child and Maternal Welfare in England, 1900–39* (London: Croom Helm, 1980).

Lewis, M. "The 'Health of the Race' and Infant Health in New South Wales: Perspectives on Medicine and Empire," in R. MacLeod and M. Lewis (eds), *Disease, Medicine and Empire. Perspectives on Western Medicine and the Experience of European Expansion* (London and New York: Routledge, 1988), pp. 301–15.

Lewson, P. *John X. Merriman* (New Haven: Yale University Press, 1982).

Lock, M. and P. Kaufert, "Introduction," in M. Lock and P. Kaufert, *Pragmatic Women and Body Politics* (Cambridge: Cambridge University Press, 1998), pp. 1–27.

Lodge, T. *Black Politics in South Africa Since 1945* (London: Longman, 1983).

Longmore, L. *The Dispossessed: A Study of the Sex-Life of Bantu Women in Urban Areas In and Around Johannesburg* (London: Jonathan Cape, 1959).

Loudon, I. "Some International Features of Maternal Mortality, 1880–1950," in V. Fildes, L. Marks and H. Marland (eds) *Women and Children First: International Maternal and Infant Welfare 1870–1945* (London and New York: Routledge, 1992).

Ludmerer, K. *Genetics and American Society* (Baltimore: Johns Hopkins University Press, 1972).

Macmillan, W. *Complex South Africa* (London: Faber and Faber, 1930).

Macnab, R. *The Story of South Africa House: South Africa in Britain – The Changing Pattern* (Johannesburg: Jonathan Ball Publishers, 1983).

Malan, M. *The Quest for Health: The South African Institute for Medical Research*, (Johannesburg: Lowry Publishers, 1988).

Malherbe, E. G. *Education and the Poor White. Vol. III., The Poor White Problem in South Africa, Carnegie Commission of Investigation on the Poor White Question in South Africa* (Stellenbosch: Pro Ecclesia, 1932).

———. *Never A Dull Moment* (Cape Town: Timmins Pub., 1981).

Mallows, E.W.N. *Johannesburg: An Outline History* (Self-published, 1982).

Mandy, N. *A City Divided – Johannesburg and Soweto* (Johannesburg: Macmillan South Africa, 1984).

Manicom, L. "Ruling Relations: Rethinking State and Gender in South African History," *Journal of African History*, 33 (1992), pp. 441–65.

Marchand, L. "Obstetrics Amongst South African Natives," *South African Medical Journal*, 7 (1933), pp. 329–30.

Marks, L. *Metropolitan Maternity: Maternal and Infant Welfare Services in Early Twentieth Century London* (Amsterdam: Rodopi, 1996).

Marks, S. *Divided Sisterhood: Race, Class and Gender in the South African Nursing Profession* (London: Macmillan Press, 1994).

———. "Doctors and the State: George Gale and South Africa's Experiment in Social Medicine," in S. Dubow (ed.), *Science and Society* (Manchester: Manchester University Press, 2000), pp. 188–211.

Marks, S. "South Africa's Early Experiment in Social Medicine: Its Pioneers and Politics," *American Journal of Public Health*, 87 (1997), pp. 452–9.

Martin, E. *The Woman in the Body: A Cultural Analysis of Reproduction* (Boston, MA: Beacon Press, 1987).

Maternity and Gender Policies: Women and the Rise of the European Welfare States, 1880–1950s. G. Bock and P. Thane (eds) (New York: Routledge, 1991).

Maylam, P. "South Africa's Racial Order: Some Historical Reflections." Paper presented at The Burdens of Race? 'Whiteness' and 'Blackness' in Modern South Africa, a conference organized by History Workshop and the University of the Witwatersrand Institute for Social and Economic Research, University of the Witwatersrand, Johannesburg, July 5–8, 2001.

Mayne, A. " 'The Dreadful Scourge': Responses to Smallpox in Sydney and Melbourne, 1881–2," in R. MacLeod and M. Lewis (eds), *Disease, Medicine and Empire. Perspectives on Western Medicine and the Experience of European Expansion* (London and New York: Routledge, 1988), pp. 219–41.

Mazumdar, P. *Eugenics, Human Genetics and Human Failings: The Eugenics Society, Its Sources and Its Critics in Britain* (London and New York: Routledge, 1992).

MB, ChB. Letter in the *South African Medical Journal* November 12, 1932, p. 713.

McCann, C.R. *Birth Control Politics in the United States, 1916–45* (Ithaca: Cornell University Press, 1994).

McIlwaine, S. *The Southern Poor-white from Lubberland to Tobacco Road* (Norman, Oklahoma: University of Oklahoma Press, 1939).

McKendrick, B.W. "The Development of Social Welfare and Social Work in South Africa, " in B.W. McKendrick (ed.), *Introduction to Social Work in South Africa* (Pretoria: Haum Tertiary, 1990).

McLaren, A. *A History of Contraception: From Antiquity to the Present Day* (Oxford: Blackwell, 1990).

———. *Our Own Master Race: Eugenics in Canada, 1885–1945* (Toronto: McClelland and Stewart Inc., 1990).

Reproductive Rituals: The Perception of Fertility in England from the Sixteenth Century to the Nineteenth Century (London: Methuen and Co. Ltd., 1984).

———. *Birth Control in Nineteenth-Century England* (London: Croom Helm, 1978).

McLaren, A and A. Tigar McLaren. *The Bedroom and the State: The Changing Practices and Politics of Contraception and Abortion in Canada, 1880–1980* (Toronto: McClelland and Stewart, 1986).

"Medical and Ethical Aspects of Abortion," Notes from a symposium presented at the Northern Transvaal Branch of the South African Medical Association (BMA). *South African Medical Journal*, 6 (1932), pp. 471–7.

"Minutes of the Meeting of the Cape Town Division of the Cape Western Branch of the Medical Association of South Africa (BMA)," *South African Medical Journal*, 6 (1932), pp. 303–7.

"Minutes of the Meeting of the Northern Transvaal Branch of the Medical Association of South Africa (BMA)," *South African Medical Journal*, 6 (1932), pp. 471–7.

Mitchinson, W. and J.D. McGinnis. "Introduction," in W. Mitchinson and J. Dickin McGinnis (eds), *Essays in the History of Canadian Medicine* (Toronto: McClelland and Stewart, 1988).

Mohr, J.C. *Abortion in America: The Origins and Evolution of National Policy, 1800–1900* (New York: Oxford University Press, 1978).

Moodie, T.D. *The Rise of Afrikanerdom: Power, Apartheid, and the Afrikaner Civil Religion* (Berkeley: University of California Press, 1975).

Morrell, R. "The Poor Whites of Middelburg," in R. Morrell (ed.), *White But Poor: Essays on the History of the Poor Whites in Southern Africa, 1880–1940* (Pretoria: University of South Africa, 1992), pp. 1–28.

"The Mothers' Clinic," *South African Medical Journal*, 10 (1936), p. 385.

"The Mothers' Clinic," *South African Medical Journal*, 11 (1937), p. 504.

Mothers of a New World: Maternalist Politics and the Origins of Welfare States. S. Koven and S. Michel (eds) (New York: Routledge, 1993).

C. Clayton (ed.), *Olive Schreiner* (Johannesburg and New York: McGraw Hill, 1983).

O'Meara, D. *Forty Lost Years: The Apartheid State and the Politics of the National Party 1948–94* (Randburg, South Africa: Ravan Press, 1996).

——. *Volkskapitalisme: Class, Capital and Ideology in the Development of Afrikaner Nationalism 1934–48* (Cambridge: Cambridge University Press, 1983).

Owen, C. *The South African Medal Roll of the 1935 Jubilee Medal and the 1937 and 1953 Coronation Medals as Issued to South Africans* (Somerset West: Chimperie Pubs., 1982).

Packard, R. *White Plague, Black Labor: Tuberculosis and the Political Economy of Health and Disease in South Africa* (Berkeley: University of California Press, 1989).

Paton, A. *Hofmeyr* (Cape Town: Oxford University Press, 1964).

Parnell, S. "Public Housing as a Device for White Residential Segregation in Johannesburg," *Urban Geography*, 9 (1988), pp. 584–602.

——. "Slums, Segregation and Poor Whites in Johannesburg, 1920–34," in R. Morrell (ed.), *White But Poor: Essays on the History of the Poor Whites in Southern Africa, 1880–1940* (Pretoria: University of South Africa, 1992), pp. 115–29.

Petchesky, R. *Abortion and Woman's Choice: The State, Sexuality, and Reproductive Freedom* 2nd edn (Boston: Northwestern University Press, 1990).

Phillips, H. "The 1945 Gluckman Report and the Establishment of South Africa's Health Centres,"*American Journal of Public Health*, 83 (1993), pp. 1037–9.

Plaatje, S. *Native Life in South Africa* London: P.S. King and Son, 1916).

Porter, A. "Eugenics From a Woman's Point of View," *Child Welfare*, 10, 2 (1931), pp. 2–5.

Posel, D. *The Making of Apartheid, 1948–61: Conflict and Compromise* (Oxford: Clarendon Press, 1991).

——. "Rethinking the Race-Class Debate in South African Historiography," *Social Dynamics*, 9, 1 (1983), pp. 50–66.

——. "State, Power and Gender: Conflict over the Registration of African Customary Marriage in South Africa c. 1910–70," *Journal of Historical Sociology*, 8, 3 (1995), pp. 223–56.

Proctor, A. "Class Struggle, Segregation and the City: A History of Sophiatown, 1905–40," in B. Bozzoli (ed.), *Labour, Townships and Protest: Studies in the Social History of the Witwatersrand* (Johannesburg: Ravan Press, 1979), pp. 49–89.

Proctor, R. *Racial Hygiene: Medicine Under the Nazis* (Cambridge, MA: Harvard University Press, 1986).

Pyrah, G.B. *Imperial Policy and South Africa, 1902–10* (Oxford: Clarendon Press, 1955).

Quine, M.S. *Population Politics in Twentieth Century Europe: Fascist Dictatorships and Liberal Democracies* (London and New York: Routledge, 1996).

"Race Welfare in South Africa." Pamphlet, 1940. NASA, SAB GES 2281 85/38, Vol. 2.

Ramírez de Arellano, A.B. and C. Seipp. *Colonialism, Catholicism, and Contraception: A History of Birth Control in Puerto Rico* (Chapel Hill: University of North Carolina Press, 1983).

Reed, J. *From Private to Public Virtue: The Birth Control Movement and American Society Since 1830* (New York: Basic Books, 1978).

Rich, P. "Ministering to the White Man's Needs: The Development of Urban Segregation in South Africa, 1913–23," *African Studies*, 37 (1978), pp. 177–91.

———. *White Power and the Liberal Conscience: Racial Segregation and South African Liberalism* (Manchester: Manchester University Press, 1984).

Riddle, J. *Contraception and Abortion from the Ancient World to the Renaissance* (Cambridge, MA: Harvard University Press, 1992).

———. *Eve's Herbs: A History of Contraception and Abortion in the West* (Cambridge, MA: Harvard University Press, 1997).

Robinson, J. "Johannesburg's 1936 Empire Exhibition: Interaction, Segregation and Modernity in a South African City," *Journal of Southern African Studies*, 29, 3 (2003), pp. 759–89.

Rodrique, J. "The Black Community and the Birth Control Movement," in E.C. Dubois and V.L. Ruiz (eds), *Unequal Sisters: A Multicultural Reader in U.S. Women's History* (New York: Routledge, 1990), pp. 333–44.

Roediger, D. *The Wages of Whiteness: Race and the Making of the American Working Class* (London and New York: Verso, 1991).

Rose, J. *Marie Stopes and the Sexual Revolution* (London: Faber and Faber, 1992).

Ross, L. "African American Women and Abortion, 1800–1970," in S.M. James and A.P.A. Busia (eds), *Theorizing Black Feminisms*, (New York: Routledge, 1994, pp. 141–59).

Rothmann, M.E. *The Mother and Daughter of the Poor Family. Vol. V. The Poor White Problem in South Africa. Carnegie Commission of Investigation on the Poor White Question in South Africa* (Stellenbosch: Pro Ecclesia, 1932).

Roux, E. *Time Longer Than Rope: A History of the Black Man's Struggle for Freedom in South Africa* (Madison: University of Wisconsin Press, 1964).

Ryan, M.P. *Civic Wars: Democracy and Public Life in the American City during the Nineteenth Century* (Berkeley: University of California Press, 1997).

Sadie, J.L. "The Costs of Population Growth in South Africa," *South African Journal of Economics*, 40 (1972), pp. 107–18.

———. "Population and Economic Development in South Africa," *South African Journal of Economics*, 39 (1971), pp. 205–22.

Salo, E. "Birth Control, Contraception and Women's Rights in South Africa A Cape Town Case Study." Unpublished paper, 1993.

Schapera, I. *Married Life in an African Tribe* (London: Faber and Faber, 1939).

Schneider, W. *Quality and Quantity: The Quest for Biological Regeneration in Twentieth-Century France* (Cambridge: Cambridge University Press, 1990).

Scully, P. "White Maternity and Black Infancy: The Rhetoric of Race in the South African Women's Suffrage Movement, 1895–1930," in C. Fletcher, L.E. Nym Mayhall, and P. Levine (eds), *Women's Suffrage in the British Empire: Citizenship, Nation and Race* (London and New York: Routledge, 2000), pp. 68–83.

Searle, G.R. *The Quest for National Efficiency. A Study in British Politics and Political Thought, 1899–1914* (Berkeley: University of California Press, 1971).

Semmel, B. *Imperialism and Social Reform: English Social-Imperial Thought, 1895–1914* (London: Allen and Unwin, 1960).

Shapiro, J. "Political and Economic Organization of Women in South Africa – the Limitations of a Notion of 'Sisterhood' as a Basis for Solidarity," *Africa Perspective* (Autumn 1980), pp. 1–15.

Siedlecky, S. and D. Wyndham. *Populate and Perish: Australian Women's Fight for Birth Control* (Sydney: Allen and Unwin, 1990).

Sinha, M. *Colonial Masculinity: The 'Manly Englishman' and the 'Effeminate Bengali' in the Late Nineteenth Century* (Manchester: Manchester University Press, 1995).

Smyth, H. *Rocking the Cradle: Contraception, Sex, and Politics in New Zealand* (Wellington: Steele Roberts Ltd., 2000).

Soloway, R.A. *Birth Control and the Population Question in England, 1877–1930* (Chapel Hill: University of North Carolina, 1982).

——. *Demography and Degeneration: Eugenics and the Declining Birthrate in Twentieth-Century Britain* (Chapel Hill: University of North Carolina Press, 1990).

Stadler, A. "Birds in the Cornfield: Squatter Movements in Johannesburg, 1944–47," *Journal of Southern African Studies,* 6 (1979), pp. 93–123.

Standard Encyclopedia of Southern Africa 1st edn (London: Nasionale Boekhanel Pub., Ltd., 1972).

Stepan, N.L. *"The Hour of Eugenics:" Race, Gender and Nation in Latin America* (Ithaca: Cornell University Press, 1991).

——. *The Idea of Race in Science: Great Britain 1800–1960* (London: Macmillan, 1982).

Stopes, M. *Married Love: A New Contribution to the Solution of Sex Difficulties* (London: Putnam, 1918).

Stoler, A.L. *Carnal Knowledge and Imperial Power: Race and the Intimate in Colonial Rule* (Berkeley: University of California Press, 2002).

——. "Making Empire Respectable: The Politics of Race and Sexual Morality in Twentieth-Century Colonial Cultures," *American Ethnologist,* 16, 4 (1989), pp. 634–60.

——. *Race and the Education of Desire: Foucault's History of Sexuality and the Colonial Order of Things* (Durham: Duke University Press, 1995).

——. " 'Tense and Tender Ties': The Politics of Comparison in North American History and (Post) Colonial Studies." *The Journal of American History* 88, 3 (2001), pp. 829–65.

Stoler, A.L. and F. Cooper. "Between Metropole and Colony: Rethinking a Research Agenda," in F. Cooper and A.L. Stoler (eds), *Tensions of Empire: Colonial Cultures in a Bourgeois World* (Berkeley: University of California Press, 1997).

Sullivan, R. "Cholera and Colonialism in the Philippines, 1899–1903," in R. MacLeod and M. Lewis (eds), *Disease, Medicine and Empire. Perspectives on Western Medicine and the Experience of European Expansion* (London and New York: Routledge, 1988), pp. 285–300.

Swanson, M. "The Sanitation Syndrome: Bubonic Plague and the Urban Native Policy in the Cape Colony, 1900–09," *Journal of African History,* 18, 3 (1977), pp. 387–410.

Thane, P. "Women in the British Labour Party and the Construction of State Welfare, 1906–39," in S. Koven and S. Michel (eds), *Mothers of a New World:*

Maternalist Politics and the Origins of Welfare States (New York: Routledge, 1993), pp. 343–77.

Thompson, L. *A History of South Africa* (New Haven: Yale University Press, 1990).

Thornton, E. "Some Problems of Preventive Medicine," *South African Medical Journal,* 8 (1934), pp. 743–7.

Tone, A. *Devices and Desires: A History of Contraceptives in America* (New York: Hill and Wang, 2001).

Trant, H. "Modern Contraceptive Methods," *South African Medical Journal,* 9 (1935), pp. 407–14.

Unterhalter, B. "Inequalities in Health and Disease: The Case of Mortality Rates for the City of Johannesburg, South Africa, 1910–1979." *International Journal of Health Services,* 12, 4 (1982), pp. 617–36.

Vail L. (ed.), *The Creation of Tribalism in Southern African* (Berkeley: University of California Press, 1991).

Van Onselen, C. *Studies in the Social and Economic History of Witwatersrand, 1886–1914* (London: Longman, 1982).

Walker, C. "Gender and the Development of the Migrant Labour System, c. 1850–1930," in C. Walker (ed.), *Women and Gender in Southern Africa to 1945* (London: James Currey, 1990), pp. 168–96.

——. "The Women's Suffrage Movement: The Politics of Gender, Race and Class," in C. Walker (ed.), *Women and Gender in Southern Africa* (Cape Town: David Philip, 1990), pp. 313–45.

——. *Women and Resistance in South Africa* 2nd edn (Cape Town: David Philip, 1991).

Walker, L. "The Colour of White: Race, Gender and South African Medical Women." Unpublished paper presented at "The Burden of Race? 'Whiteness' and 'Blackness' in Modern South Africa," Conference held at the University of the Witwatersrand, July 2001.

Walshe, P. *The Rise of African Nationalism in South Africa: The ANC, 1915–1952* (Berkeley: University of California Press, 1971).

Ward, D. *Poverty, Ethnicity, and the American City, 1840–1925* (Cambridge: Cambridge University Press, 1989).

Warwick, P. *Black People and the South African War, 1899–1902* (London: Longman, 1983).

——. *The South African War: The Anglo-Boer War, 1899–1902* (Harlow, Essex: Longman, 1980).

Watkins, E. *On the Pill: A Social History of Oral Contraceptives, 1950–1970* (Baltimore: Johns Hopkins University Press, 1998).

Webster, C. (ed.), *Biology, Medicine and Society 1840–1940* (Cambridge: Cambridge University Press, 1981).

Webster, C. "Introduction," in C. Webster (ed.), *Biology, Medicine and Society 1840–1940* (Cambridge: Cambridge University Press, 1981).

Weeks, J. *Sex, Politics and Society: The Regulation of Sexuality Since 1800* (London and New York: Longman, 1981).

Weiss, S.F. *Race Hygiene and National Efficiency: The Eugenics of Wilhelm Schallmayer* (Berkeley: University of California Press, 1987).

Western, J. *Outcast Cape Town* (Minneapolis: University of Minnesota Press, 1981).

Wilcocks, R.W. *The Poor White. Vol. II. The Poor White Problem in South Africa. Carnegie Commission Investigation on the Poor White Question in South Africa* (Stellenbosch: Pro Ecclesia, 1932).

Woodrow, E. "Contraception: Its Justification and Practice," *South African Medical Journal,* 6 (1932), pp. 653–7.

——. "Family Planning in South Africa: A Review," *South African Medical Journal,* 50 (1976), pp. 2101–3.

——. "Golden Jubilee," Unpublished paper, April 1982. In author's possession.

——. "The Start of the Family Planning Movement in Cape Town," Unpublished paper, 1972 in author's possession.

Worden, N. *The Making of Modern South Africa: Conquest, Segregation and Apartheid* (Oxford: Blackwell Publishers, 1994).

Theses

Adler, M. "The Literary, Personal, and Socio-Political Background of William Plomer's *Turbott Wolfe*." MA thesis, University of the Witwatersrand, 1988.

Berger, D. "White Poverty and Government Policy in South Africa, 1892–1934." PhD thesis, Temple University, 1983.

Brink, E. "The Afrikaner Women of the Garment Workers' Union, 1918–38." MA thesis, University of the Witwatersrand, 1986.

Burns, C. "Reproductive Labours: The Politics of Women's Health in South Africa, 1900 to 1960." PhD thesis, Northwestern University, 1995.

Clynick, T. "Afrikaner Political Mobilization in the Western Transvaal: Popular Consciousness in the State, 1920–30." PhD thesis, Queen's University at Kingston, 1996.

Collins, C.L. "Women and Labour Politics in Britain, 1893–1932." PhD thesis, London School of Economics, 1991.

Du Toit, M. "Women, Welfare and the Nurturing of Afrikaner Nationalism: A Social History of the Afrikaans Christelike Vroue Vereniging, *c.* 1870–1939." PhD thesis, University of Cape Town, 1996.

Klugman, B. "Decision-Making on Contraception Amongst a Sample of Urban African Working Women." MA thesis, University of the Witwatersrand, 1988.

——. "The Political Economy of Population Control in South Africa." BA thesis, University of the Witwatersrand, 1980.

Koch, E. "Doornfontein and its African Working Class, 1914–35; A Study of Popular Culture in Johannesburg." MA thesis, University of the Witwatersrand, 1983.

Martens, J. " 'An Easy Prey to Temptation': White South African Perceptions of 'Coloured' People in the Era of Segregation, 1928–1945," MA thesis, Queen's University at Kingston, 1997.

Newton-Thompson, L. "Birth Control Clinics in the Western Cape, c. 1932 to c. 1974: A History." BA thesis, University of Cape Town, 1992.

Nicol, M. "A History of Garment and Tailoring Workers in Cape Town, 1900–39." PhD thesis, University of Cape Town, 1984.

Roos, N. "From Workplace to War: Class, Race and Gender amongst White Volunteers, 1939–1953." PhD thesis, University of North West, 2001.

Wagner, O.J.M. "Poverty and Dependency in Cape Town: A Sociological Study of 3300 Dependents Receiving Assistance from the Cape Town General Board of Aid." PhD thesis, University of Stellenbosch, 1936.

Walker, L. "Feminism, a Theory of Practice for Personal and Political Liberation." BA thesis, University of the Witwatersrand, 1988.

Interviews

Interview with Dr. Geoffrey Scott, Cape Town, April 1997.
Interview with Dr. Patricia Massey, Cape Town, April 1997.
Interview with Dr. Dorothea Douglas-Henry, Vishoek, April 1997.

Index

Page numbers in italics refer to tables in the text.

DATE DUE